LEGENDARY LOCALS

OF

EUNICE
LOUISIANA

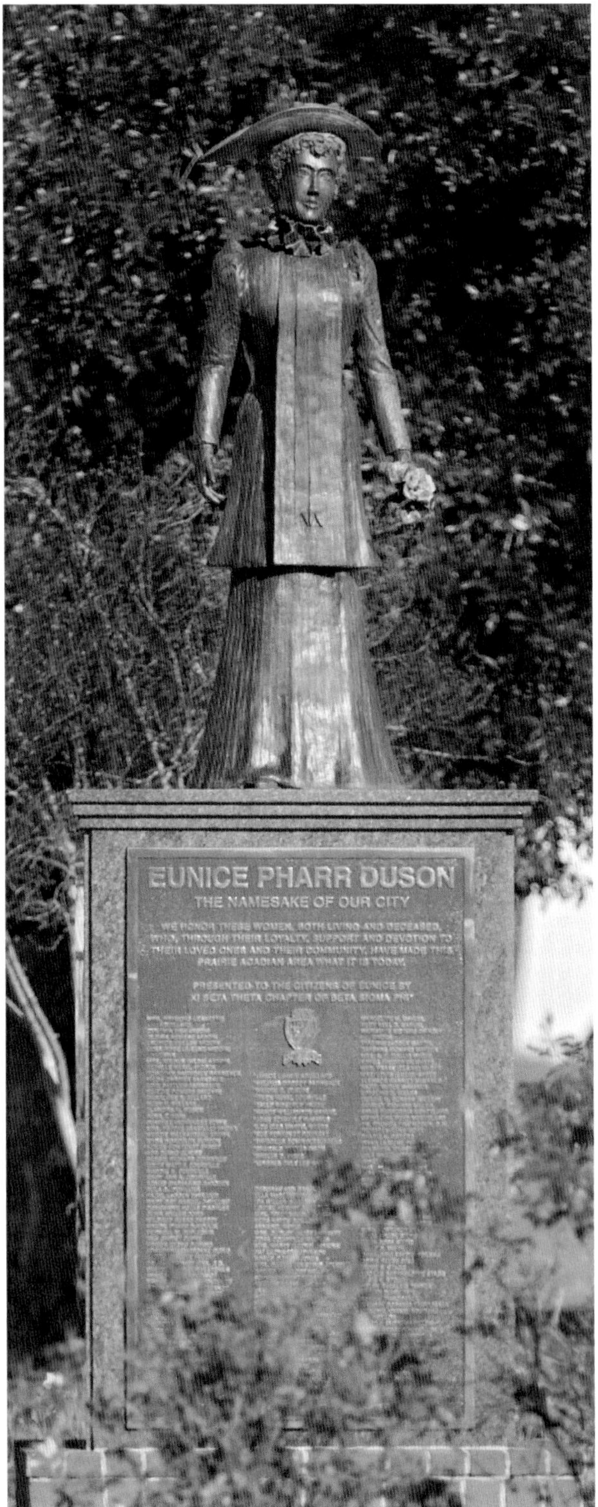

Page 1: **Road through the Cajun Prairie**
A sign on Highway 13 South is pictured as the road cuts across the Cajun prairie, providing a picturesque drive and a hurricane evacuation route through the rice and crawfish fields and the bird habitats of the flat, grassy ecological region. "The Cajun Prairie is not only a biogeographical and ecological region, but also a cultural region—it is obvious in its name." —Dr. Malcolm Vidrine. (Courtesy of authors' collection.)

Page 2: **First Lady of the Cajun Prairie**
The Xi Beta Theta chapter of Delta Sigma Phi sorority presented this statue of C. C. Duson's wife and Eunice's namesake, Mary Eunice Pharr Duson, in honor of the women of Eunice who contributed significantly to the progress and beauty of the city. The statue was dedicated on the city's 100th birthday in 1994. The sculptor, Jerry Gorum, attended the dedication for Eunice's "First Lady of the Cajun Prairie." (Courtesy of Van Reed.)

LEGENDARY LOCALS

OF

EUNICE

LOUISIANA

ALMA BRUNSON REED AND VAN REED

LEGENDARY LOCALS

ISBN 978-1-4671-0024-3

Published by Legendary Locals, an imprint of Arcadia Publishing
Charleston, South Carolina

Printed in the United States of America

Library of Congress Control Number: 2012930848L

For all general information, please contact Arcadia Publishing:
Telephone 843-853-2070
Fax 843-853-0044
E-mail sales@arcadiapublishing.com
For customer service and orders:
Toll-Free 1-888-313-2665

Visit us on the Internet at www.arcadiapublishing.com

Dedication

To the courageous and visionary folks who carved Eunice out of the prairie wilderness and to their descendants who have made the city thrive.

On the Cover: From left to right:
(TOP ROW) Clara Carrell Gray, early settler, teacher (Courtesy of Wilda Brunson Gregory; p. 23), S.Sgt. Donald Wayne Sistrunk, KIA Vietnam (Courtesy of Cat Jamison; page 105), Jonas E. Mason, principal (Courtesy of Rev. James Edwards; page 34), Allen Horton, teacher and coach (Courtesy of Allen Horton; page 52), Aurelie Roi Bergeron, pioneer wife (Courtesy of Marty Bergeron Dupuis and Lane Bergeron Olivier; page 31).
(MIDDLE ROW) B. Rodney Reed, physician (Courtesy of John I. Reed; page 38), Michelle LaFleur MacFadyen, NASA engineer (Courtesy of Michelle MacFadyen; page 47), Felix Mire, US Army, World War II translator (Courtesy of Patrick Mire; page 102), Alice Foster Cottrell, elementary teacher (Courtesy of Joyce W. Thibodeaux; page 35), Shelton Manuel, Cajun musician (Courtesy of Dr. David Simpson; page 75).
(BOTTOM ROW) Jerold "Jerry" Hoffpauir, journalist (Courtesy of Myra Miller; page 100), Catherine Leona Bonvillain Jenkins, school board member (Courtesy of Eunice Public Library; page 45), Greg "Honey Bee" Bollich, rodeo champion, farmer (Courtesy of Greg and Pat Bollich; page 76), Jimmie E. Edwards, St. Landry Parish councilman (Courtesy of Jimmie E. and Lea Edwards; page 42), Gilliam McLane, boxer (Courtesy of *Boxing: Louisiana's Forgotten Sport*; page 95).

CONTENTS

ACKNOWLEDGMENTS

Once again, Dr. Ron Harris has generously allowed us to use images from the historic collection of Tom and George Bevan, who along with their nephew, Leonard Thompson, visually recorded the meaningful life events of Eunice residents. The Bevan Brothers Historic Collection will be cited as BBHC.

Since this book is a collective effort, we also thank the following people who supplied collections of images: Bettie Brunson Jenkins, Audrey Milner, Kakie McGee Manuel, Jesse Breaux, Lennie Parrott Buller, the staff of the Eunice Public Library, Tom Morris, *Boxing: Louisiana's Forgotten Sport*, Bill Wimberly and Post 129 American Legion, Helen Claire Mahfouz, Dr. David Simpson, fire chief Michael Arnold, Fred and Gloria Byars, Harold Gournay, Allen Horton, Arnette Tyson Reese, DeVonne Reese, Rowland Jackson, Janet Heinen Martel, Daine Devillier, Ann Rozas Frugé, Rick Nesbitt and KEUN radio station, John E. LeDoux Sr., Kenneth Pitre and the Lakeview Park staff, Fr. Thomas Voohries, William "Mac" Atteberry, and the Louisiana Maneuvers and Military Museum. For the loan of her collection of the Pharr family photographs, particularly the image of a youthful Eunice Pharr, we are extremely grateful to Linda Carson.

For invaluable information: Matthias J. "Jimmy" Frugé Jr., Helen Wyble, Floyd Young, Stephanie Richard Boone, Gary Bult, Hilda Bollich, Charlie Wine and Linda Manuel Thibodeaux, Trudy Jenkins Patterson, Jackie Jenkins Choate, Gloria O'Brien Fontenot, "Chookie" and Judy Derbes, Deen Thompson, Dr. Richard Lowe, Fr. Paul Thibodeaux, John "Randy" Vidrine, Margaret McWhorter, Chris Brown Carrier, Kathy Lowe, Cinderella Hayes, Pat Sittig Bollich, James "Tee" Leger, Garland "Bully" Arnold, Dr. Gary and Amanda Rozas LaFleur, Dr. Barbara Lyman, and Camille Reed.

For leadership, advice, and guidance, we are indebted to our editors, Tiffany Frary and Erin Vosgien.

For the individual images used, we have acknowledged all of you who donated your photographs in the images' credit lines, but our gratitude is far greater than the few words there, for this book would never have been published without your contributions. Thank you sincerely.

INTRODUCTION

Initially, *Legendary Locals of Eunice* presented a problem. How could anyone select just a few people out of the richness of the past and the variety of the present for inclusion in one small volume? Eunice has had and presently has so many successful and interesting people to consider. Despite inevitable and regrettable omissions, *Legendary Locals of Eunice* contains many images and stories of Eunice residents who were unique, or were in the vanguard of movements—business, social, political, educational, scientific, religious—during the past 150 years.

Countless stories were offered about people who built the city from the prairie. Others told about turning points in individual lives. However, often there was no image to match a wonderful story. Many times, there were myriad images of an individual and it was difficult selecting just the right one to include. Each story and image, then, provides a brief insight into the important experiences and significant life events of Eunice's men and women.

Legendary Locals of Eunice includes stories about women because the history of women's experiences in male-defined society, although not without hardships and struggles, is a positive story of progress that mirrors the city's history. Eunice women have advanced from being "only housewives" to controlling the space shuttle's flights with computers. This book illustrates the ways local women have adapted to life's changes and, therefore, gained a greater mobility in life and also a larger role in the city's functions.

Eunice's men have shown unusual courage and strength too. Images of local men reflect the skills they needed to lead their lives and support their families on a semi-isolated prairie through the decades. War, depressions, irrigation challenges, sporting events, diseases, economic turmoil, boom times, outlaw activities, nature's fury, and life's ceremonies have etched the faces in these images.

Eunice's ethnic diversity also played an important part in the composition of the little city. Although Eunice's culture may seem exotic when compared to other American cities, it reflects the mixture of nationalities that populated the little village on the prairie: Native Americans, Anglo-Saxons, Irish, Lebanese, Jewish, Italians, Germans, African Americans, Greeks, Slavs, French, Cajuns, and numerous others. Eunice grew richer as the cultures blended, yet yielded to the dominance of the Cajun culture. Each generation has also added its knowledge and talents to the aggregate of Eunice experiences, with immigrants bringing their old-world values and institutions with them. The people of Eunice have, over time, shaped history through their community-building. Their stories present a rich record of their community activities and the pride they derived from molding their town into a progressive place to live.

With culture in mind, we looked toward our churches because portraits of the clergy or lay ministers of various religions are legion. Selecting images that show something definitive about Eunice's religious leaders was sometimes difficult. Would the priest who met Pope John Paul II be meaningful to readers? What about a Sunday school teacher? Though interesting tales abound, only a few clergy could be included.

People who lived in scattered homesteads prior to Eunice's founding treasured their old photographs and some have been made available for this collection. Civil War photographs show a young man who proudly displayed his uniform, a man who was considered the enemy by his wife's family, a poor farmer who weathered the destruction of his land, and an outlaw who worked both sides of the conflict against the other. Serious young men wearing World War I military uniforms were ready to "go over there" to fight the "war to end all wars." Young women dressed in their best posed for the photographer in every decade. Brave American fighters in World War II and our nation's other conflicts, and the women who awaited them on the home front smile from the pages of this book.

Teachers, nurses, doctors, businesspeople, and politicians all share their stories. Businessmen whose enterprises had new life breathed into them with the discovery of the nearby Tepetate oil field are pictured showing off their new prosperity. Because it is located on a major east-west highway with passenger train service, Eunice has also had its share of entertainers, from those who put on the Buster Brown Shoe puppet shows to big-name musicians like Fats Domino and the Harry James Big Band.

Over the years notable visitors have brought new ideas to locals. Several persons have been drawn to the new frontier—space. Eunice has had its share of notorious locals and visitors as well, including a citizen who had advance warning from an unwilling and disreputable visitor of one of the nation's most heinous crimes, the assassination of Pres. John F. Kennedy.

Here are the nostalgic stories of Eunice's legendary locals.

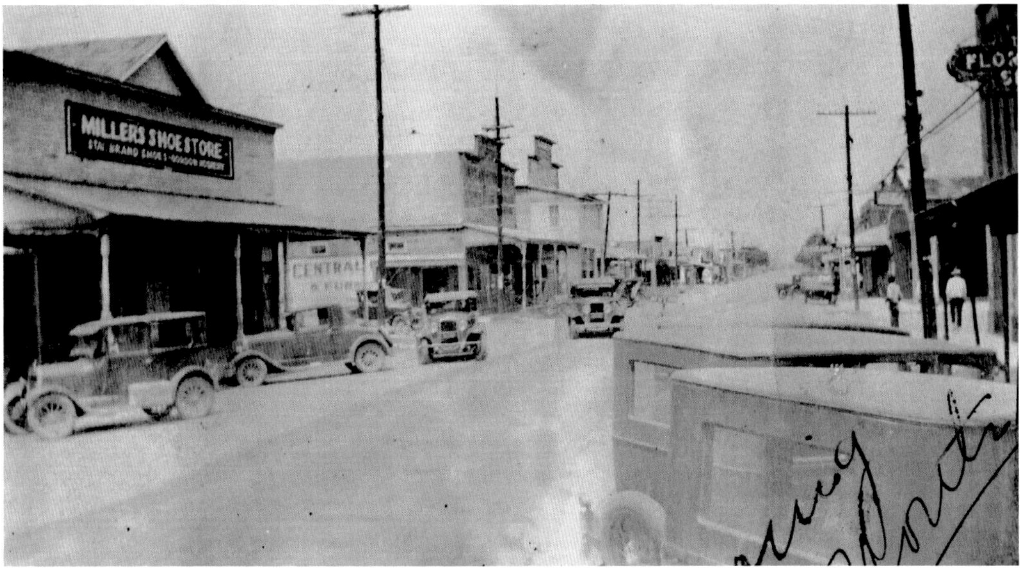

Eunice in 1936

The main shopping area in 1936 showed the north view of Second Street at its juncture with Highway 190 looking toward the Missouri Pacific railway station. Two long-lived businesses that were visible were Miller's Shoe Store, established by Emile Miller, and the Central Hardware. (Courtesy of Allen Horton.)

CHAPTER ONE

Before Eunice's Founding

Prior to C.C. Duson's arrival, the area around the proposed town of Eunice had scattered settlers that preceded the city, and many of those old family names can be found in a current telephone directory. Cajun cattle herders, African Americans, Native American hunters, a few relics from the days of Imperial Spanish colonization, and a small number of Frenchmen forged homesteads on the isolated prairie. Some Union soldiers, lured by the mild climate and fertile land, returned to establish their homes in this area after the Civil War. A number of freed slaves and free *gens de couleur* found the prairie to be hospitable. Life was not easy, however, since the war left everyone, except a few speculators, in poor financial condition. The Civil War devastated the entire southwestern Louisiana area, particularly in the Cajun prairie where settlers were caught in a vise-grip between the two warring armies with their scavengers and the murderous and bloodthirsty bands of Jayhawkers who were pursued by equally violent vigilante groups under the guise of the Home Guard. The economy flatlined after foragers repeatedly raided area farms and businesses. With the men at war, killed, or hiding in the wilderness, women struggled to produce crops without laborers. The lack of livestock, which usually was confiscated for army use or stolen by Jayhawkers, was a hindrance. Some historians point out that it took 50 years for the area to become productive after the war. Several Civil War soldiers are buried in the city. Henry Young, a cavalryman with the 4th Texas Cavalry, is interred at St. Paul Cemetery. Young's headstone is carved with a rifle and flag prominently displayed. Franklin Reed, an area farmer and woodworker, was a sharpshooter with the Consolidated Crescent Regiment. James Arnaud, Eunice's only Union soldier with a visible grave, is buried at St. Louis Cemetery. However, there are rumors that other Union soldiers were buried in a common grave along the edge of the "Headless Cemetery" north of town. Ozemé Carrier, called the "King of the Jayhawkers," roamed this area causing havoc and destruction. Moreover, several local families are reputed to have had a Civil War ancestor who deserted to follow Carrier, and some locals are related to Carrier. Despite war and poverty, the Duson brothers managed to cling to their finances and soon owned massive amounts of land. Then, they branched out into real estate and founding towns on the Cajun prairie.

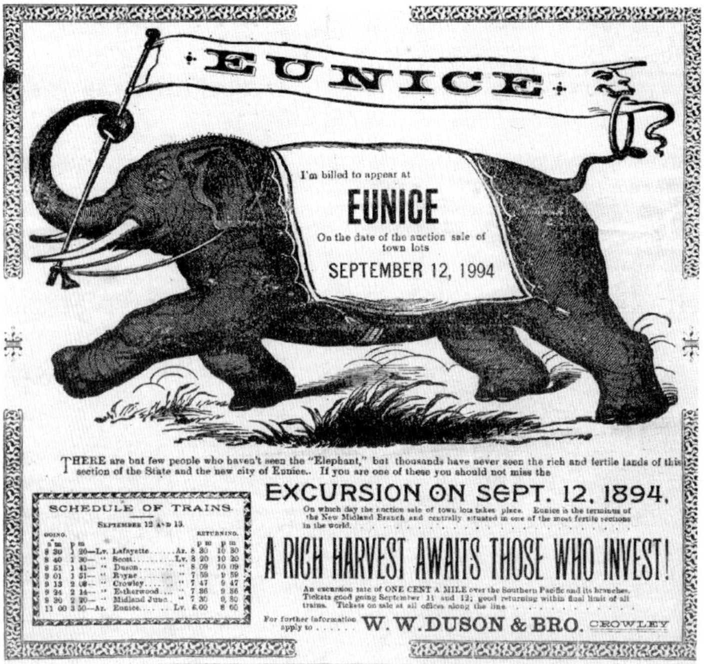

Newspaper Ads
This newspaper advertisement touting the Dusons' city lots auction was one of C.C. Duson's attempts to lure bidders with a circus-like, festive atmosphere as well as with inexpensive excursion train fares. Duson, the quintessential salesman, set out to market the prairie. Apparently, the printer's mistake in recording the date of the planned event on the elephant's blanket did not affect the attendance. It was estimated that over 3,000 people flooded into the area for Duson's sale and the founding of the city of Eunice. (Courtesy of the authors' collection.)

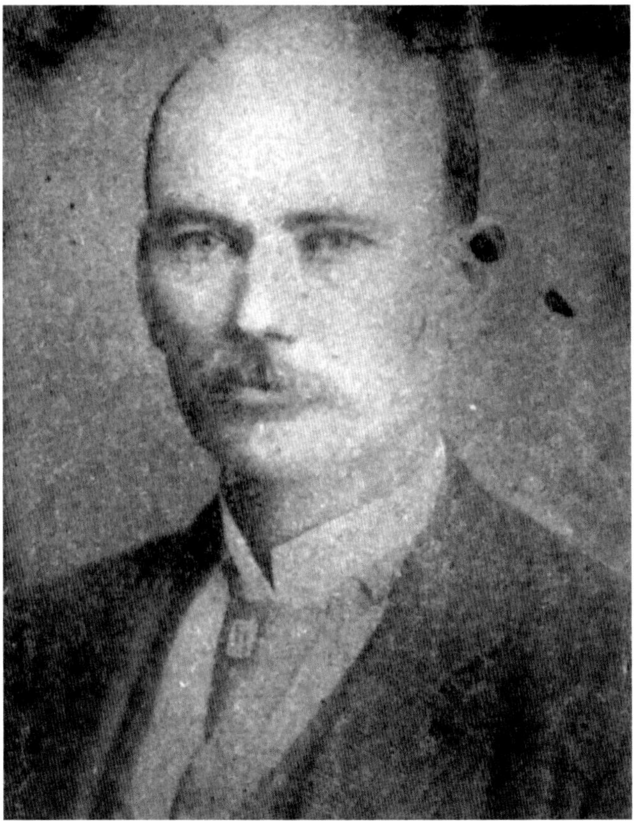

C.C. Duson
Cornelius C. Duson, a former St. Landry Parish sheriff and Louisiana state senator, is seen in his younger days. He was given his nickname, "Curley," early in his life. Duson was born in Webb's Cove on the Mermentau River. His parents had come to Louisiana from Canada to escape political persecution. It would be many years until Duson learned that his father had changed his surname from McNaughton to Duson because of the political troubles. He was recognized in later years as a shrewd businessman and real estate promoter, and his fame as a federal marshal "who always got his man" is legendary. (Courtesy of Acadia Parish Library.)

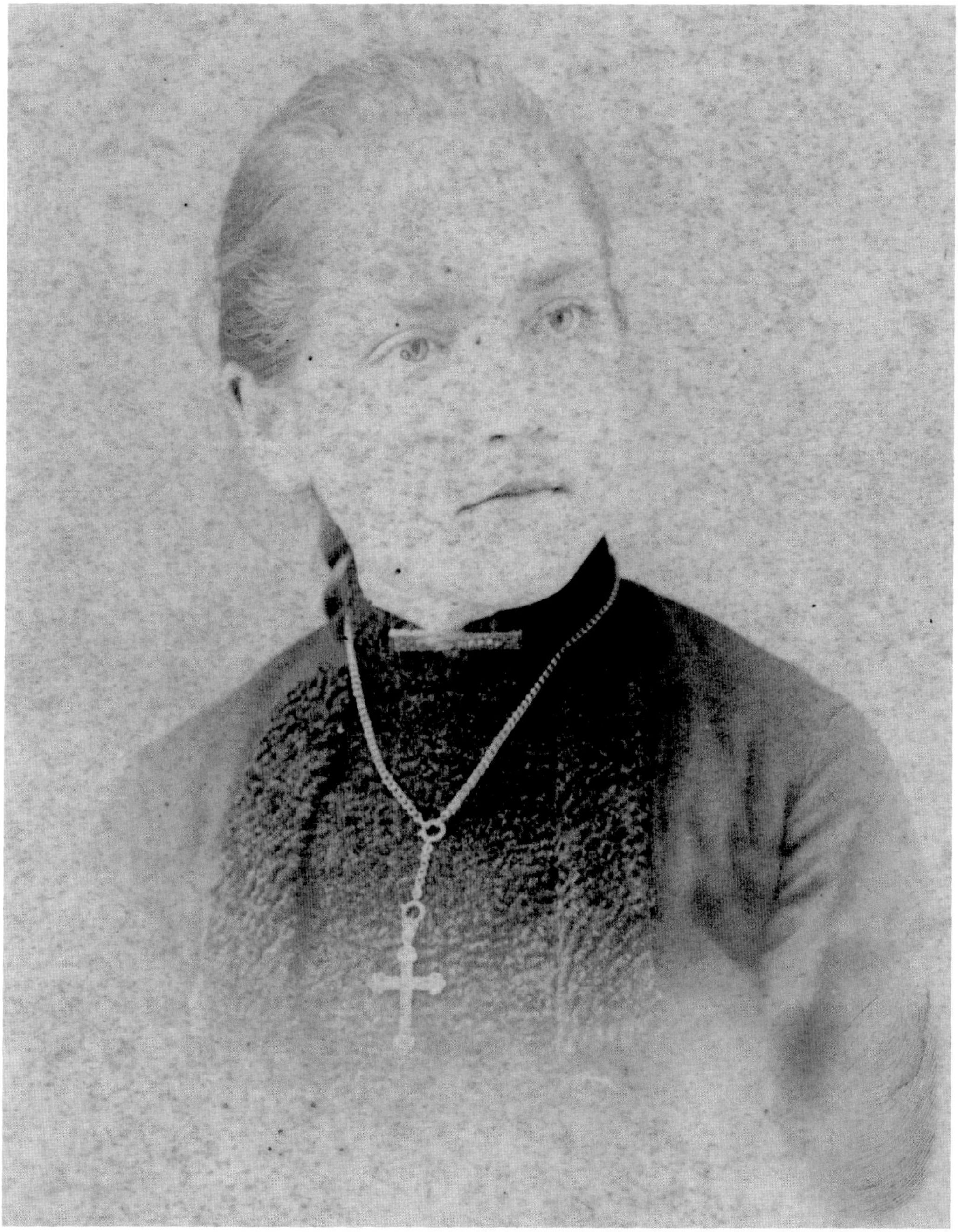

Mary Eunice Pharr Duson
Mary Eunice Pharr Duson, born January 20, 1872, was C. C. Duson's second wife, the mother of two of his children, and the namesake of the city of Eunice. A native of New Iberia, Louisiana, Eunice was the daughter of Elias Albertus Henry and Amelia Gall Pharr, a prominent family. Eunice died from tuberculosis in September 1908 in Alpine, Texas, and is buried among the Pharrs at Roselawn Cemetery in her hometown.

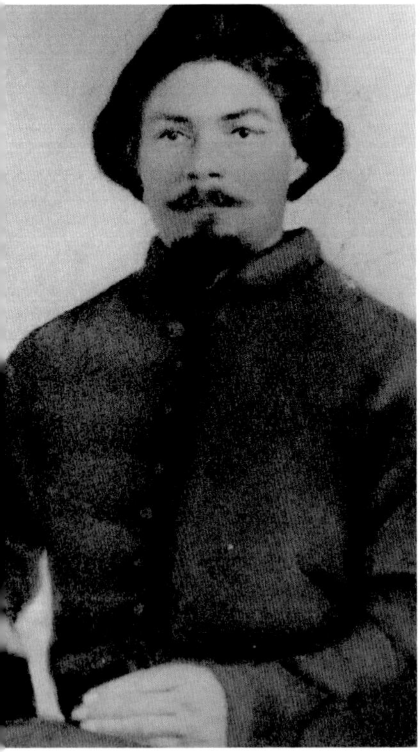

Henry Young, CSA

Young was 24 years old when he served in the Confederate Army as a member of the 4th Texas Cavalry, Company A. He claimed to have seen Robert E. Lee's surrender at Appomattox, and he participated in the Red River Campaign in Louisiana. Young was discharged in northern Arkansas in 1865 and made his way to the Louisiana prairie. He married four times—Valentene McGee, Erene Smith, Mary Hickman, and Mary Ida Brown. He lived to be 90 years old and is buried at St. Paul's Cemetery in Eunice. (Courtesy of Clifton Miller.)

James Arnaud/Arnow

James Arnaud/Arnow, 18 years old, was a shoemaker by trade when he enlisted in the US Army for the $100 bounty as a private in Company H, First Regular New Orleans Infantry. He was born near Natchitoches. His parents were born in France, but tradition tells that they died in a yellow fever epidemic and Arnaud was placed in an orphanage. He ended up in Mallet Woods, east of Eunice, where he married Ruth Goss, daughter of John Goss. They had 11 children. Left to right are (standing in back) Chester, unidentified, unidentified, unidentified, Teresa, Dora, Arthur Andrus holding Alton and John Goss; (second row, left to right) W.T. Miles holding Bill, Anna Miles, James and Ruth Goss Arnaud, George McHenry, and Walter Cecelus; (front row, left to right) Ella Miles, John Ivy Miles, David Arnaud, Ruth Miles, and Maude Andrus. (Courtesy of Richard and Jo-Anne Arnaud.)

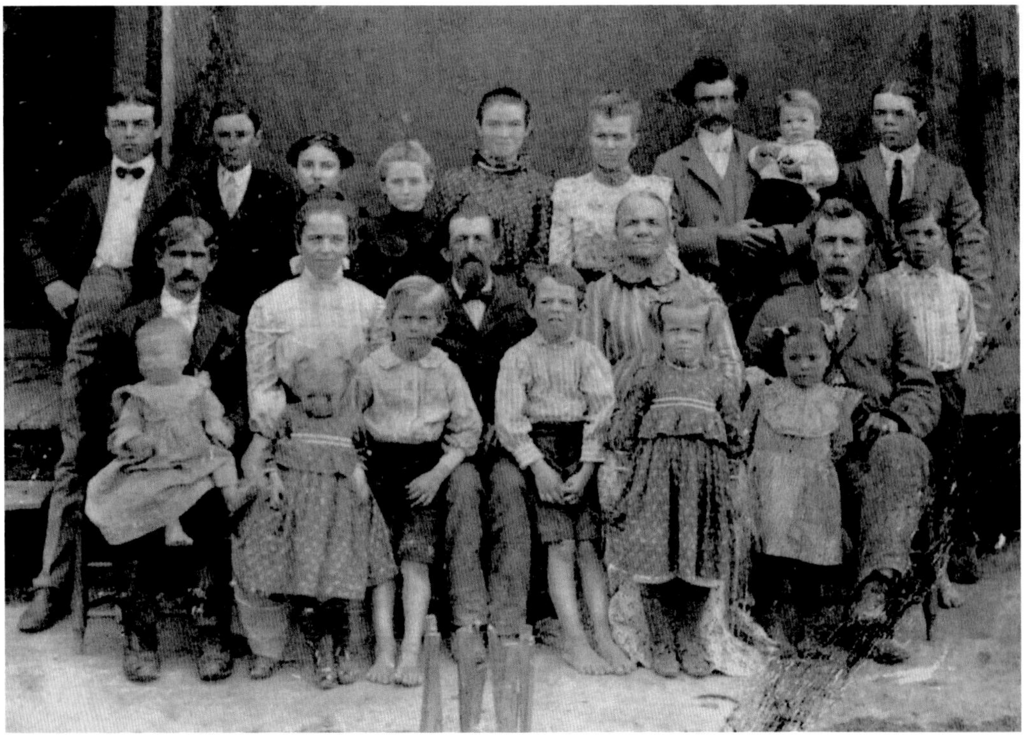

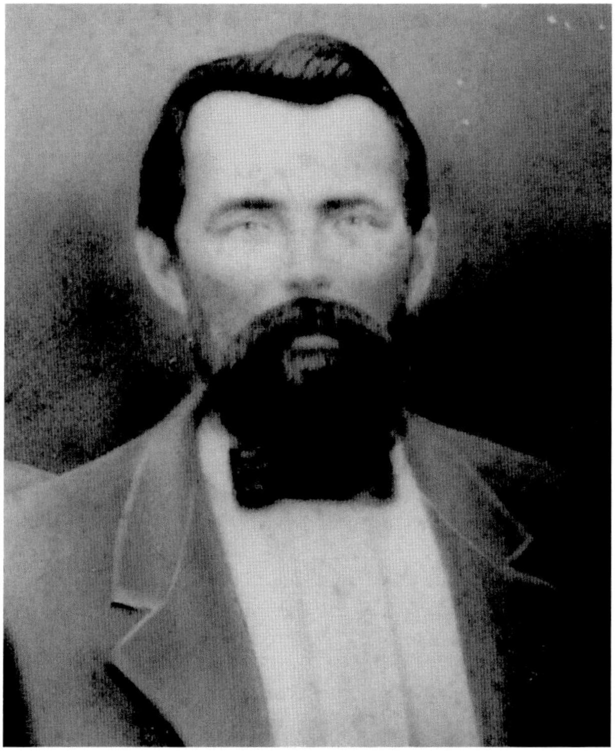

Franklin Reed
Reed was a farmer, cattle herder, and woodworker on his farm north of the proposed city of Eunice. He was married to Anastasia McGee, daughter of John Hugo McGee, an Irish immigrant. Reed was drafted into the Consolidated Crescent Regiment, Company C, as a rifleman in the Civil War. After the war, he returned to his farm to rebuild his property. (Courtesy of Dr. B. Rodney Reed.)

Robin Hood or Outlaw
Ozemé Carrier was a resident of "Bois Mallet" in St. Landry Parish. He was the youngest of eight children of Ursin Carrier and Emilite La Cosse, both descendants of French-Canadian immigrants. He was nearly 29 years old when western St. Landry Parish became the scene of roving bands of brigands and vigilante groups engaged in guerrilla-like warfare. In 1863, Carrier recruited disgruntled deserters, draft dodgers, runaway slaves, and criminals to his band of approximately 1,000 outlaws. Some people called him "Robin Hood of Mallet's Woods," but he changed from a young man who helped the poor to one engaged in guerrilla fighting and terrorizing settlers. His gang stole horses, saddles, and weapons from Confederate camps, burned homes of innocent settlers, and stole from Union Army wagon trains. He was confronted by Lt. Amedé Bringier, CSA, in Mallet Woods. Carrier was left dead and his right hand man, Martin Guillory, was wounded. (Courtesy of LSU Eunice Library.)

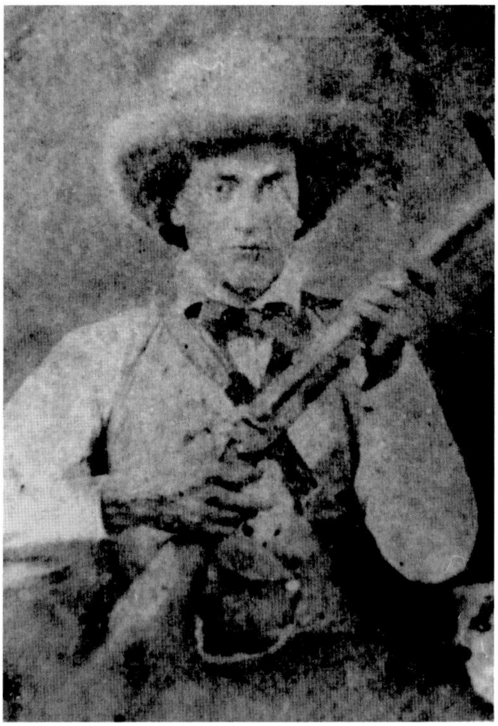

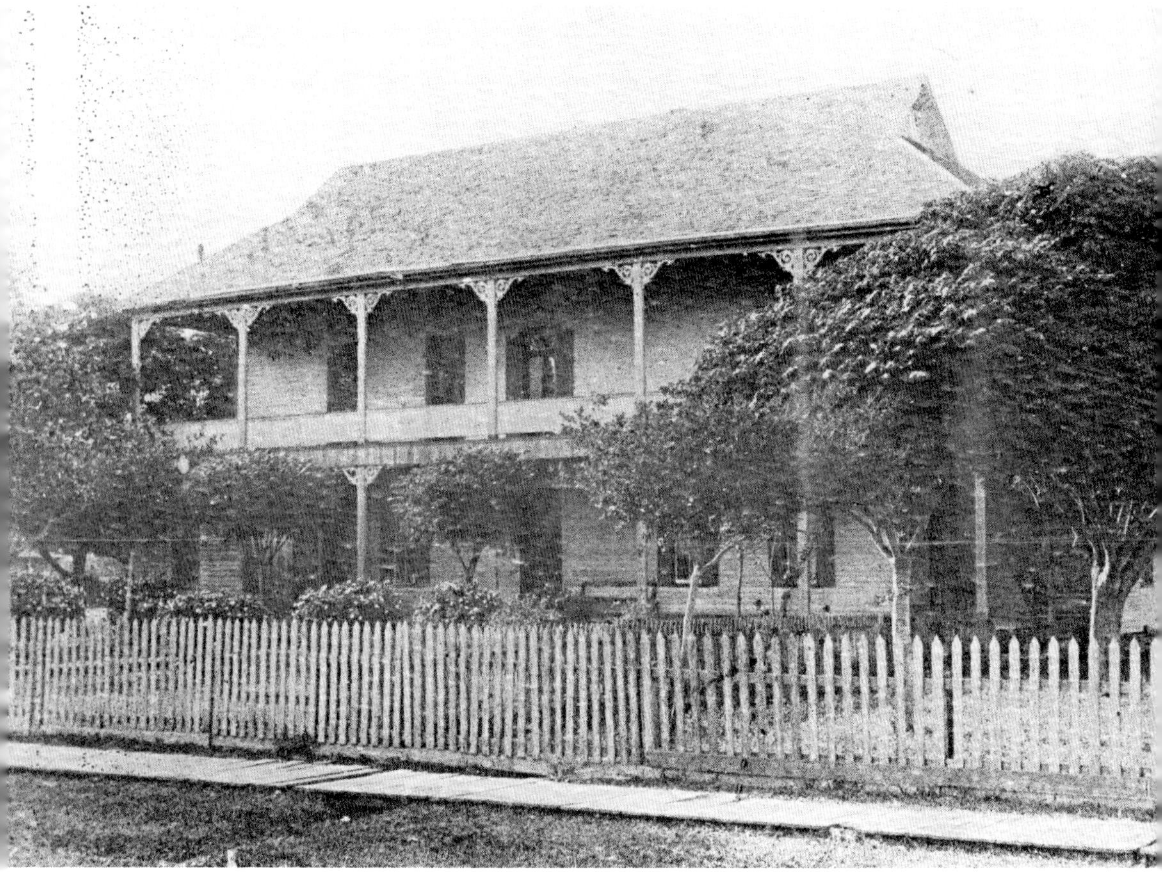

Duson Home

Cornelius C. "Curley" Duson, Eunice's founder, built this palatial home on the entire block at Seventh Street and Park Avenue, overlooking the Circle Park in 1894. His family lived in the 12-room home for several years prior to moving to Crowley, where Mrs. Duson preferred to live. Duson's friend, Joseph Bergeron, purchased the home. During the time that C.C. and Mary Eunice Pharr Duson resided in the home, the landmark became a place of many social gatherings. The Crowley newspaper of January 1895 published the following statement: "Dance at the Duson home and 'all who participated had a pleasant time'." Another mention was made of the Dusons' New Year's Eve ball. (Courtesy of Dr. B. Rodney Reed.)

CHAPTER TWO

Pioneers and Early Settlers

Some Cajun cattle herders, trappers, homesteaders, and Native Americans were lured to the prairie land before Eunice's founding by its fertile soil, abundant wildlife, and balmy weather. Before the Dusons purchased land as stockholders in the Southwest Louisiana Land Company, August Constant Pierrotti, Ursin Miller, Valentin Savoie, Louis Lavergne, Andre Miller, Joseph Z. Frugé, and other families had settled within the borders of Duson's proposed city. Papers in the State Land Office indicate that Louis Lavergne may have lived in the area first. He did register his land ownership at a date prior to all others who came to own land in the proposed boundaries of the new town and within several miles adjacent to that plot of land. Numerous other pioneers including, but not limited to, Gus Fusilier, Franklin Reed, Stephen Martel, John Hugo McGee, Onezippe LeDoux, and Mentor Guillory, settled in the adjacent area. Duson's highly advertised city sale on September 12, 1894, brought more people of all races and nationalities to the future town of Eunice. Jews, Lebanese, Germans, Canadians, a few Orientals, and a Greek family saw opportunity in the new town and added their particular traditions to the cultural gumbo of the area. Streets had been graded and as soon as the sales were finalized, sounds of saws and hammers were heard. Christian Ruppert and the Goss Brothers were running their respective sawmills at full force to furnish lumber to meet the demand for houses and buildings. Carpenters flooded into the village knowing that work was readily available. George O'Brien and Stephen and Balthazar Martel were among these workers who tried to meet the settlers' needs for housing and business accommodations. It was said that the young city sprang up on the prairie like a mushroom.

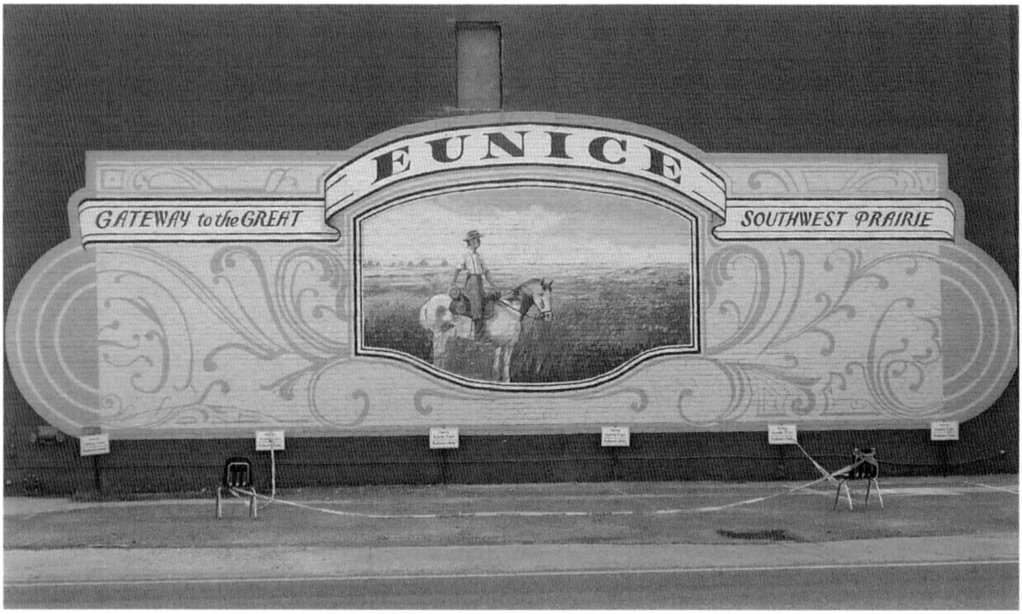

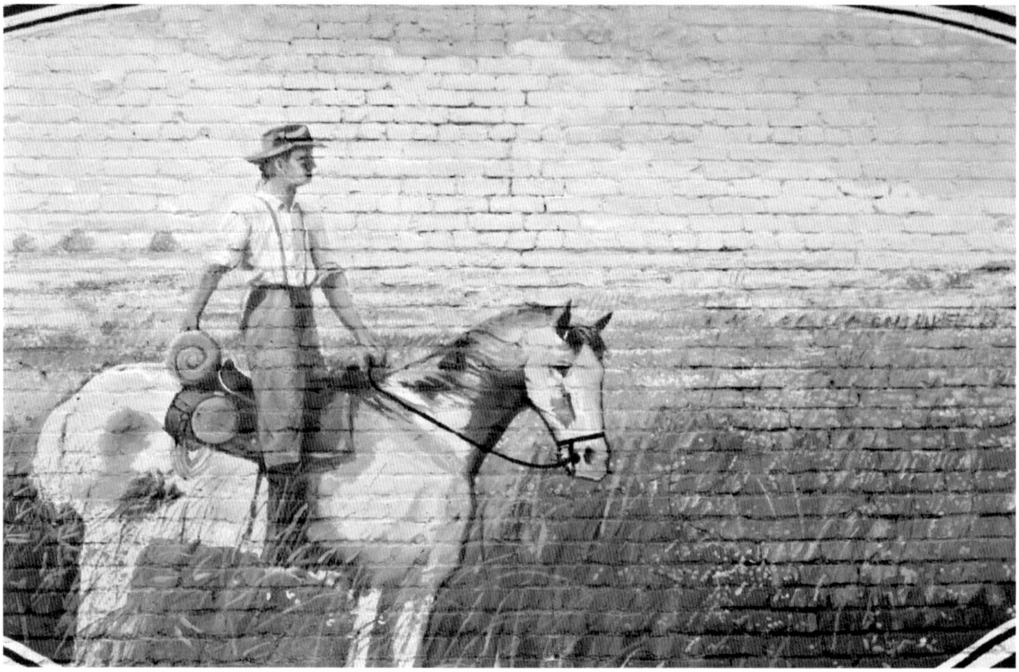

Gateway Mural
Robert Dafford of Lafayette, a prolific and successful historical muralist with over 350 large-scale works gracing structures in the United States, Canada, France, and Europe, was commissioned to depict the vast Cajun prairie. The old Ardoin Store building in downtown Eunice, which has a long unobstructed wall facing Highway 190, was selected for the painting with the purpose of boosting downtown development. A pioneer settler is shown looking out over the Cajun prairie where the *paille jaune* (yellow grass or straw) indicates a late fall or winter day. (Courtesy of Van Reed.)

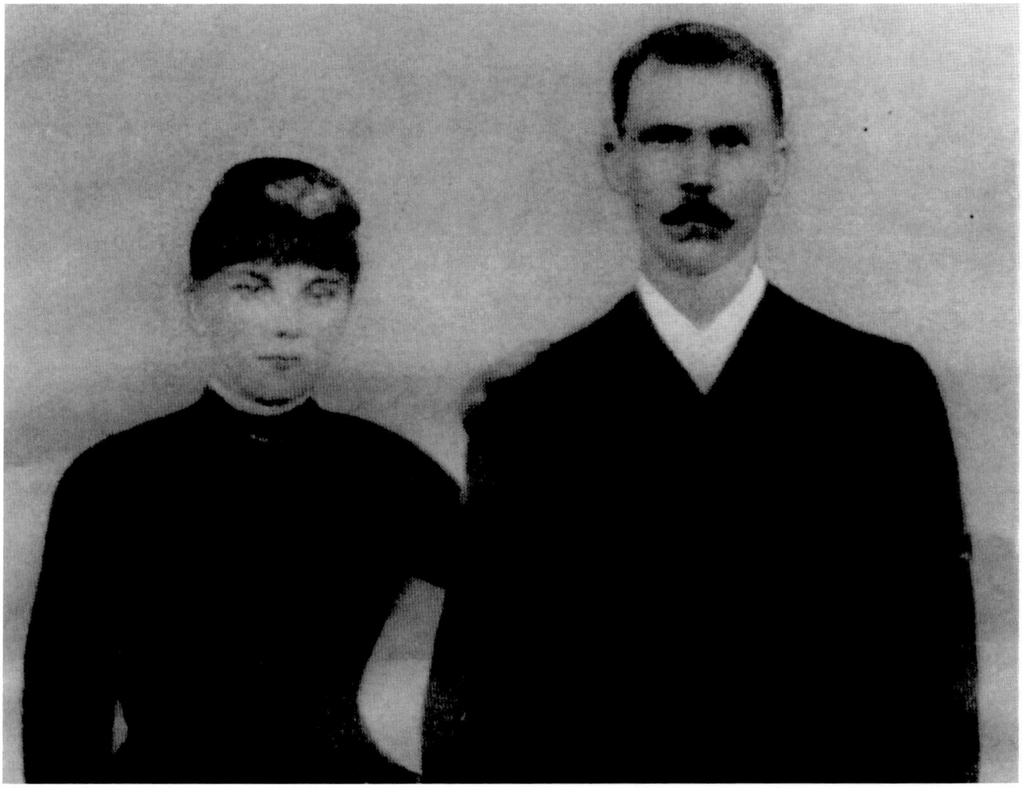

Eunice's First Merchant
Gustave Fusilier, married to Marie Louise Courville, operated a store and saloon in the Eunice area years before the town auction. Some believe that he, not Duson, was the actual founder of Eunice. Nevertheless, Fusilier was a driving force in the town's development. (Courtesy of authors' collection.)

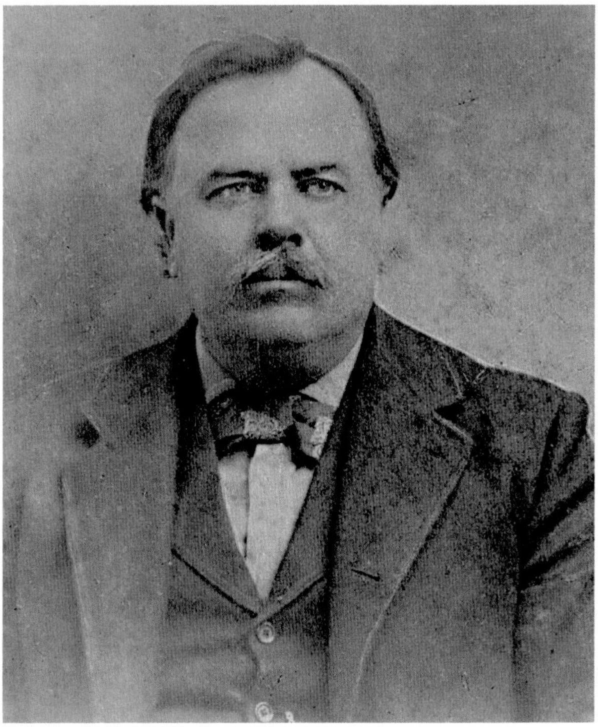

Eunice's Third Merchant
Theogene Reed built a mercantile on Park Avenue at Third Street. He was Eunice's first school board member, St. Anthony Parish trustee from 1908 to 1911 and 1920 to 1923, officer of the Catholic Cemetery Association, and fundraiser for the new church building. In his eulogy, Father Daull called Reed "one of our foremost citizens. . . ." (Courtesy of Dr. B. Rodney Reed.)

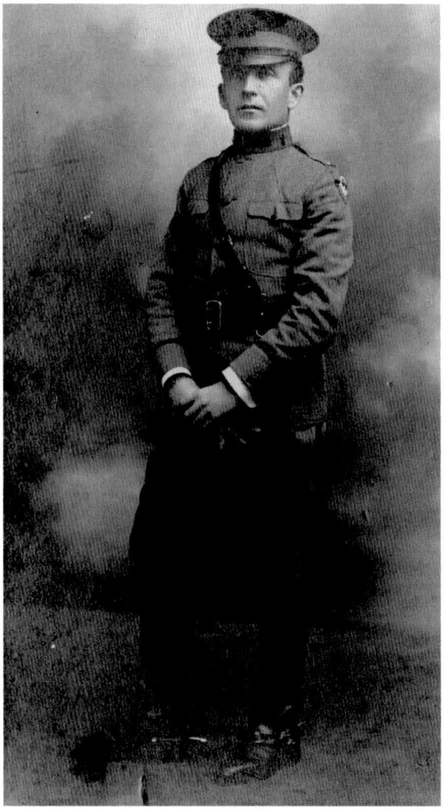

French Priest at Catholic Church

Fr. Celestin Marie Chambon-Grange was a native of Lyon, France, and served in the French military in North Africa, causing rumors that he was in the French Foreign Legion. The priest wrote a book entitled *In and Around the Cathedral,* about New Orleans's parishioners. He was the pastor at St. Anthony's Parish from 1910 to 1916. In World War I, he was a chaplain with the 113th Ammunition Train in the American Expeditionary Force in France. Appointed "Aide-de-Camp" to the Louisiana governor in 1952, he retired to St. Joseph Abbey in Covington. (Courtesy of St. Anthony Parish.)

An Educator

Dr. Gladys Peck (second from left), daughter of Charles and Amelia Andrews Peck, was principal at St. Edmund School, Louisiana state supervisor of business education in 1960, and donor of the Peck Building to the school. Pictured on her father's taxicab in 1921 were, from left to right, ? Gardiner, Gladys Peck, Marie Louise Gardiner, unidentified, unidentified, Aline Richard, Theo Richard, and four unidentified individuals. (Courtesy of Dr. B. Rodney Reed.)

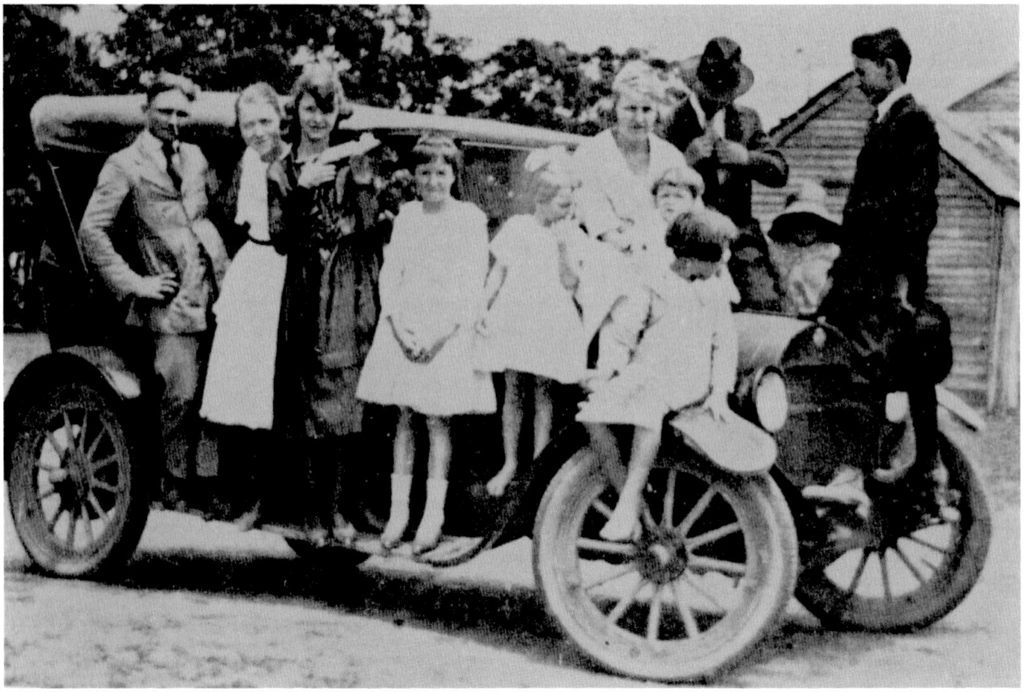

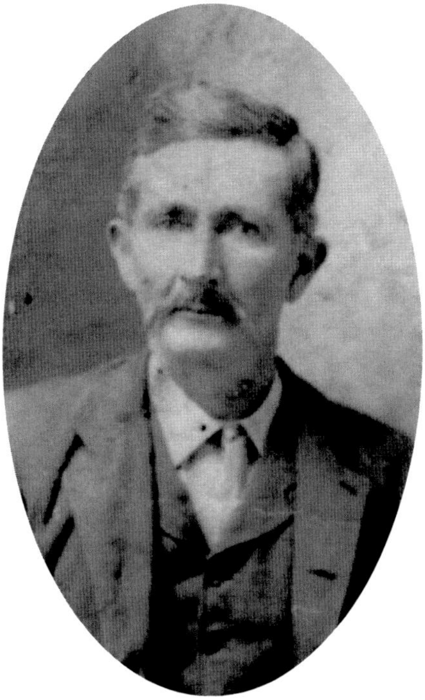

Well-Known Carpenter
Stephen Martel worked with his brother, Balthazar, and was responsible for building many of the original structures in the new town of Eunice. The Martels were some of the first settlers in the Patasa community. Stephen was married to Ann Elizabeth Moore. (Courtesy of Sylvia Martel Boyér.)

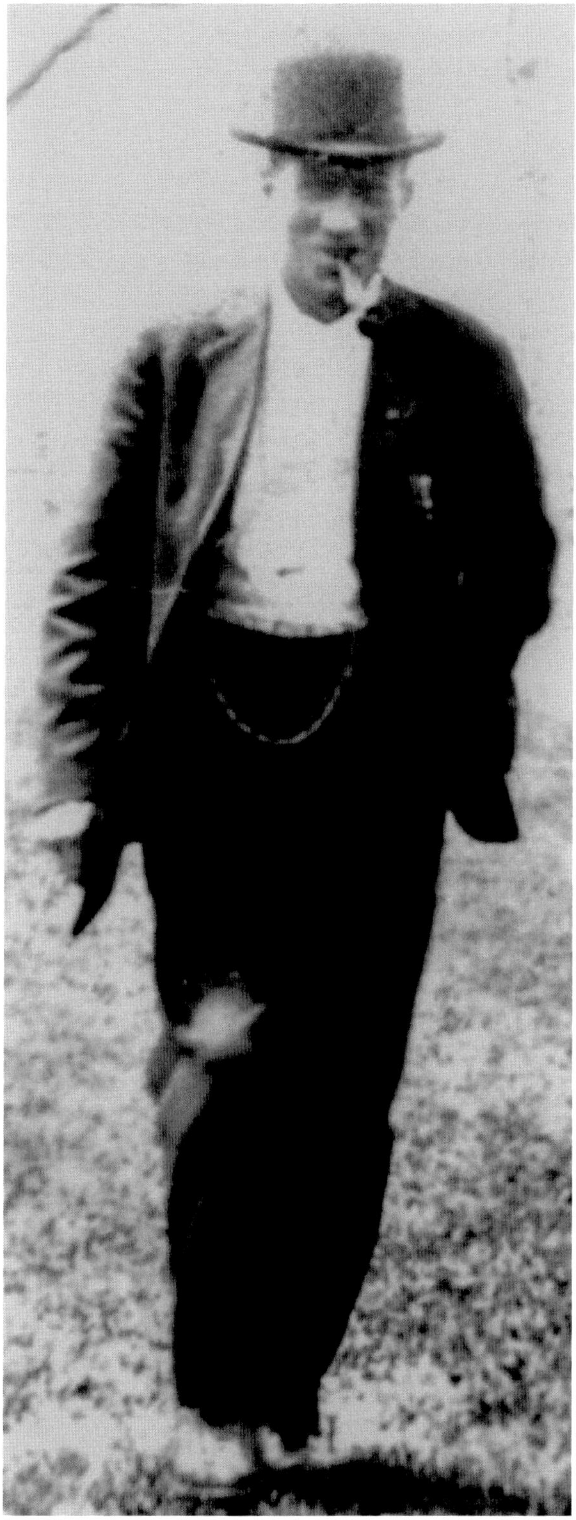

English Immigrant
George F. Bult, born in Essex, England, in 1874 to George and Lenae Milford Bult, arrived at Ellis Island from Southampton, England, aboard the ship *Berlin* in 1894. Making his way to Eunice where his brother, James, lived, Bult married Laura "Sallie" Sanders. He owned the large Eunice Red Dairy, which stretched from Park Avenue to Maple Avenue. Bult died at the age of 47. (Courtesy of Gary Bult.)

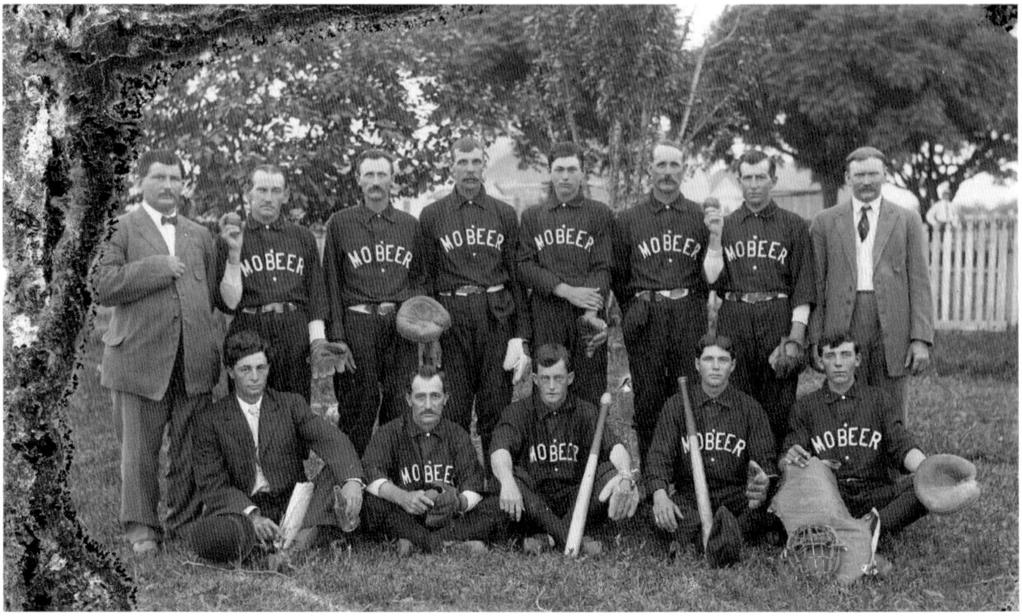

German Community Baseball Team
The Mo-Beer baseball team, composed of Germans from the Mowata community, provided sports entertainment for settlers. In this 1911 photograph, from left to right, were (first row) Walter Williams, Anthony "Tony" Bollich, Frank Brossart, Wentzel, and Joe Ohlenforst; (back row) Lorenz Zaunbrecher, Will Bollich, Ben Cramer, Albert LaFrantz, Ralph Schoney, Joseph Klausen, Frank Bollich, and Conrad Hensgens. (Courtesy of Alfred Bollich and BBHC.)

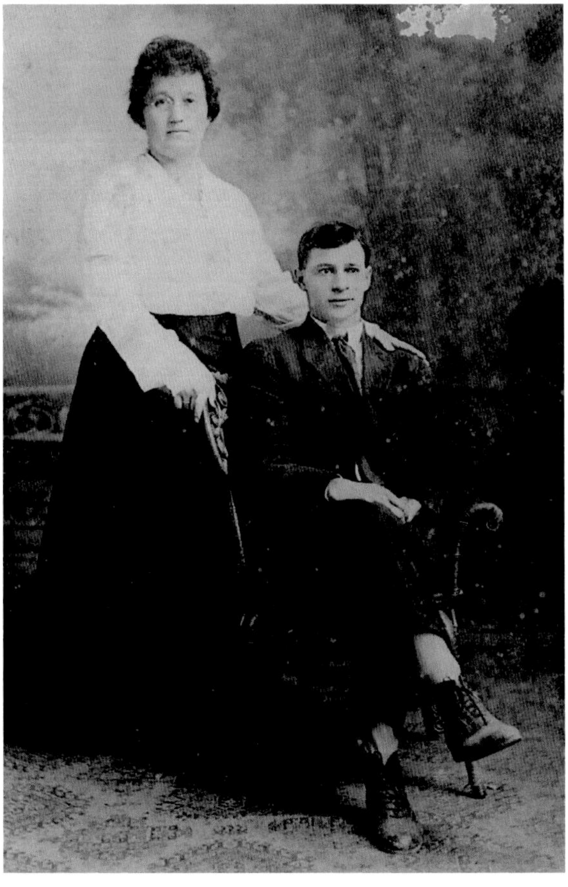

Knapp Shoe Salesman and Barber
Howard McManus, seated with wife Lucilla, was Henry Harrison and Colastie David McManus's son and a Knapp Shoes door-to-door salesman. He opened a barbershop, but sold it to D.J. "Cat" Doucet, legendary St. Landry Parish sheriff, who tried and hated barbering before being elected sheriff. (Courtesy of David and Patricia Darbonne McManus.)

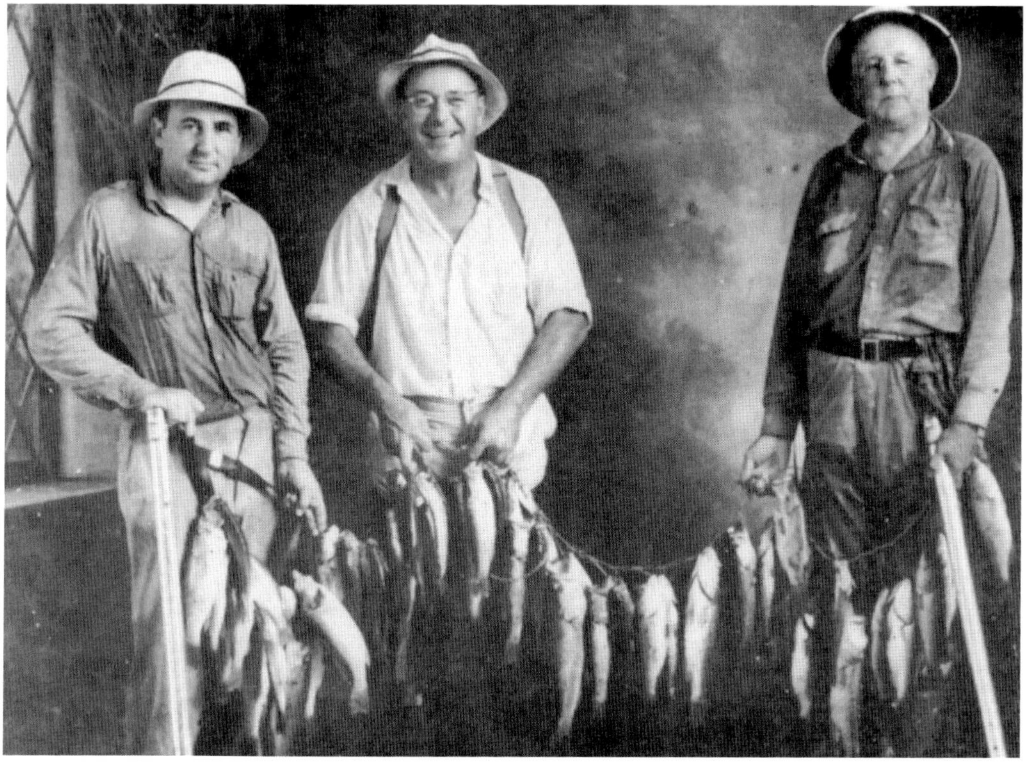

Progressive Mayor
Dudley Berwick, right, with Dr. Charles Lewis Jr., left, and Gerald Parrott, an avid outdoorsman and conservationist, was appointed state commissioner of conservation in 1920. Berwick came to Eunice in 1907 with his wife Martha "Mattie" Banyon. He was elected mayor in 1919, with a plan for cleaning up the town both behavior-wise with Sunday laws and health-wise with sanitary requirements. Mayor Berwick was credited with giving Eunice the slogan, "Eunice—A City with a Future." He began a street repair program and citizens remarked, "Berwick took the country out of Eunice." (Courtesy of authors' collection.)

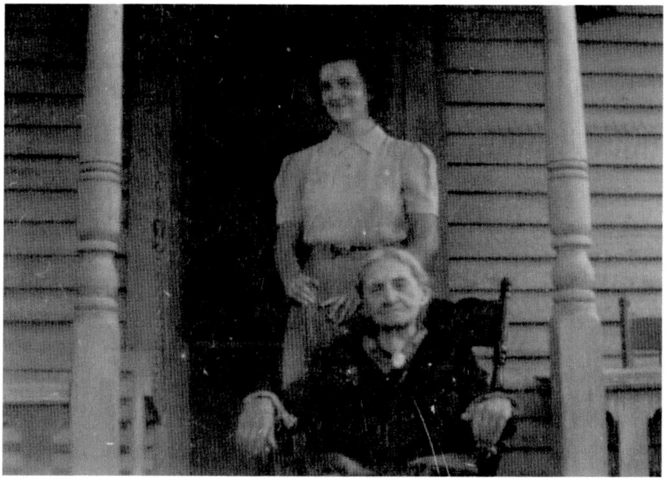

Independent Female
Mary Ann Young Prudhomme Rasberry Miller was born in 1853 to Stephen Madison and Marianne Richard Young/LeJeune. Independent and business-wise, Miller bought one of the first lots at Duson's auction. She built her home on Maple Avenue and later sold it to Dr. A.B. Childs, father of her niece, Wanda, standing behind her. Outliving three husbands, she died in 1943, leaving a legacy of female independence. (Courtesy of Wanda Childs Rense.)

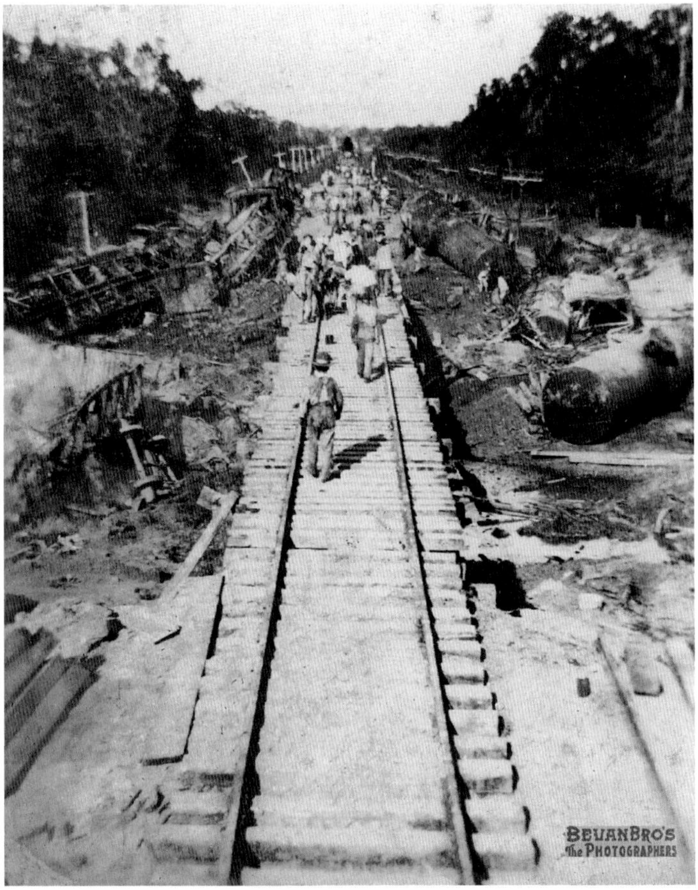

Train Wreck, Murder, and Mayhem
Auguste and Octave Thibodeaux, brothers who lived five miles south of Eunice near Bayou Mallet, had a longstanding dispute with the Southern Pacific Railroad over the question of a right-of-way through their property. Southern Pacific's Midland-to-Eunice branch train, the one Eunice's founder C.C. Duson had convinced the railway to construct so that buyers could travel to the Southwest Louisiana Land Company's auction of city lots in 1894, was targeted by the Thibodeaux men as encroaching on their land. They argued that the train caused their cattle to die because the engines ran over the beeves. The men had tried building a wire fence across the tracks, but that proved useless, so they threw switches and blocked rails to cause mayhem. Death and destruction resulted when a Southern Pacific passenger train wrecked on November 24, 1894, just about a month after the lots auction in the new town of Eunice. Some passengers transported the injured train engineer, Joseph Mauldin, to Eunice on a hand car. Hugh Geiger, the fireman, was killed when the switch lock was partially thrown and the rails were blocked with wooden blocks driven between rails. William Jackson, the brakeman, ran about four and a half miles to Eunice in 32 minutes to get a doctor. Dr. Joseph was dispatched to the wreck on a hand car, but the fireman was dead when he reached the scene. The Thibodeaux men were arrested and tried for murder in Judge Perrault's court. They were sentenced to Angola State Prison. But the Thibodeaux brothers' convictions were overturned by the Louisiana Supreme Court, which ordered them retried on perjury charges. They were convicted of perjury and sentenced to five years hard labor. It is likely that pictures of the men are not extant, but a photographer recorded the destruction of the train wreck in this image. (Courtesy of BBHC.)

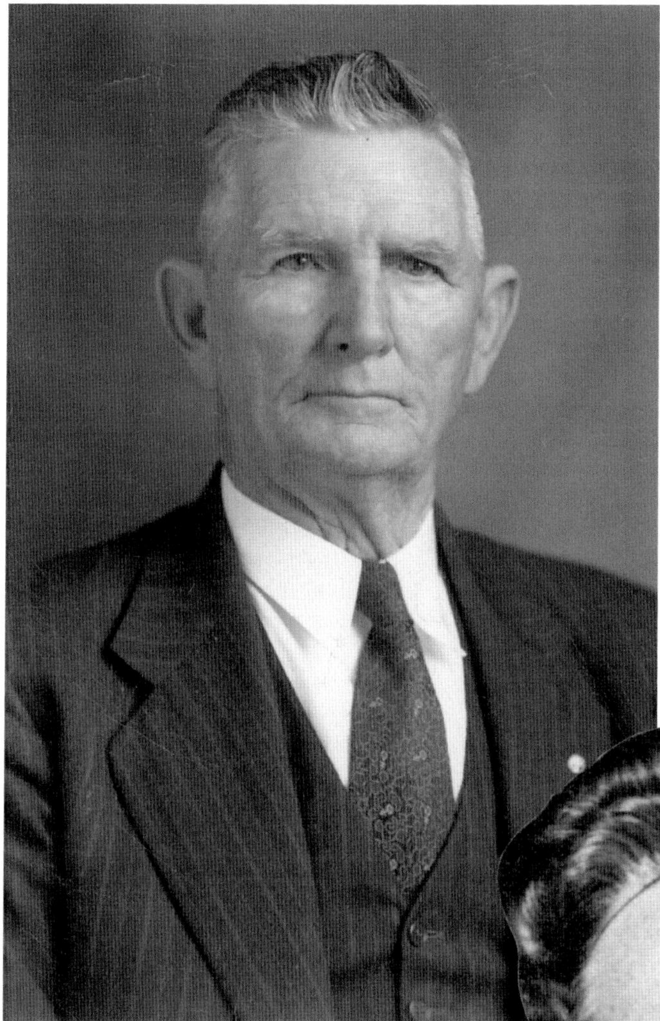

Sunday School Superintendent
Charles Jesse Sanders Sr. was 29 years old when he arrived with C.C. Duson, his real estate associate. Sanders and his wife Sallie Culberson participated in Masons, Eastern Star, and Woodmen of the World activities. He is remembered for serving over 25 years as Sunday school superintendent of the First Methodist Church. In 1941, Sanders's funeral drew an overflowing crowd to his beloved church. (Courtesy of William F. Sanders.)

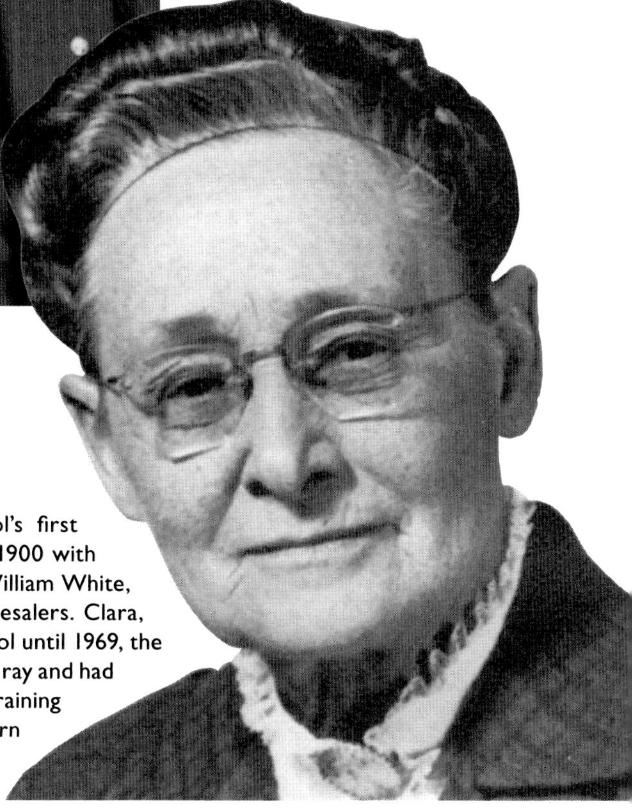

In First Graduation Class
Clara Carrell Gray was in Eunice High School's first graduation class of 1910. She came to Eunice in 1900 with her mother, Tommie Stell, and stepfather, John William White, a partner with Joe Lyman in Lyman-White Wholesalers. Clara, born in Texas in 1892, taught at Eunice High School until 1969, the year of her death. She married George A. "Gus" Gray and had two sons, one of whom was killed in 1944 while training as a Class 44E pilot. She was active in the Eastern Star and First Baptist Church. (Courtesy of Wilda Brunson Gregory.)

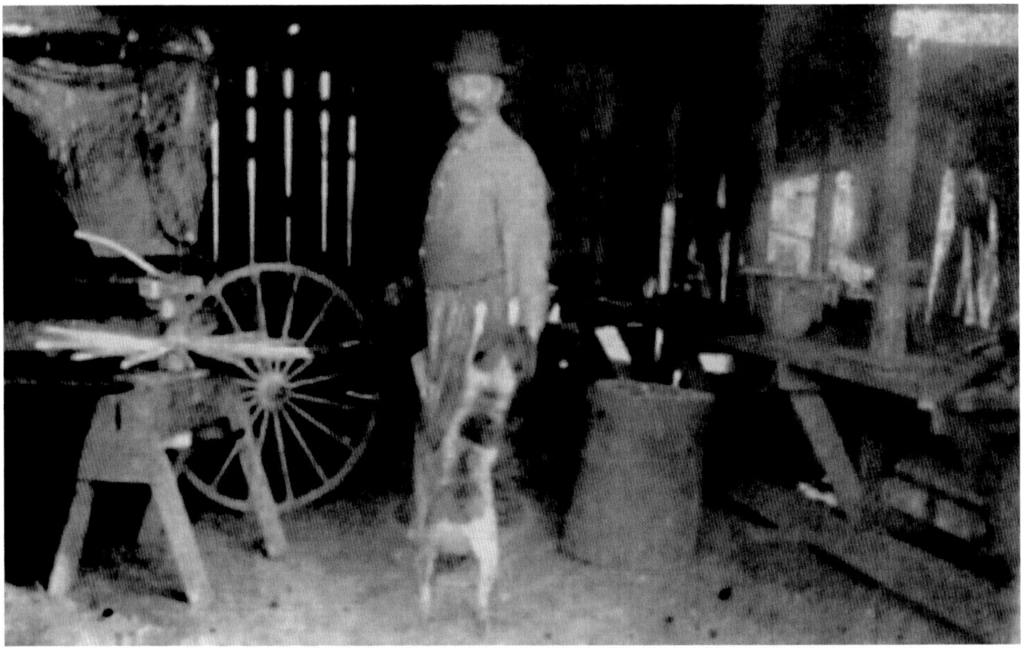

Early Blacksmith
Yves "Bebe" Savoy, son of Eloy Pierre Valcour Savoy, was a blacksmith. Married to Amelia Ardoin, they were parents of much-elected St. Landry Parish tax assessor Lennie Savoy. In the 1920s, Yves and his dog were photographed in his blacksmith shop, which was a popular gathering place for men of the community. (Courtesy of Lennie Parrott Buller.)

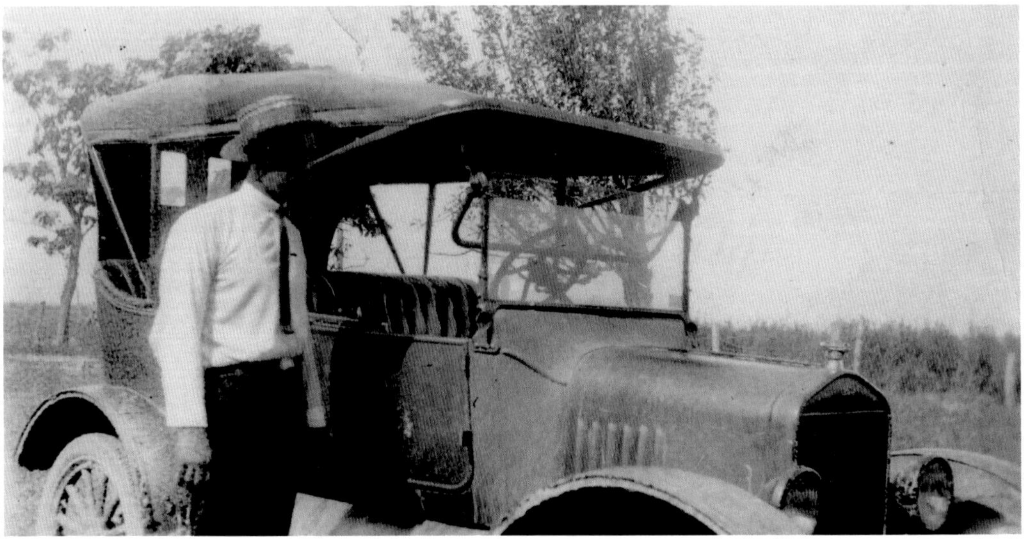

Respected Mechanic
Garnett A. Milner I. married Lillian Brunson in 1923. A respected mechanic who owned a garage/service station in Rayne and worked at Odom's Garage, he opened a motorcycle repair shop in the 1950s. Milner was the son of William and Millie Jane Tobey Milner of Ellis. (Courtesy of Audrey Clayton Milner.)

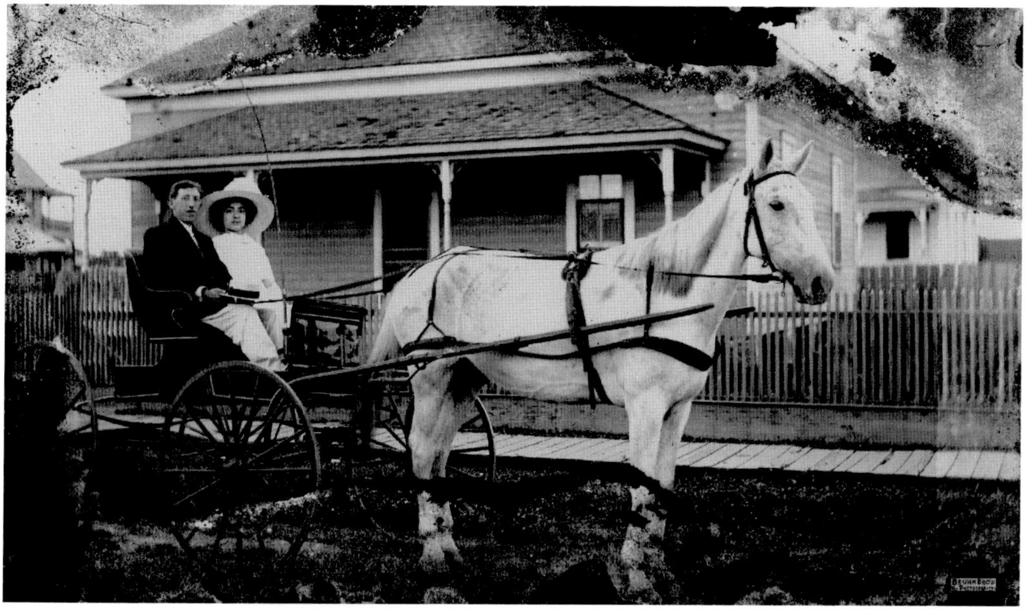

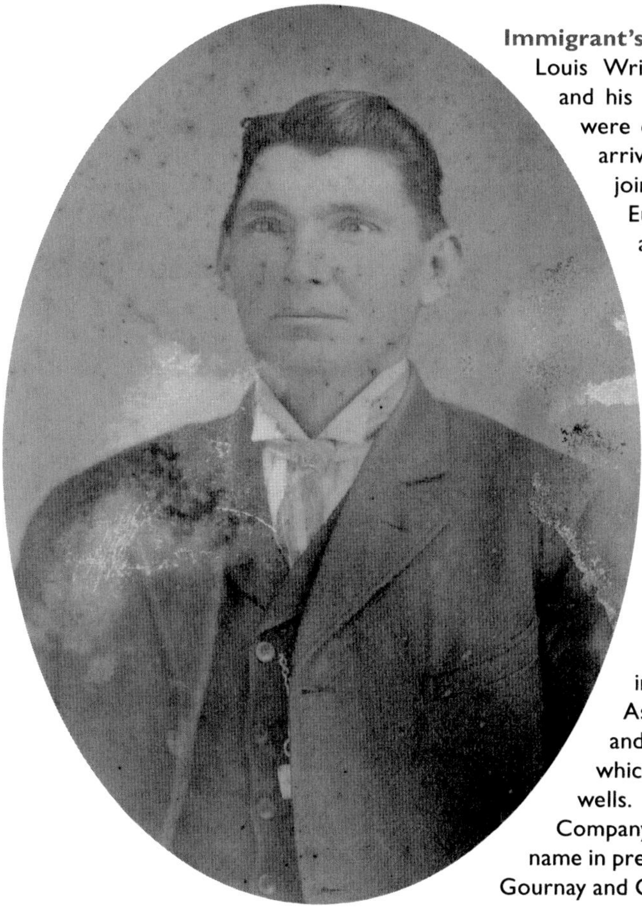

Immigrant's Clothing Store

Louis Wright, a native of Dembica, Austria, and his wife Sadie Kreinik, from Manhattan, were early settlers in the young town. He arrived in New York in 1900 and later joined a small core of Jewish citizens in Eunice. The couple was pictured on an afternoon drive in 1912. Wright opened Louis Wright's Store in 1911, where three generations of the family were managers for nearly 100 years. (Courtesy of BBHC.)

Blacksmith and Realtor

Sceavola A. Gournay was born in New Orleans in 1866. He married Armide Ardoin. A blacksmith who ventured into real estate, Gournay served on several boards of directors including the Eunice Homestead Association, the Eunice State Bank, and the Eunice Deep Well Company, which was formed to drill farm irrigation wells. He also owned Gournay Motor Company. A subdivision bears the Gournay name in present-day Eunice. (Courtesy of Harold Gournay and Gloria Wilkins Byars.)

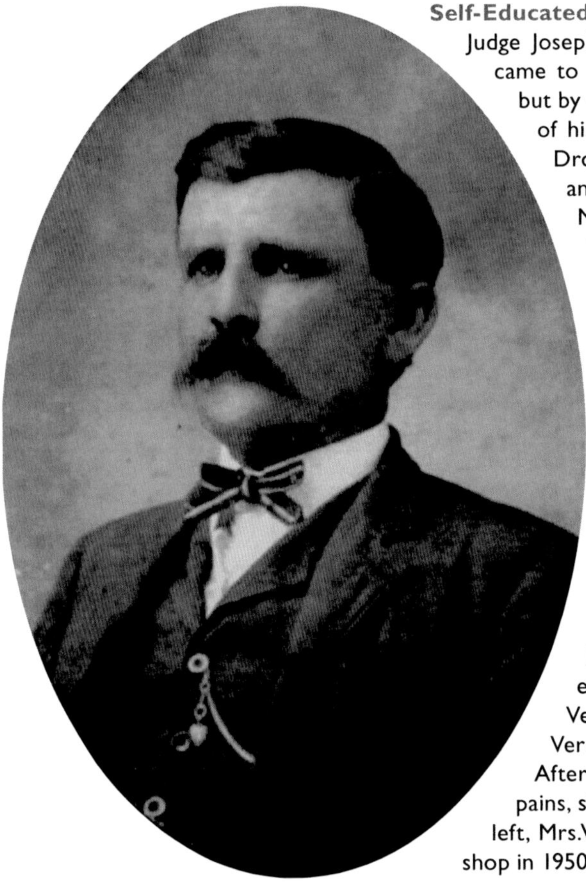

Self-Educated Judge

Judge Joseph McGee, a St. Landry Parish magistrate, came to his position not by education or training, but by determination. McGee, the first generation of his family born in America, was the son of Droheda, Ireland, native John Hugo McGee and his Louisiana-born wife, Anastasie Savoie. McGee was self-taught, yet he passed the bar exam. He married Domecile Miller, whose uncle was the infamous Civil War "jayhawker," Ozemé Carrier. (Courtesy of Charlie Thibodeaux.)

Opened a Hat Shop

Mari Camelia O'Brien Verret, the daughter of J. Edward and Caroline Mendoza O'Brien, came during the town's infant days. As a very young lady, she opened her millinery shop on Park Avenue. For decades, nearly every female living in the city entered her shop to see her exquisite handmade hats or to watch Mrs. Verret construct them. Married to Achille Verret, she had two daughters and three sons. After being rushed to the hospital with chest pains, she died at the age of 50. Pictured third from left, Mrs.Verret posed with unidentified clerks in her shop in 1950. (Courtesy of Peter Vidrine.)

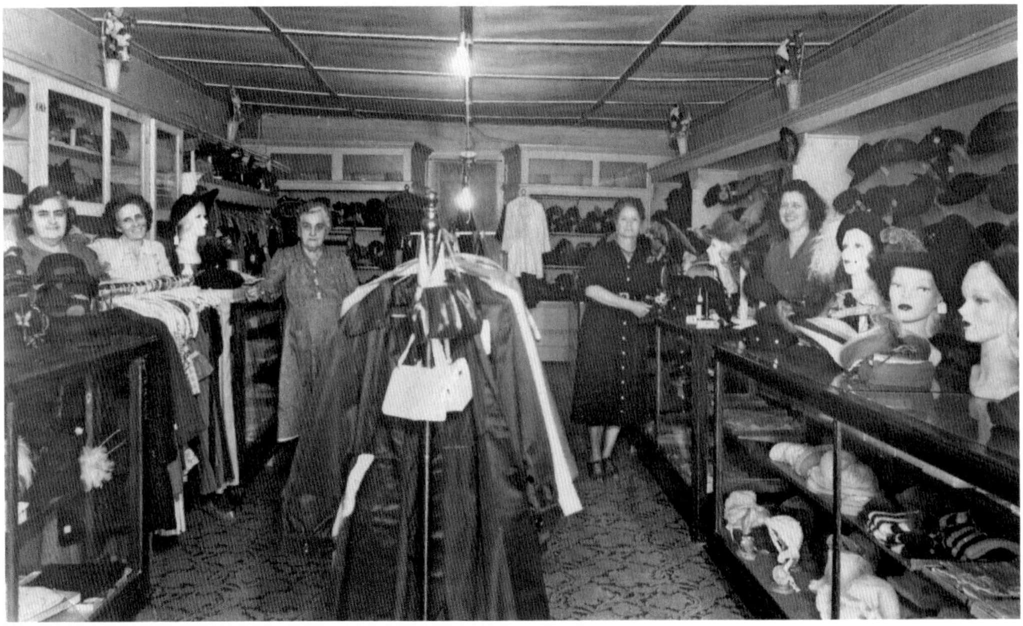

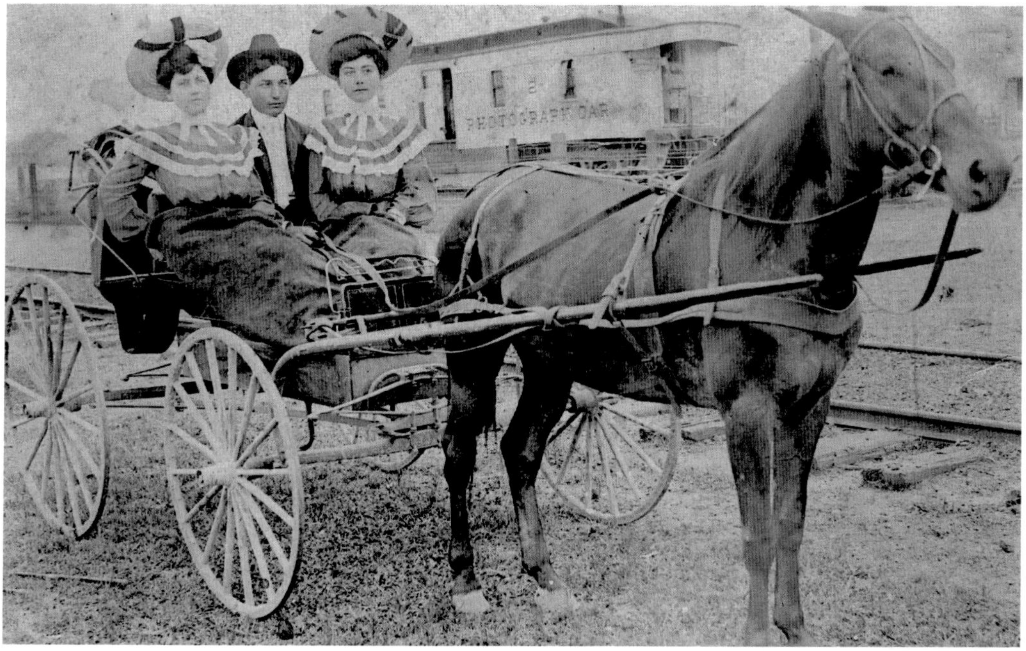

Bayou Drowning

Sidney Sittig, center, with his wife, Julia Goss Sittig, left, and his sister, right, Maud Sittig Goss, wife of Julia's brother, John Goss, waited to be photographed at McGee's photographic railroad car. In 1917, Sydney, aged 37, drowned when the logs he was hauling for Newell Lumber Company toppled into Bayou de Cannes near Jelk's Mill. Unable to swim, Sittig tried to ride a mule as it swam across the bayou, but it became entangled in debris. Rumors said Sittig carried an unrecovered payroll. His business partner ran off with the wagon leaving Julia without support for her five children, so she opened a boardinghouse. (Courtesy of Pat Sittig Bollich.)

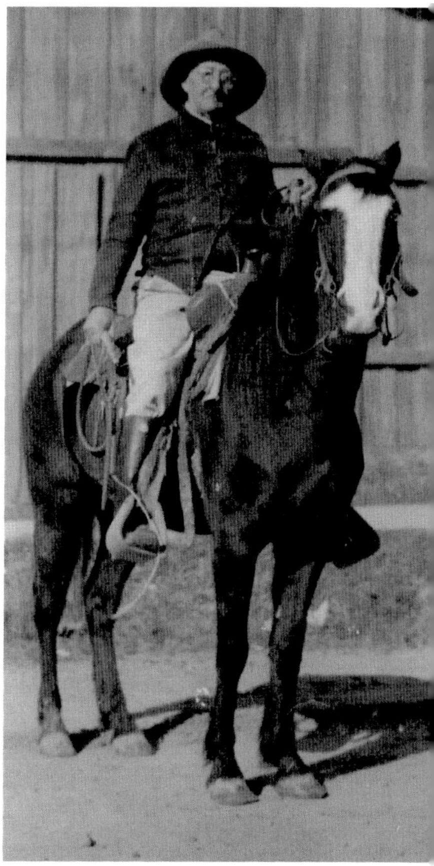

Home on the Prairie

Alexander "Nonc Alec" Miller lived on the southwestern Louisiana prairie before the founding of Eunice. His family was one with the oldest roots in the prairie soil. Born in 1861 to Ursan Miller, he was educated at home by an itinerant teacher, Julian Provant, a French expatriate. He married Alida Frugé in 1888. They had three children, but a case of shingles caused Alida's death in 1894. Miller's second wife, Bertha Guillory, was the mother of A.C. Miller Sr. "Nonc Alec" acquired his land, about 1,300 acres at one time, from homestead grants. On that acreage, he built his own home from hand-hewn cypress lumber and lived there for 44 years. A kindly gentleman, he entertained children by "popping his whip" when children called to him to do so as he rode his favorite horse into town. Although three railroads, the Missouri Pacific, the Rock Island, and the Texas Pacific, cut through his land, he never objected to anything that meant progress for Eunice and its trade area. (Courtesy of Joseph "Joe" and Beverly Mudd Miller.)

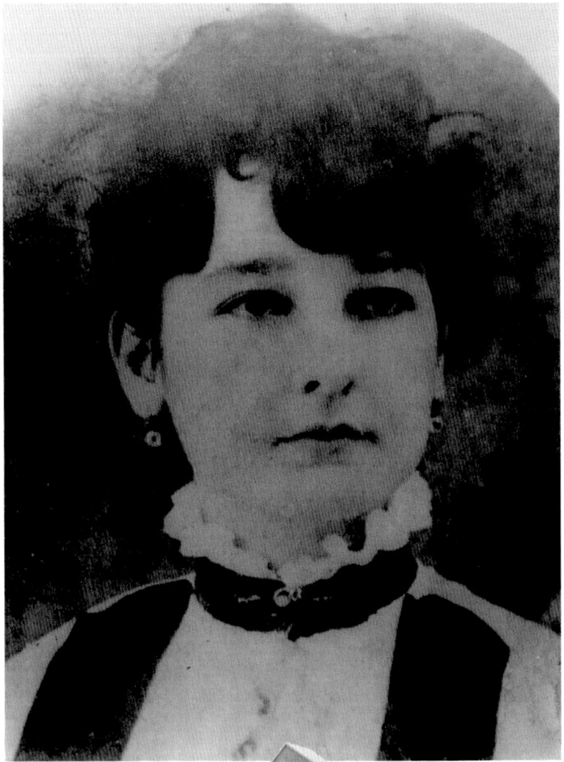

Dance Hall Owner
Cora Stagg Parrott Long, daughter of Confederate captain Louis and Laure Lise LaTour Stagg, was born in 1868 near Ville Platte. With her husband William H. Parrott, she opened a hotel and dance hall in the new town on the location of the Mayer Hotel in 1894. When Parrott died in 1902, Cora continued operating both of her businesses. She married John Long in 1930 and died nine years later. (Courtesy of Lennie Parrott Buller.)

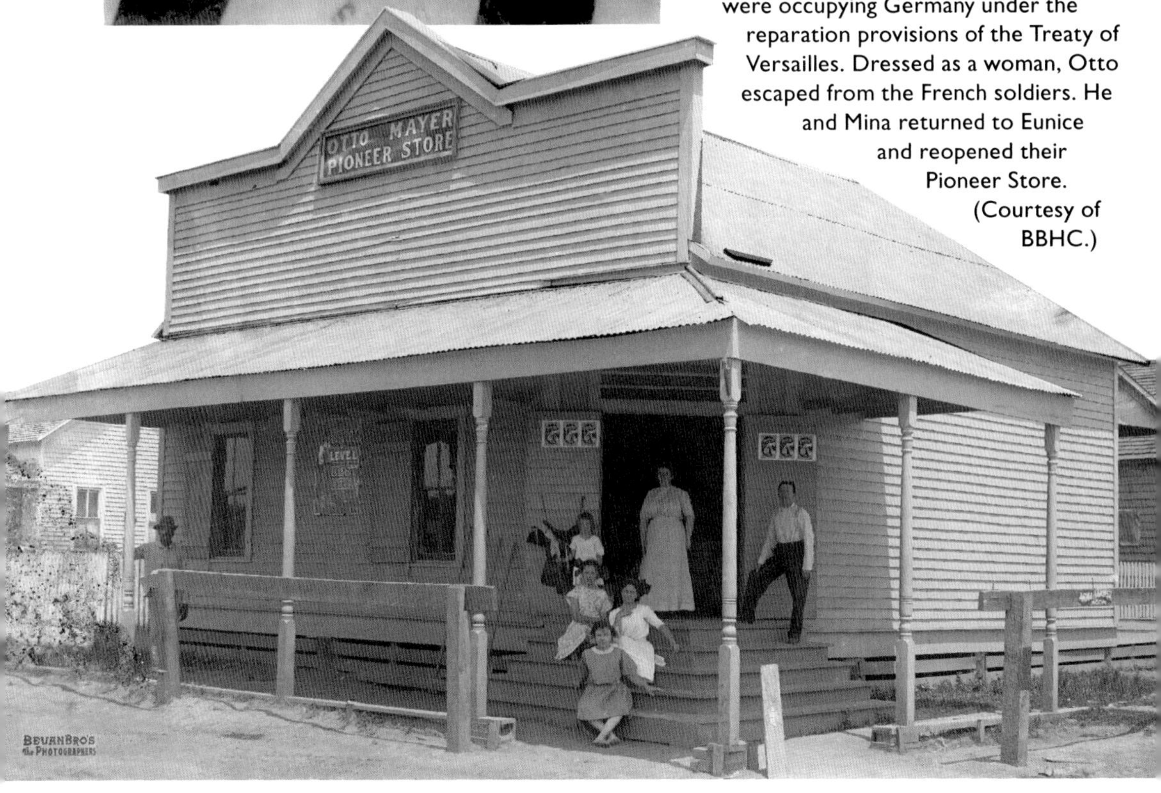

Escaped from Germany
Otto Mayer immigrated to New Orleans from Germany in 1899 when he was 22 years old. He married Mina Feitel in Acadia Parish before they moved to Eunice to establish a sawmill and lumber business that he sold to Dudley Berwick about 1907. After World War I, the couple went to Germany to settle his father's estate, but they were held under house arrest in his father's building by French troops who were occupying Germany under the reparation provisions of the Treaty of Versailles. Dressed as a woman, Otto escaped from the French soldiers. He and Mina returned to Eunice and reopened their Pioneer Store. (Courtesy of BBHC.)

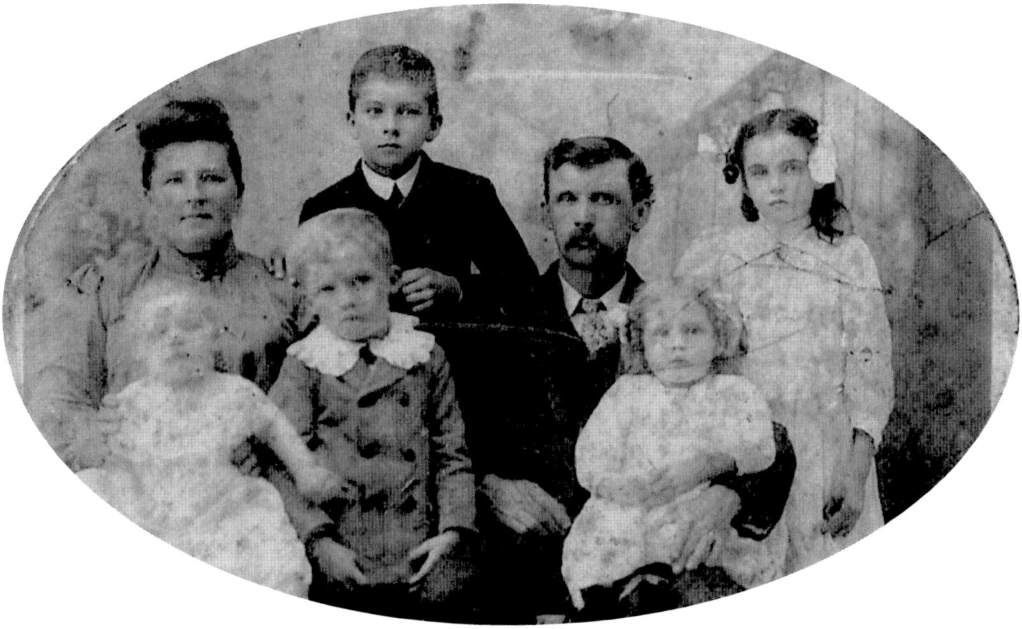

A Colorful Character

Judge Otha Key "OK" Brunson, born in 1867 in Edgefield, South Carolina, came in a wagon train with his parents James Oscar and Emily Frances "Fanny" Burton Brunson after the Civil War. He married Mary Eva, daughter of Houston and Mary Elizabeth Hopkins Young, in 1893. A period newspaper article described their wedding and also stated that "Brunson is a pushing, energetic young man who made good the old saying 'get your cage ready before you catch the bird,' as he has built his house and furnished it complete to receive his bride." Described as "a colorful character," the judge was a deacon at First Baptist Church, served on the city council for a two-year term from 1921 to 1923, and was one of the founders of St. Louis Cemetery. Apparently, Brunson and his wife enjoyed entertaining young people as the same newspaper reported a year later that "A ball that night after a picnic in the woods at the schoolhouse was held at Mr. Andrepont's and a sociable at Otha Brunson's, which the young folks report as a pleasant ending to the picnic." The judge wrote that he never traveled across the prairie without carrying a pistol because gangs of thugs and outlaws roamed the area. He described seeing cattle skinned alive and left to die by these gangs. Prior to becoming the city magistrate, Brunson was a self-employed surveyor and notary. The Brunson family posed together in 1904. Standing, left to right, were (back row) James Houston and Lillian. Seated, Mary Eva Young Brunson holding Otha Key Jr., Hugh Gordon (standing), and Judge Brunson, seated, with Fanny on his lap. (Courtesy of Judge and Mrs. Hugh E. Brunson.)

Businessman

Samuel "Sam" McManus was born in 1874 in Prudhomme City. McManus married Alice Eleanor Merritt. He owned stores at the Light 'N Tie community and other enterprises in Eunice. A leader in establishing the Acadia Baptist Academy, he served on the city council in 1922 and 1925. Along with Judge Otha Key Brunson and a Mr. Oliver, McManus established St. Louis Cemetery. (Courtesy of Myrtis Smith and Bob Butler.)

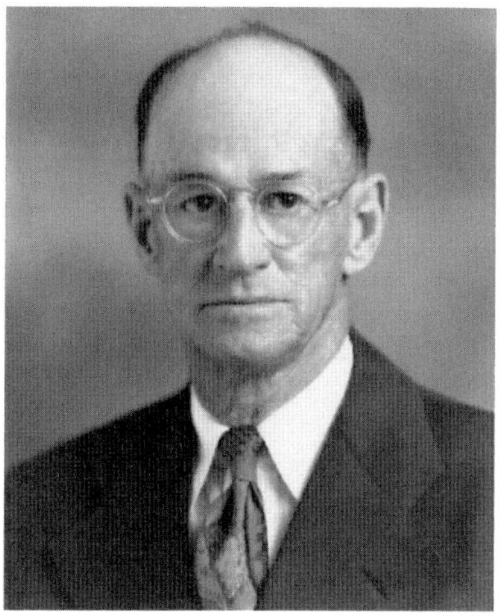

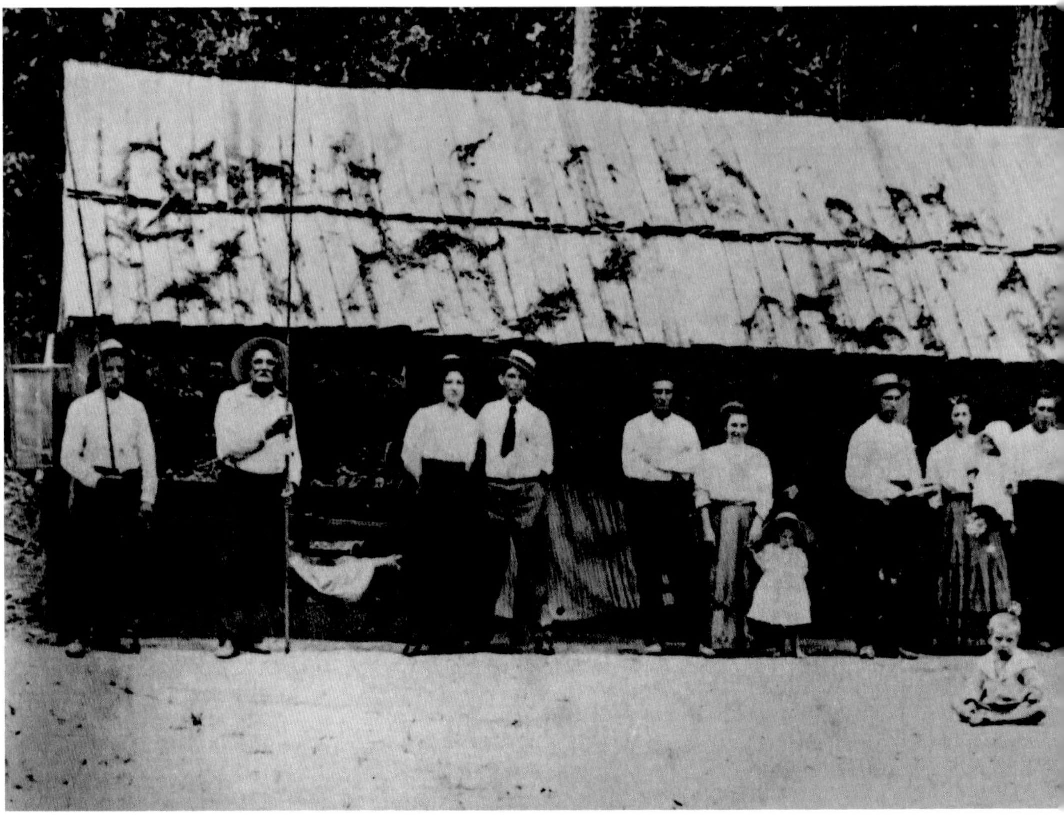

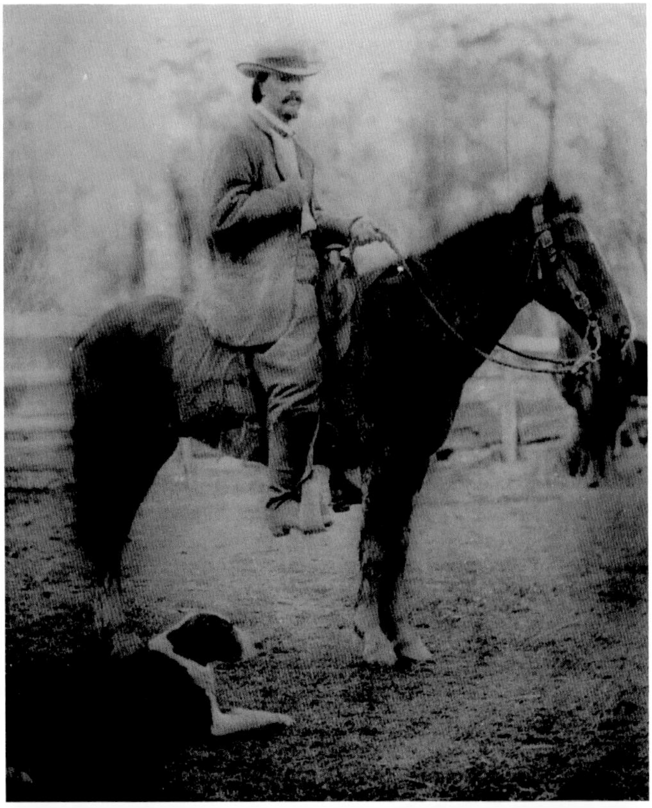

A Noted "Jayhawker"
Onezippe "Papa Blanc" LeDoux, an early prairie settler who attended Duson's town auction, was claimed by his grandson in his book, *Cowboy Tales*, to have been a "noted Jayhawker" during the Civil War. After the war, LeDoux was a respected resident who fathered a large family. (Courtesy of Ray and Audrey Biessenberger.)

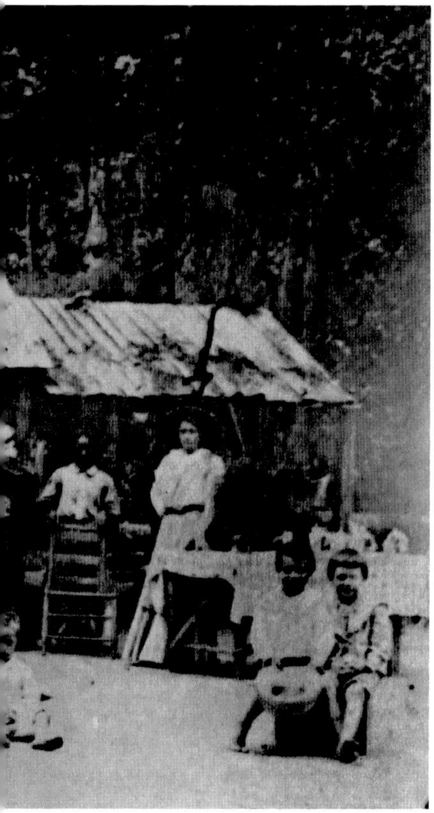

At Bayou Blue Camp

Camps dotted the stream banks where residents spent carefree weekends fishing. The Mentor Guillory family posed in 1908 at his camp on Bayou Blue, north of Eunice. From left to right are (standing) Mentor, ? Fuselier, Claude and Regina Keller, Adius Guillory, ? and Bertha Guillory, Frank and Marceline Fusilier and Carrie, Omar "Black" and Lucille Guillory, Genevieve Duplechain Guillory who was Mentor's first wife, the cook and Lydia Guillory Bergeaux. In the foreground, seated left to right, are Francis "Brother" Guillory and Osman Fuselier. Seated on a log are Stewart Rozas and Paul Fuselier. Mentor Guillory served in the 2nd Louisiana Reserve Corps Company B, which conducted raids against Civil War Jayhawkers. He died at 90 years of age. (Courtesy of Ann Rozas Frugé.)

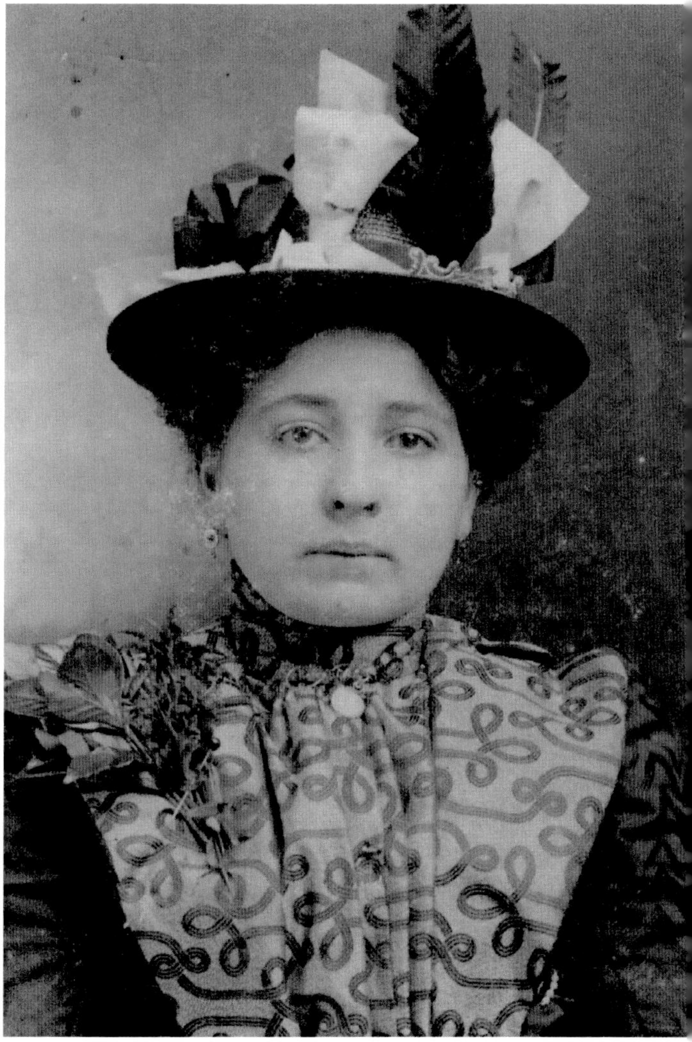

Bought Duson's Mansion

Aureline Roi Bergeron, a Canadian, married Joseph Bergeron and moved to Eunice where her husband, an associate of C.C. Duson, had purchased the first lot at the city auction. Having 12 children, the Bergerons bought the Duson's mansion to accommodate their family. (Courtesy of Marty Bergeron Dupuis and Lane Bergeron Oliver.)

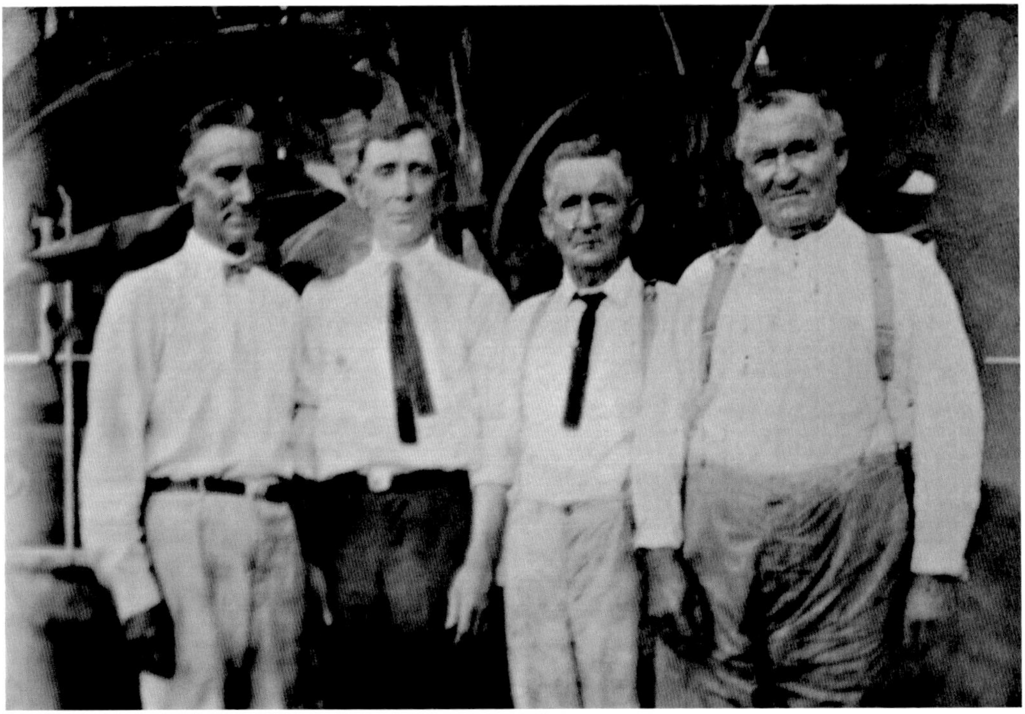

A Noble Family

At a Chachere family reunion in 1931 in the Prudhomme community were, left to right, Gaines, Aaron Marie, Theodosius Jr. and Jackson "Buddy" Chachere, all descendants of Louis Chachere, the progenitor of the Chachere family in Louisiana. He arrived at the *Poste des Opelousas* during "The Reign of Terror" in France. Rumors are that he was of noble blood, and had changed his name to Louis in honor of King Louis XVI and to Chachere from Charette. Whether noble or not, the Chachere clan was part of the political and medical elite of this area. (Courtesy of Fr. Paul Thibodeaux.)

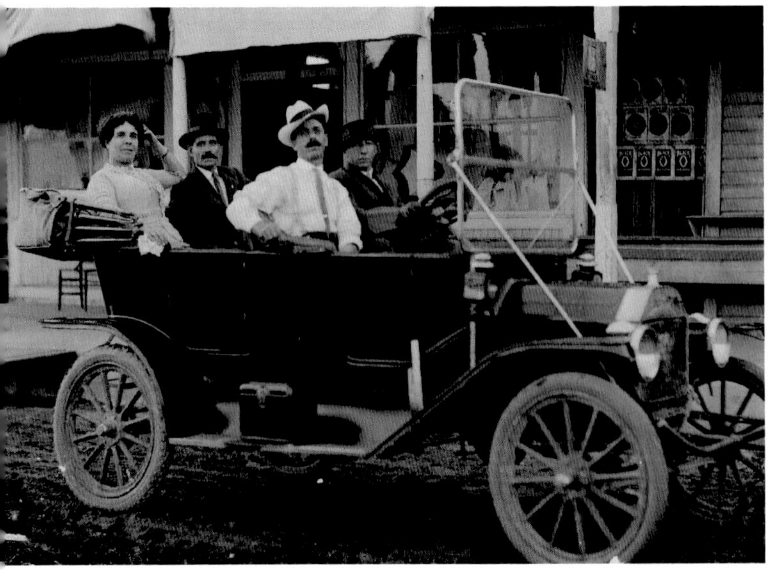

Lebanese Immigrants

The Nacol and Moosa family, immigrants from Lebanon, left their homeland in 1893 because Christians were being persecuted there. They joined into the community by their ownership of several businesses and their numerous civic activities. Pictured are some of Eunice's "firsts"—first garage owner, Theophile Moosa, driver; first auto dealer, Forest J. Nacol, front seat passenger; first volunteer fire chief, Katar Moosa, right back passenger; and first millinery shop owner, Kitty Nacol Moosa, left back. (Courtesy of BBHC.)

CHAPTER THREE

Unique and Colorful Citizens

From its earliest days, Eunice was known as a progressive town. In the 1920s, Mayor Dudley Berwick coined the phrase, "Eunice—a City with a Future" to describe the community's cutting-edge combination of natural resources and forward-looking people. Eunice has always been a beautiful city, from the large oaks that line the Park Avenue boulevard to the golden rice fields or prairie grasses that surround the city. It has been made more attractive by the efforts of its residents, civic organizations, churches, and city administrations. In 1967, library board members, particularly Matt Vernon, Mayor Moosa, and Sophie Wright, worked to obtain a modern building for the Eunice Public Library. City firefighters staff the Central Fire Station in mid-city, providing protection for the residents. African American leaders such as Jonas Mason and Jimmie E. Edwards have contributed to the city's well-being in their chosen fields. Former mayor Curtis Joubert, Charles Seale, and a cadre of volunteers worked in the 1980s to restore the Liberty Theater, to have it listed on the National Register of Historic Places, and to establish the weekly *Live Cajun Music Radio Show* to be held there. They also were instrumental in convincing the United States National Park Service to establish the Jean Lafitte Acadian Culture Center on Park Avenue. The family-oriented rural Mardi Gras parade led by *Le Capitaine* Pat Frey provides color and Cajun culture for residents and visitors alike. Whether they are pipeliners, missionaries, musicians, or pageant contestants, Eunice citizens are enthusiastic advocates for the city. Populated by fun-seeking, yet hardworking people, Eunice has come a long way since 1894, and the same spirit of progress and pride that moved the town forward since its earliest days is still evident. The common denominator of Eunice's success has been the character of its unique, colorful, and progressive people, since no town is any better than its people.

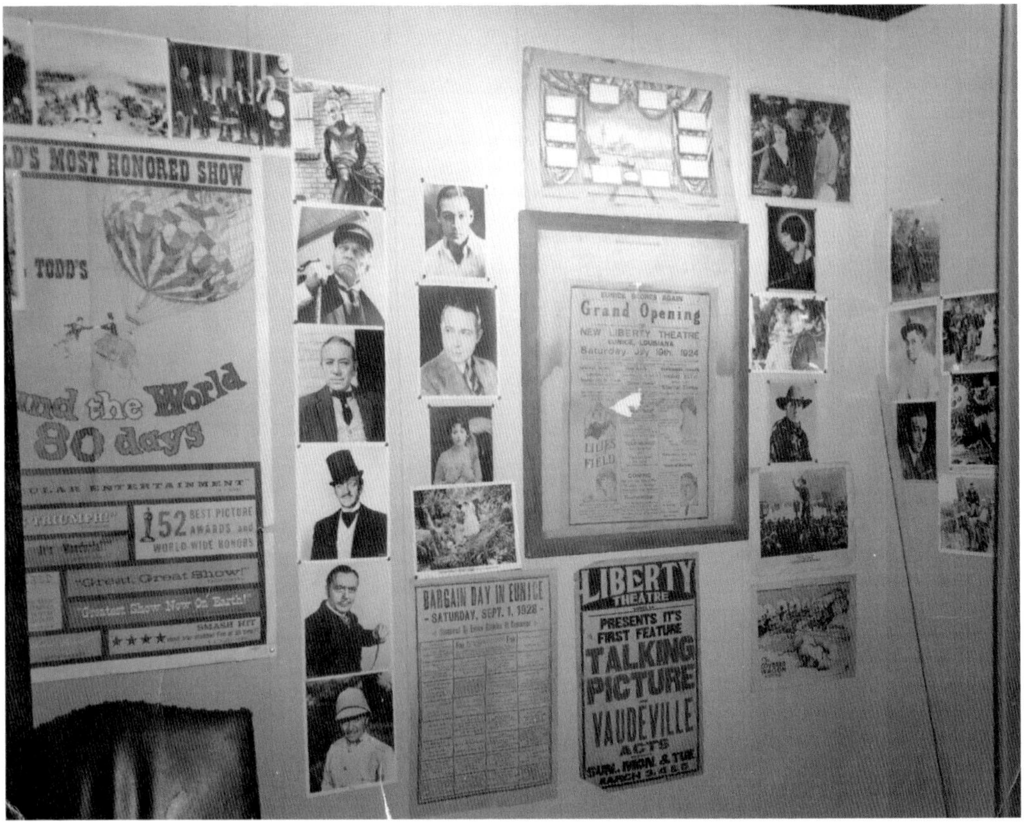

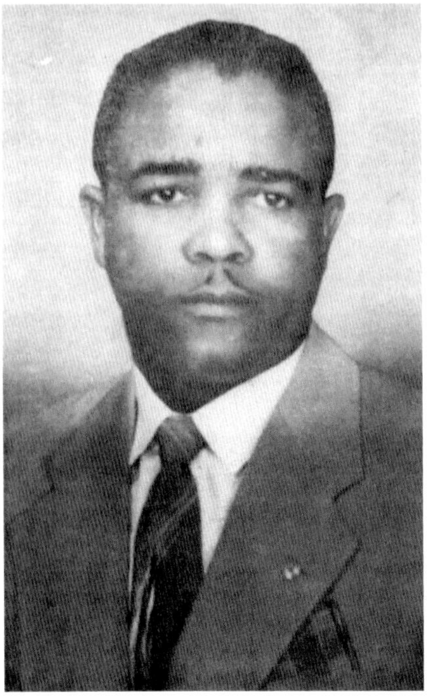

Liberty Theater Office Sign

The fun-loving nature of the citizens of Eunice was evident upon entering the business office of the Liberty Theater. Posters proclaimed "talking pictures" and coming attractions. Famous movie actors' portraits adorned the walls from 1924 until the 1980s. One of the few sources of entertainment, the theater was also a place where friendships were made and hearts were broken. (Courtesy of the authors' collection.)

African American Educator

Jonas E. Mason was instrumental in the progress of African American education. As principal of the all-black Charles Drew High School in 1951, he initiated "Youth Tutoring Youth," a program for the academically challenged, which paired them with classmate tutors who were more adjusted to school. As a Roman Catholic deacon, Mason organized the Deanery Conference at St. Anthony's in 1981. With Louise Guillory, who was administrator of Moosa Memorial Hospital, he cofounded the Charismatic Prayer group. Mason also sat on the board of directors of First National Bank in 1975. (Courtesy of Rev. James Edwards.)

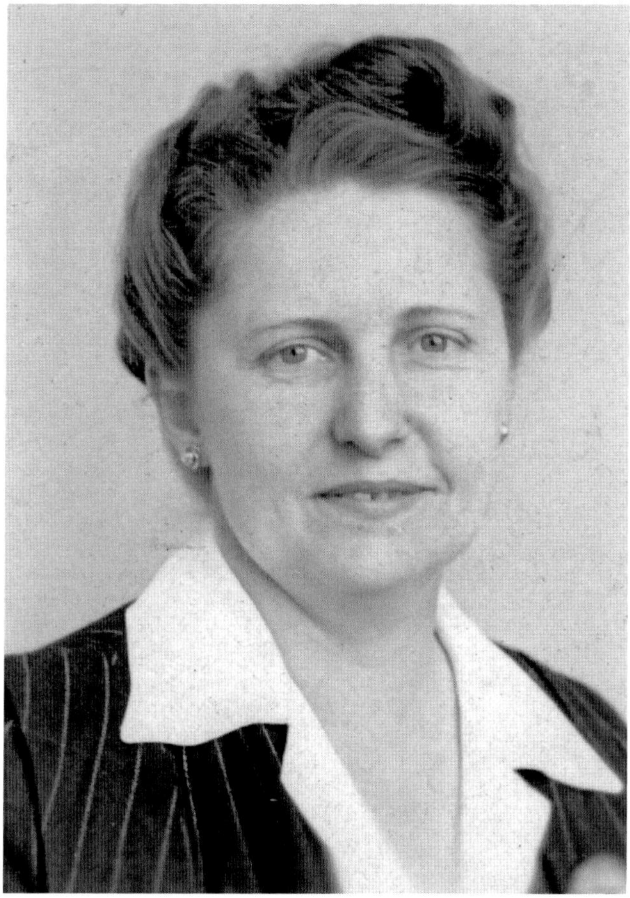

Elementary Teacher

Alice Foster Cottrell, born in 1912 in Morrow, Louisiana, to Clifton and Mary Simpson Foster, married Wesley Cottrell and was widowed early. While teaching, Cottrell received a grant to study in France. She was a member of First Methodist Church where she served faithfully for years in various leadership positions. Cottrell joined the Daughters of the American Revolution where her interest in genealogy was shared. (Courtesy of Joyce Thibodeaux.)

Medical Missionary

Sr. Isidora Bollich, nee Edna Bollich, of the religious community Medical Mission Sisters, spent the years from 1961 through 1972 as the administrator of the Leprosy Hospital in Ghana, West Africa. She is pictured with unidentified patients who brought her a native snake. Sr. Isidora is on the far right. (Courtesy of Hilda Courville Bollich.)

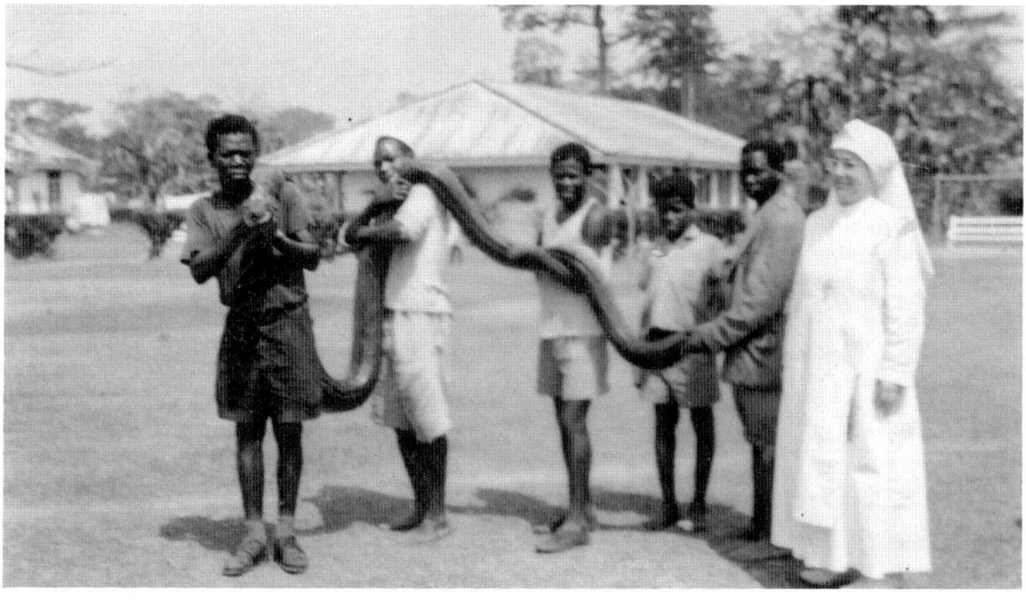

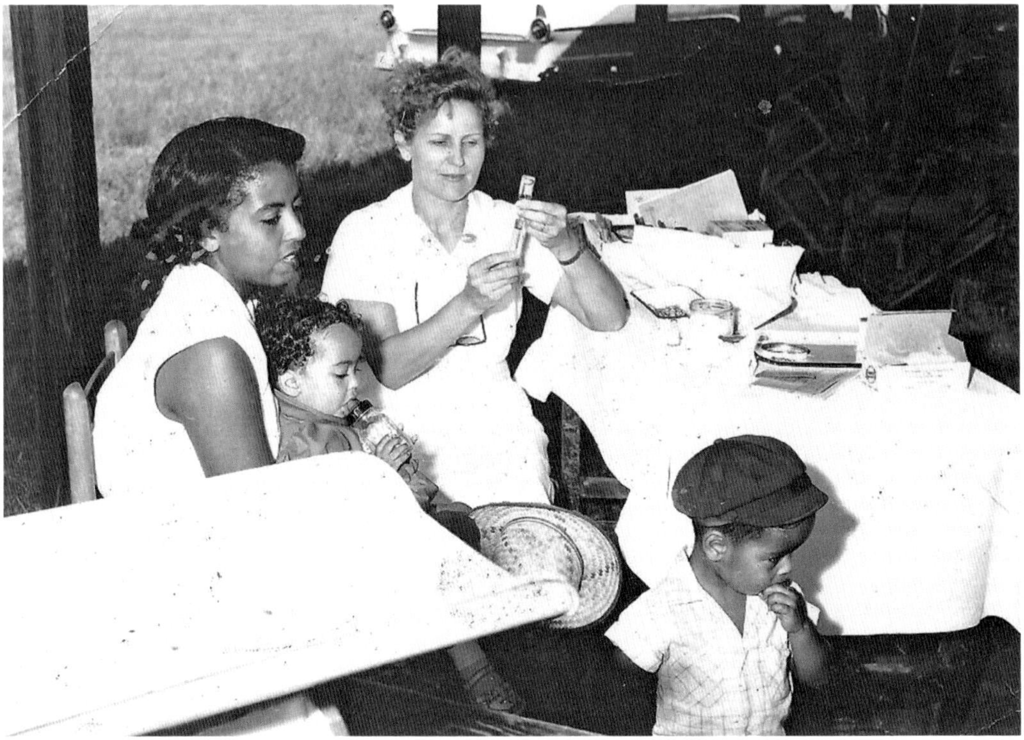

Public Health Nurse

Lily Aguillard Hebert R.N. was the daughter of Edward and Lillie Aguillard and the wife of Felix Hebert. Pictured making field calls for vaccination of common ailments, Hebert worked diligently during the years of the massive inoculations for the dreaded disease polio. In 1955, 700 Eunice children received the newly perfected polio inoculations at the Public Health Unit. Hebert was in charge of the project. In 1963, she and the public health officials administered over 24,000 doses of the polio serum on sugar cubes in a mass immunization effort at the Health Unit. (Courtesy of Felicia Hebert Wiggins.)

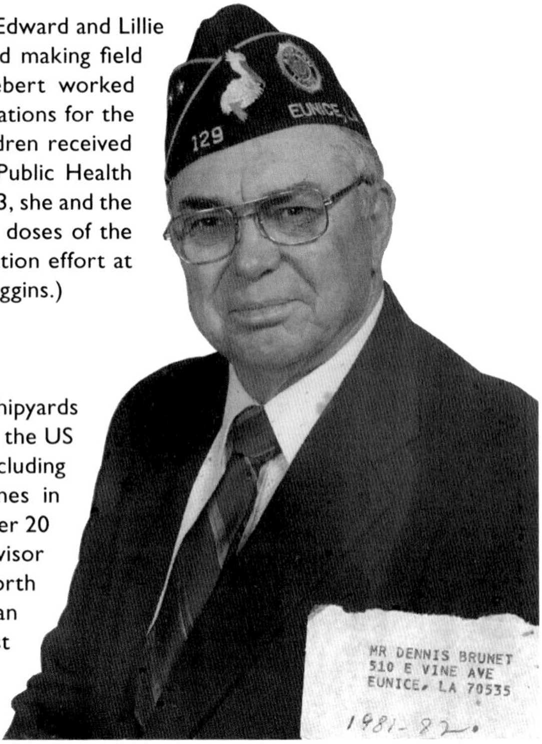

Overseas Welding Inspector

Dennis Brunet worked in the New Orleans shipyards where he honed his welding skills. As a sailor in the US Navy, he made several major beach landings including Okinawa and Iwo Jima. Brunet welded pipelines in many Louisiana and Gulf of Mexico oil fields. After 20 years, he became a welding inspector and supervisor working in Europe, Africa, Bahrain, and the North Sea. As a 60-year active member of American Legion Post 129, he held the position of post commander. He was married to Gladys Miller and the father of three children. (Courtesy of American Legion Post 129.)

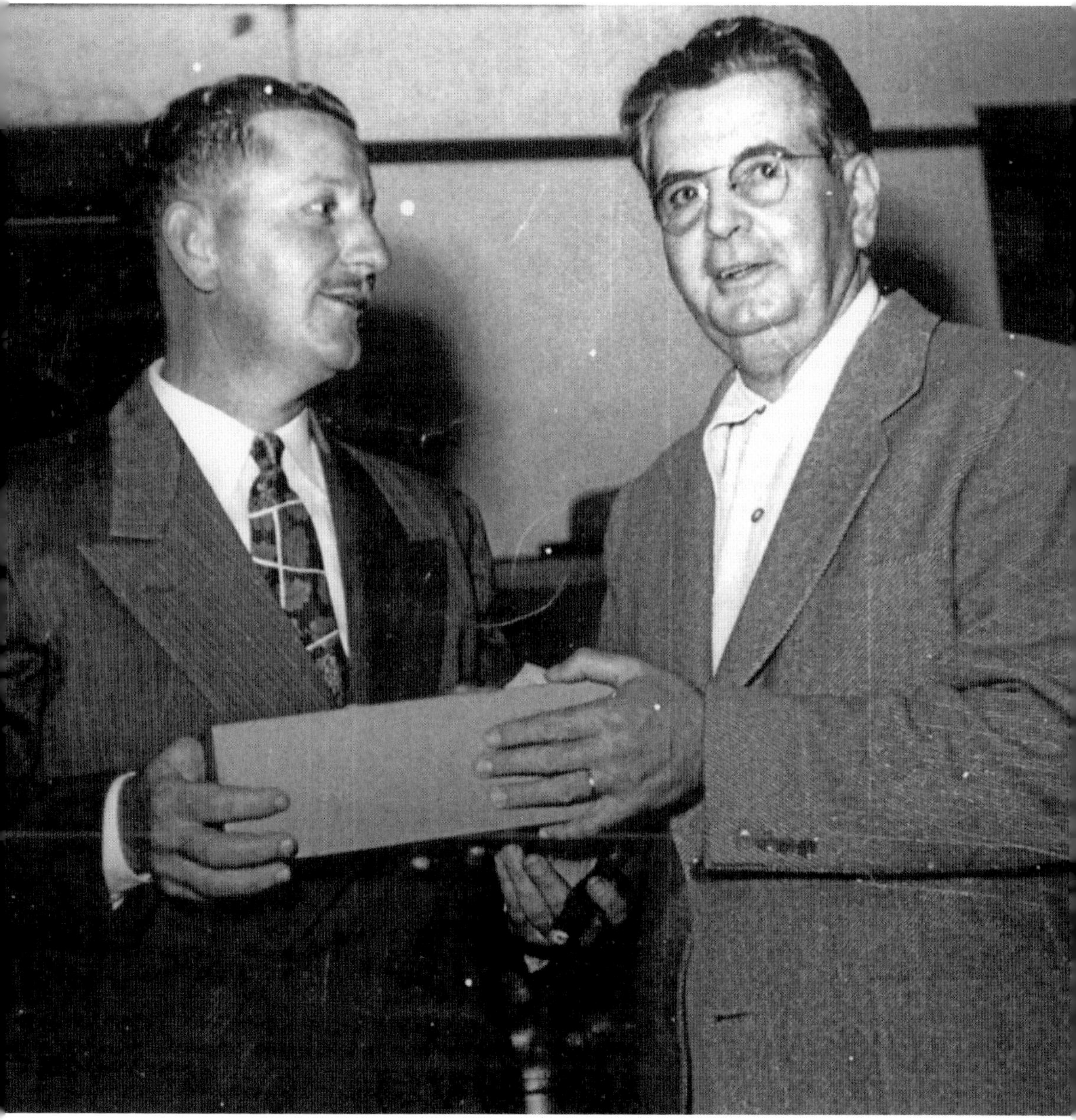

Wildlife and Flying Saucers
Coleman "Red" Fontenot, left, was photographed at the Eunice Rotary Club meeting with Matthias J. Frugé Sr. Fontenot was employed as a wildlife enforcement agent with the Louisiana Department of Wildlife and Fisheries. In January 1950, during the early space era, Fontenot reported that he and W.W. Lambert, Eston Bellow, Chester Wimberly, and Marius Garcille spotted a flying saucer streaking over Eunice about 11:00 a.m., leaving a vapor trail and a number of startled, gasping citizens. The stunned observers claimed that after the sighting, they believed such things were real and not a product of someone's imagination. The object was described as round, shiny, and moving from west to east at a terrific speed. Sightings were also made by shocked observers in both Oakdale and Opelousas. (Courtesy of Mathias J. Frugé Jr.)

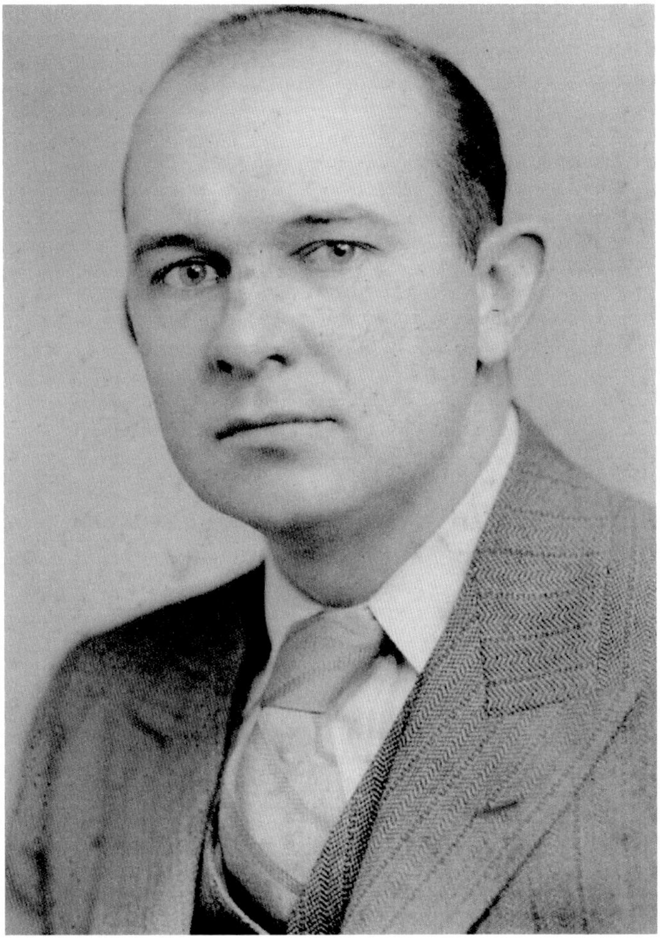

Medical Pioneer

Dr. B. Rodney Reed, son of Theogene and Emmaize Guillory Reed, attended Loyola University in 1925 where he played football before transferring to the University of Alabama for his undergraduate degree. He attended St. Louis University in Missouri before entering the Feinberg School of Medicine at Northwestern University of Chicago for his medical degree. He was a resident at the prestigious Chicago Lying-In Hospital and at Charity Hospital in New Orleans. Reed practiced in Eunice for over 40 years where he was a member of the St. Landry Parish Medical Society. Reed said he learned as much in his first year of practice as he had in medical school. Opening his office in Eunice in the 1930s, he learned how muddy roads would affect his medical practice. Reed recounted the story of his first house call to a rural home of a mother ready to give birth on a cold, rainy night. After the baby was born, the doctor charged the father $3.00. The farmer could not pay his fee, but promised he would pay as soon as he made the money. As Dr. Reed left, his car became mired in the sloppy road. The farmer gladly offered to pull the doctor's car out with his team of mules. Then he charged the doctor three dollars for the rescue! Next, the farmer paid Reed for delivering the baby. Reed built a small clinic at the corner of Vine Avenue and Third Street in the early 1940s. Prior to that, his office was upstairs over Chisholm's Drug Store on Second Street. He married Marian Frances Irving, a schoolteacher, and they had two sons, Dr. Rodney Theogene and John Irving "Johnny" Reed. Reed was a captain in the Naval Reserve and served during World War II. He managed Reedwood Farms and the T. Reed Farm where he raised registered Shorthorn cattle and rice. (Courtesy of John I. Reed.)

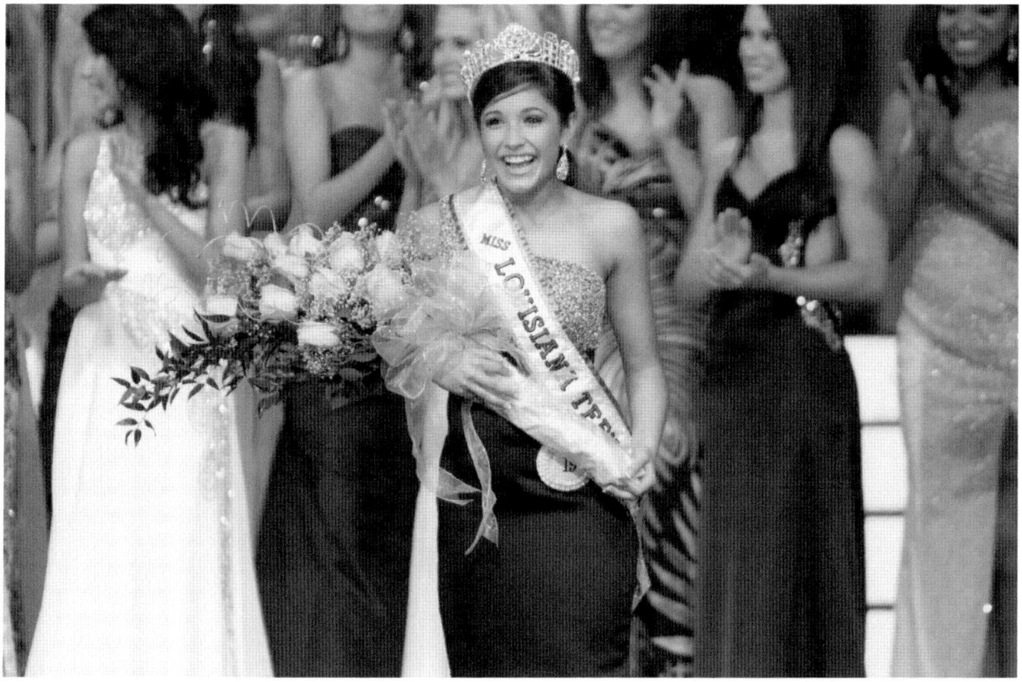

Miss Louisiana Teen USA
Elizabeth Heinen, beautiful daughter of Dr. Monty and Tiffini Powell Heinen, was crowned Miss Teen Eunice in 2010, Miss Teen Evangeline in 2011, and Miss Louisiana Teen USA in 2011. She competed in the Miss Teen USA pageant in the Bahamas in 2011. (Courtesy of Ryan Miles, Sage Media Group, LLC.)

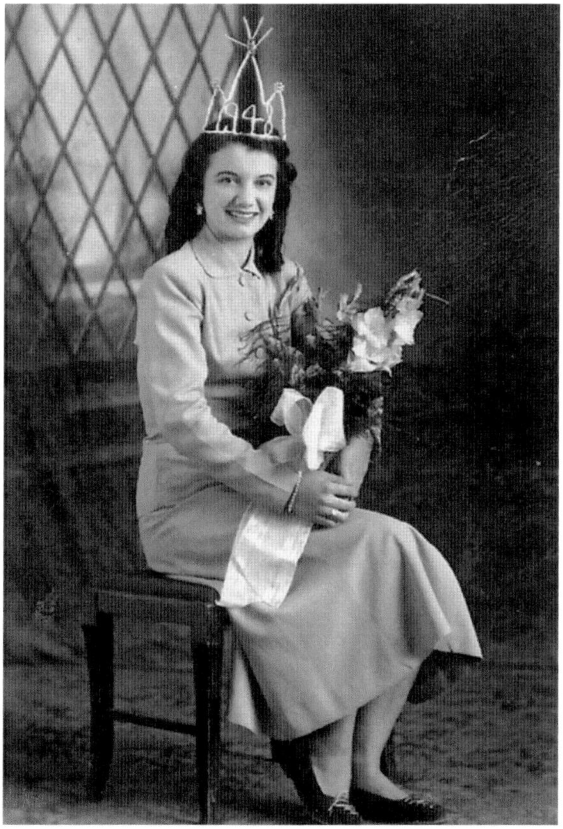

First Freshman Homecoming Queen
Anna Lois Fontenot Miller was a Cajun lady known for her grace and friendliness. She set a school record in 1948 when she was chosen Eunice High School's first freshman homecoming queen. A daughter of Eunice pioneers, Enos and Gertrude McGee Fontenot, Anna Lois married Dr. Jack Miller. (Courtesy of Dr. Jack D. Miller Jr.)

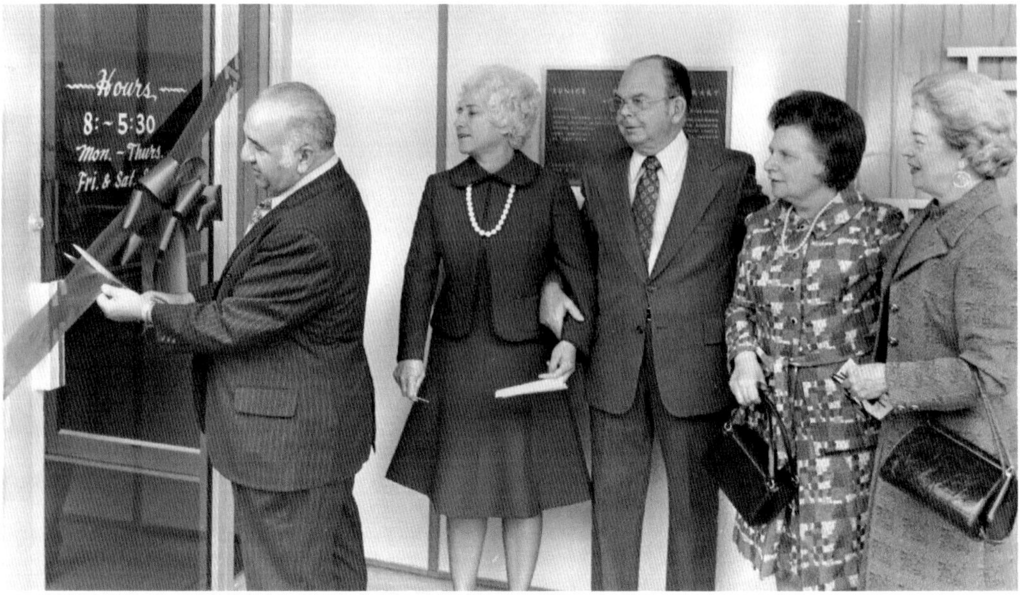

Opelousas-Eunice Library Advocates

From left to right, Mayor Wilson Moosa, Dorothy Mayer, Matt Vernon, Sophie Kerstein, and state librarian Sallie Farrell, advocates for a bi-city public library system for Opelousas and Eunice, watched as Mayor Moosa cut the ribbon dedicating the new library home in 1973. Mayer was hired as the first Opelousas-Eunice Public Library Systems director. Vernon and Kerstein were members of the library board. (Courtesy of Eunice Public Library.)

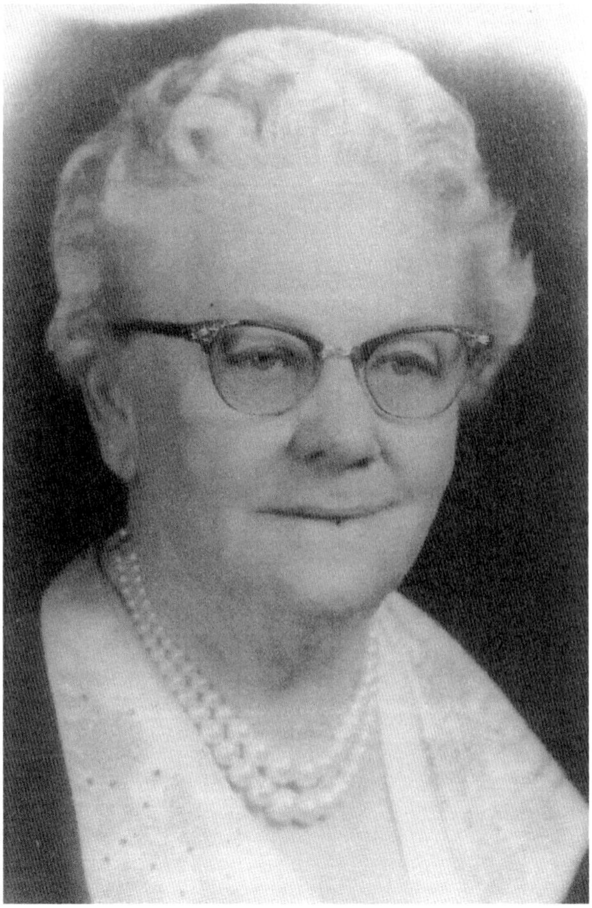

First City Librarian

Josephine Seaders Moody was Eunice's first librarian at the Woman's Club library in the 1950s. Moody, born in 1889, married Lon Moody, a sawmill operator. They came to Eunice in 1918 from Dixie, Georgia. She died at age 80, and was survived by seven adult children. (Courtesy of Ginny Moody.)

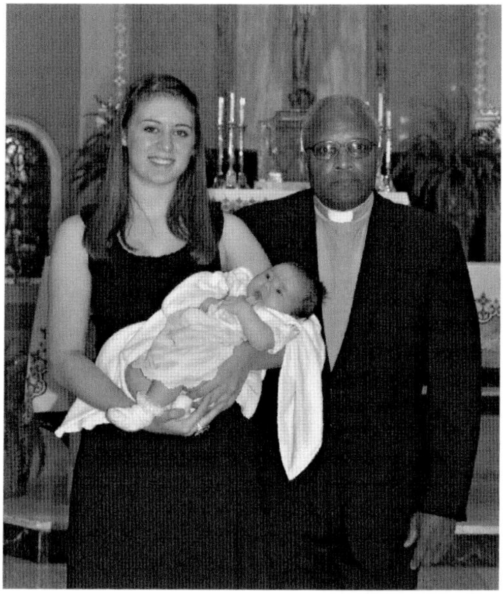

A Benedictine Monk
Fr. Joseph Alexander, a Lafayette native, became St. Anthony's pastor in 1993, after serving 30 years as a Benedictine monk, Provincial Superior of St. Mark's Priory, and president-rector of St. Mark's Seminary School of Theology. While at St. Anthony's Church, he made renovations to the building, brought the Marianite nuns back to St. Edmund School, and increased church support of the school. He is pictured with his godchild Miller-Grace Fuselier and her godmother, Catherine Fuselier. (Courtesy of Ryan and Mary Miller Fuselier.)

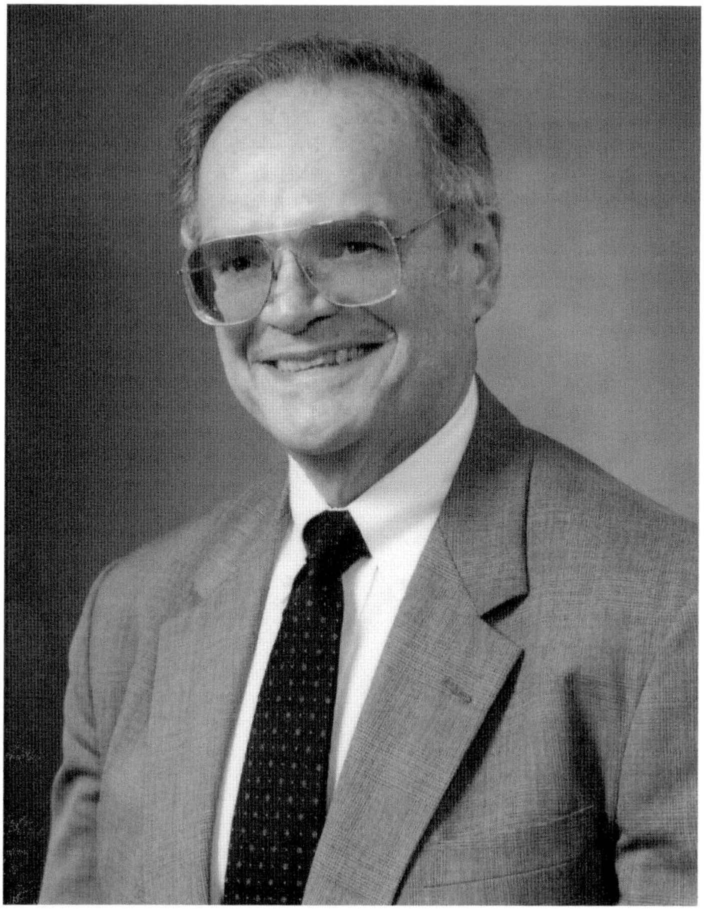

Cutting-Edge Medicine
Dr. Rodney Landreneau, son of Rodney and Blanche Savoy Landreneau, exhibited his cutting-edge medical knowledge when in 1965 he attempted to graft a teenager's left foot and a portion of her leg, which she lost in a horse-automobile accident. Landreneau worked for a full month trying to make the graft work, but despite his efforts, the young lady lost her leg. Ironically a few years in the future, medicine saw the perfection of the technique the doctor had tried in Eunice. Landreneau was a graduate of LSU Medical School, a veteran, and a recipient of many awards. (Courtesy of Melanie Landreneau Vidrine.)

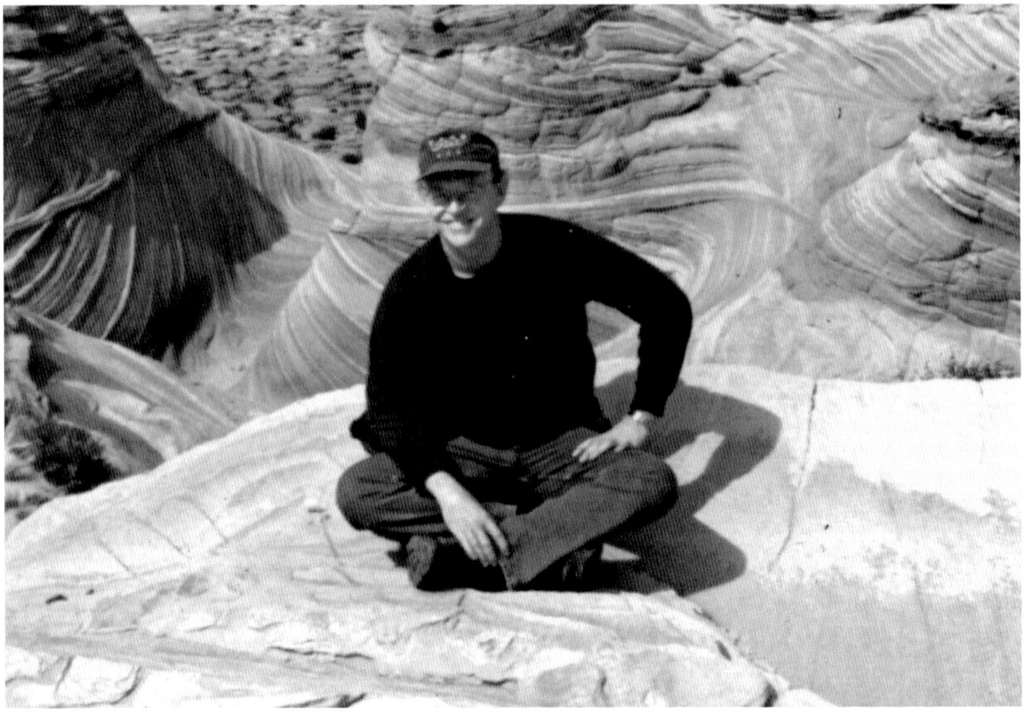

Author

Michael D. Jenkins, son of Mark and Mable Cox Jenkins, graduated from Eunice High, LSU, and Harvard Law School. He was an economic consultant, a CPA, a partner in an accounting firm, and a tax attorney in a California law firm. Jenkins authored a million-selling series of tax and legal guidebooks for small businesses. He currently writes and publishes software and e-books in Utah. (Courtesy of Michael D. Jenkins.)

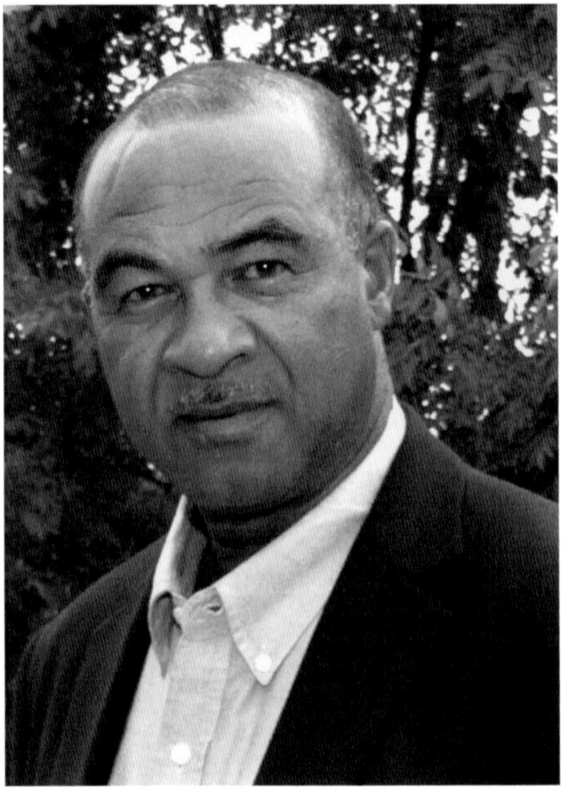

Parish Councilman

Jimmie E. Edwards, a well-known and popular St. Landry Parish councilman, worked with the city marshal's office, the US Post Office, and retired as a school bus driver. He belongs to the Progressive Brothers Social Club, Knights of Peter Claver, St. Mathilda Catholic Church, and Eunice Police Reserve. Edwards married Lea Eldren Jordan, and they have five adult children. (Courtesy of Jimmie E. and Lea Jordan Edwards.)

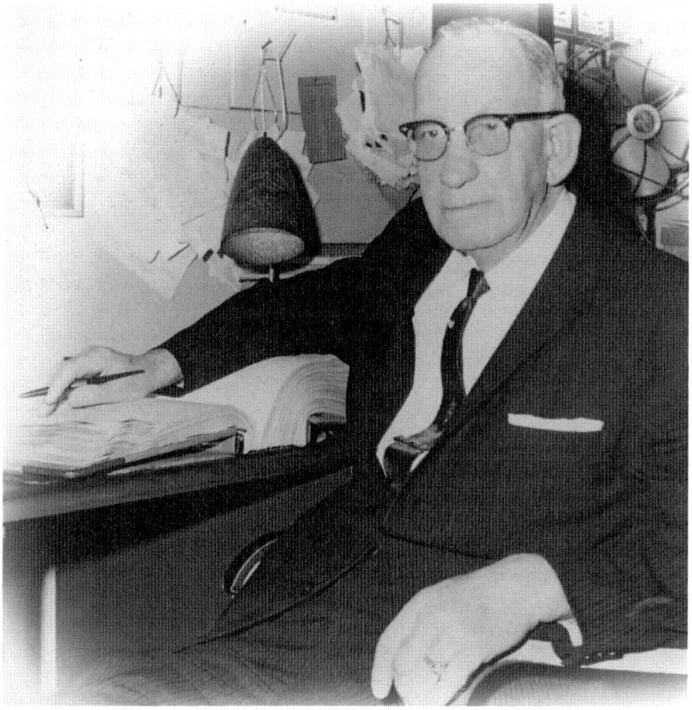

Supportive Citizen
Willis Johnson, a printer, was in 1919 the cofounder with M.V. Strother of the *New Era* newspaper, the forerunner of the *Eunice News*. Johnson was a tireless city supporter and an active civic leader. He was on the city council from 1929 until 1941, commander of American Legion Post 129, and on the St. Landry War Price and Rationing Board in 1944. (Courtesy of the American Legion Post 129.)

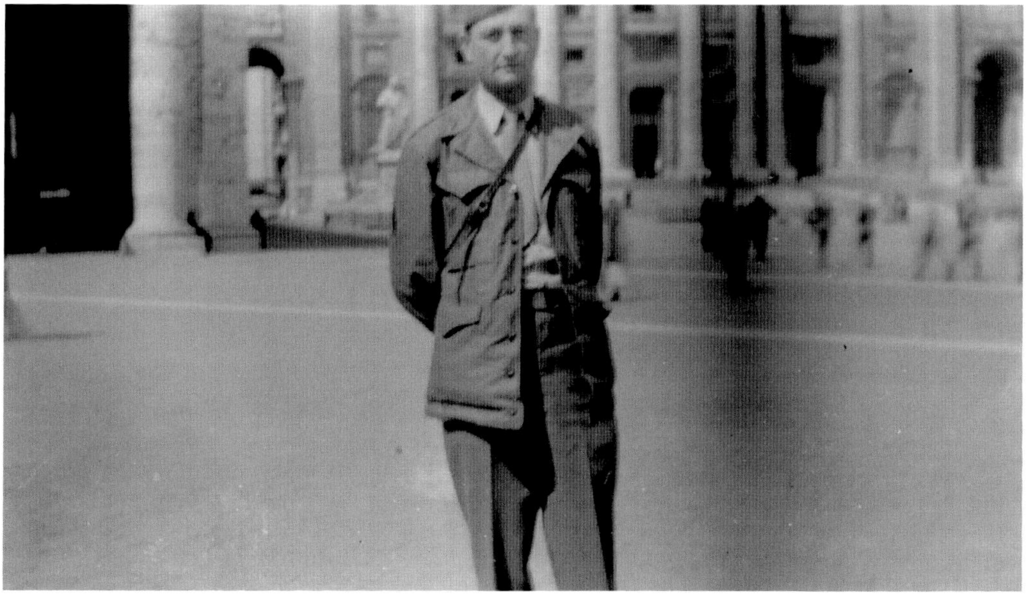

Colorful Postman
John Riley "Hooks" Roy was a colorful resident. Born in 1906 to John Pellington and Celma Peck Roy, he served in the military from 1942 to 1945 where he visited the Vatican as this image records. Returning home, Roy was employed at the post office. He is remembered fondly for always treating his visiting nieces and nephews to bottles of cold soda pop—a rare treat in the 1950s and 1960s. (Courtesy of Claire Roy Richard.)

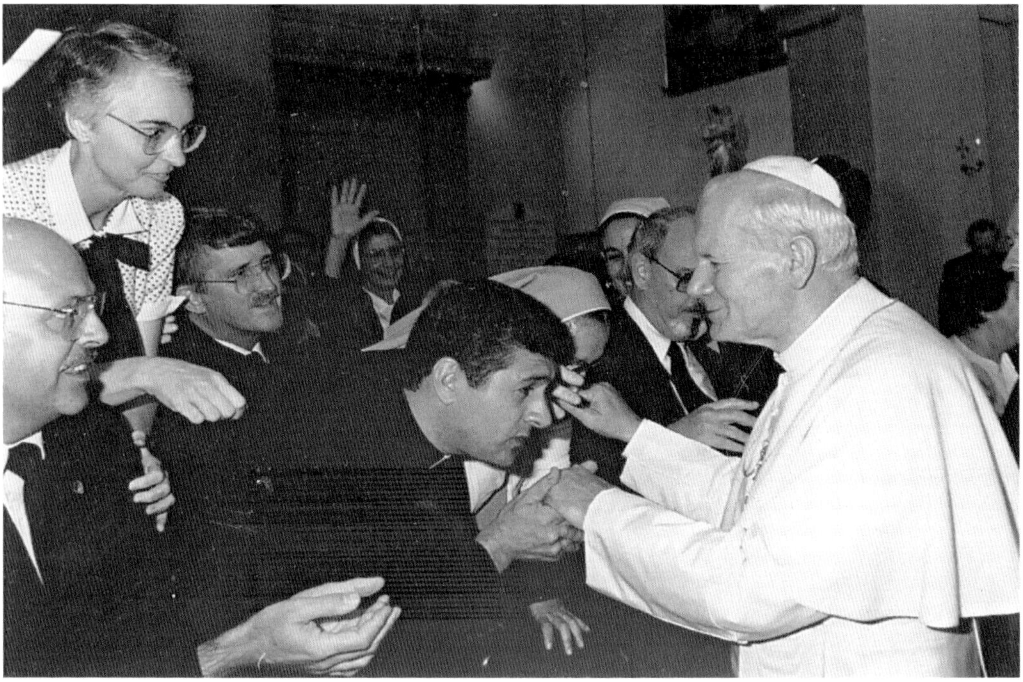

Met Pope John Paul II

Fr. Thomas Montelaro, center, son of Phillip and Annie Montelaro, was shown kissing Pope John Paul II's ring when the pontiff entered St. Louis Cathedral in New Orleans in 1987. Other people are unidentified. Father Montelaro was ordained in 1975. (Courtesy of Mary Margaret Montelaro.)

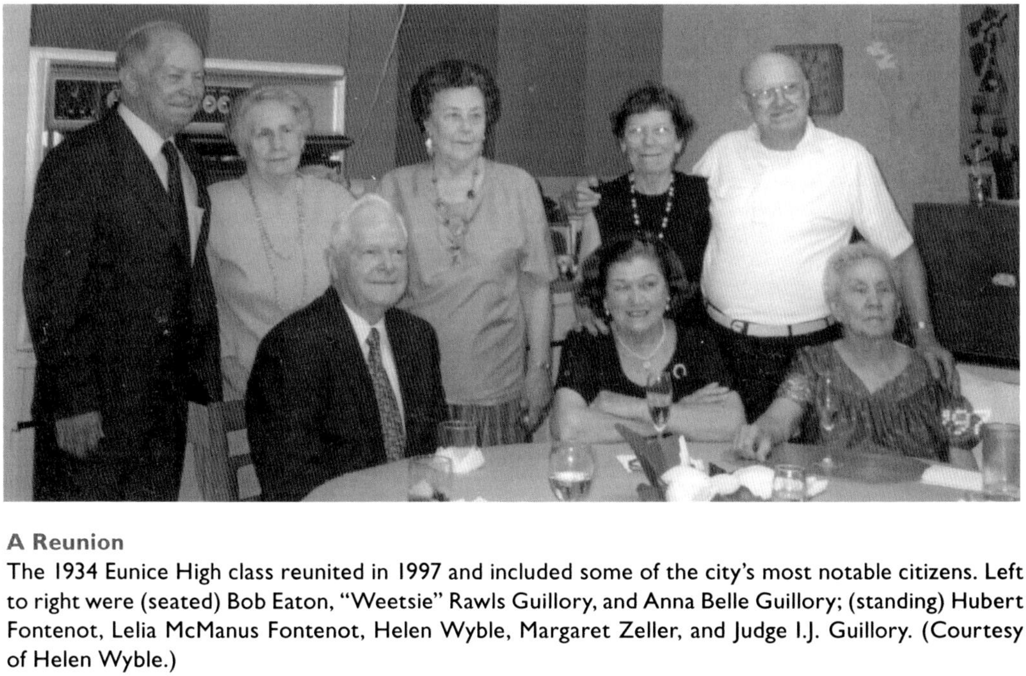

A Reunion

The 1934 Eunice High class reunited in 1997 and included some of the city's most notable citizens. Left to right were (seated) Bob Eaton, "Weetsie" Rawls Guillory, and Anna Belle Guillory; (standing) Hubert Fontenot, Lelia McManus Fontenot, Helen Wyble, Margaret Zeller, and Judge I.J. Guillory. (Courtesy of Helen Wyble.)

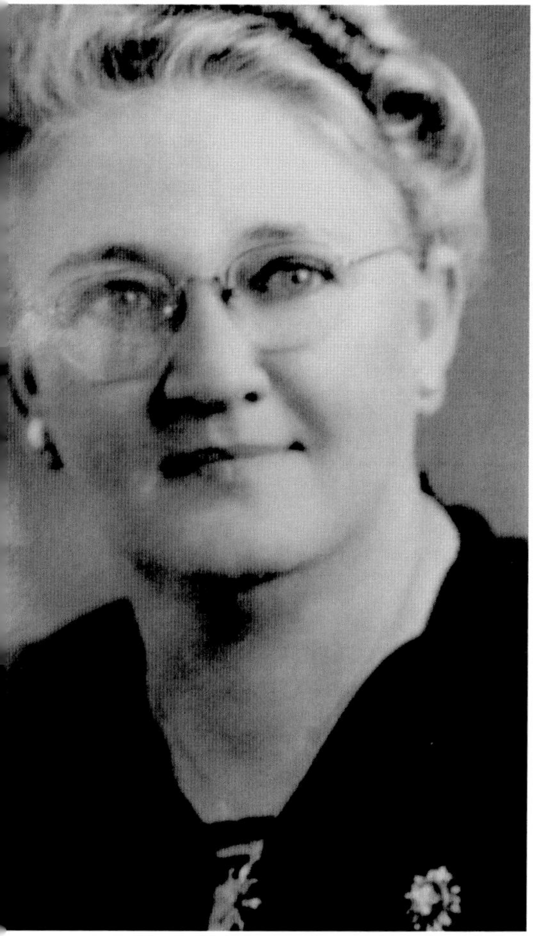

First Female School Board Member
Catherine Leona Bonvillain Jenkins was born in 1903 to Ernest Norbit and Emma D. Bonvillain of Erath, Louisiana. A nurse, she married Dr. Harry Jenkins of Eunice and had six children. In 1952, Jenkins became the first Eunice woman and the second from St. Landry Parish to serve on the St. Landry Parish School Board when she was appointed by Governor Kennon. (Courtesy of Eunice Public Library.)

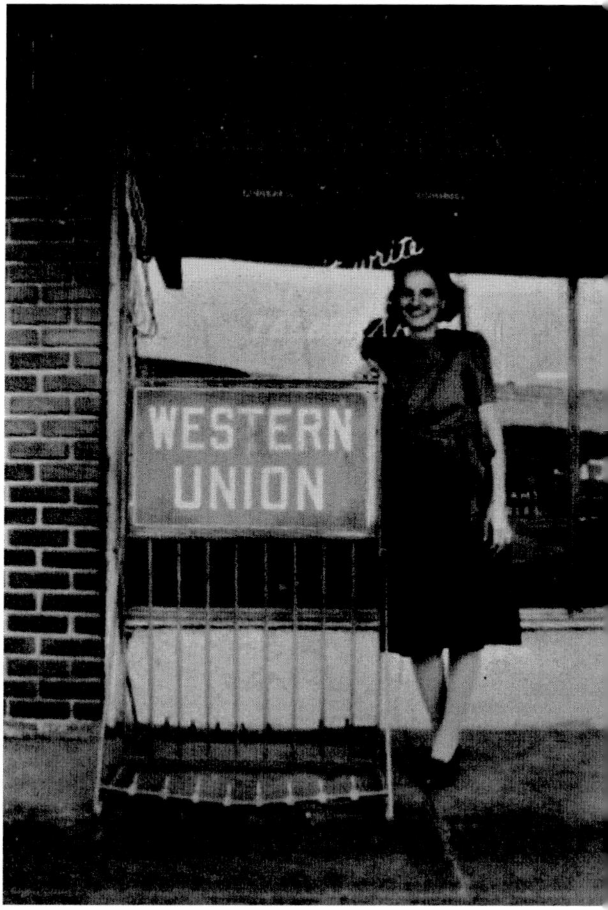

Western Union Operator
Annie Ferruggia, daughter of Philip and Annie Strangi Ferruggia, came to Eunice in 1933 as the Western Union operator. Two years later, she married Phillip Montelaro and had six children. However, marriage did not end Annie's work. She and her husband owned and managed the Mayer Hotel from 1944 to 1964. With boundless energy, she worked as the district manager for World Book Encyclopedia until 1988. (Courtesy of Frances Montelaro Frugé.)

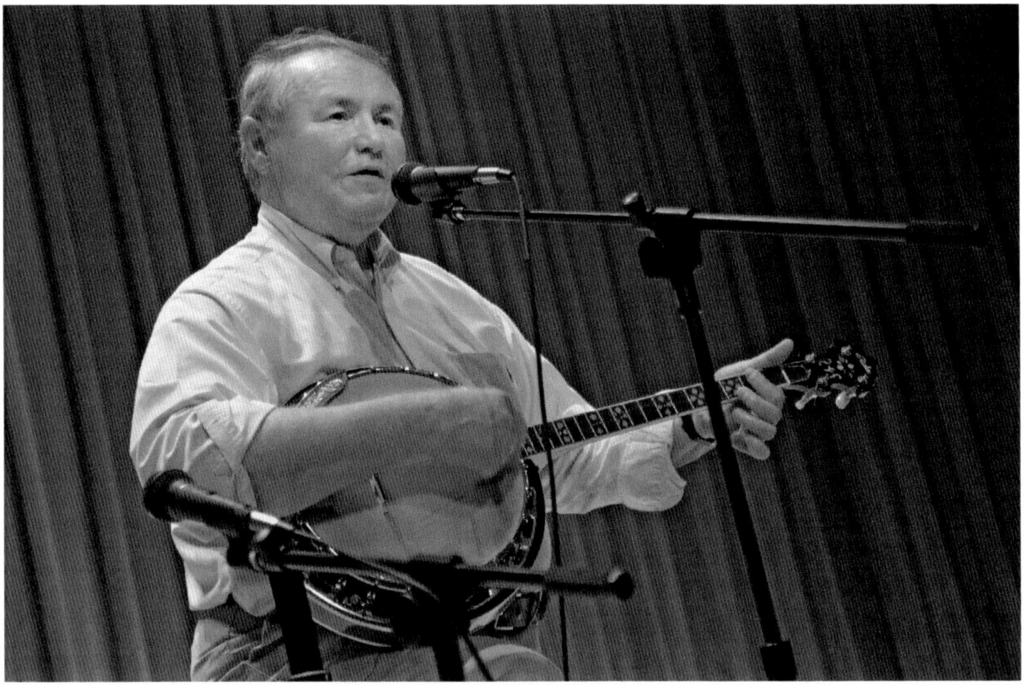

The Chancellor
Dr. William J. Nunez, selected chancellor of LSU Eunice in 1996, immediately became involved on campus and in the community. One of his most visible achievements includes the acquisition of a privatized student apartment complex. Bengal Village. He takes pride in the high ranking of LSU Eunice students on the National Board Exams for Nursing and Applied Health students. Nunez is chairman of the board of Acadian Medical Center, a member of the Eunice Rotary Club, and was Citizen of the Year in 2005. (Courtesy of LSU Eunice.)

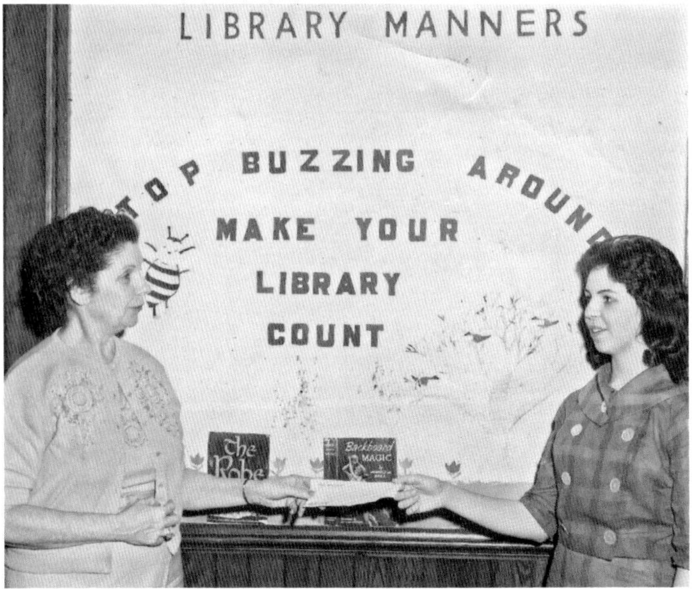

Award-Winning School Library
Mildred "Millie" Crozier Wooten came to Eunice from Whiteville where she was born in 1910. She was the daughter of Barrett and Gertrude Milburn Crozier, and the wife of Dan Wooten. Wooten, left, Eunice High School librarian, was pictured congratulating student, Donna Ardoin, for her clever bulletin board. Wooten received the coveted James O. Modisette Award for the Outstanding High School Library in Louisiana in 1964. (Courtesy of authors' collection.)

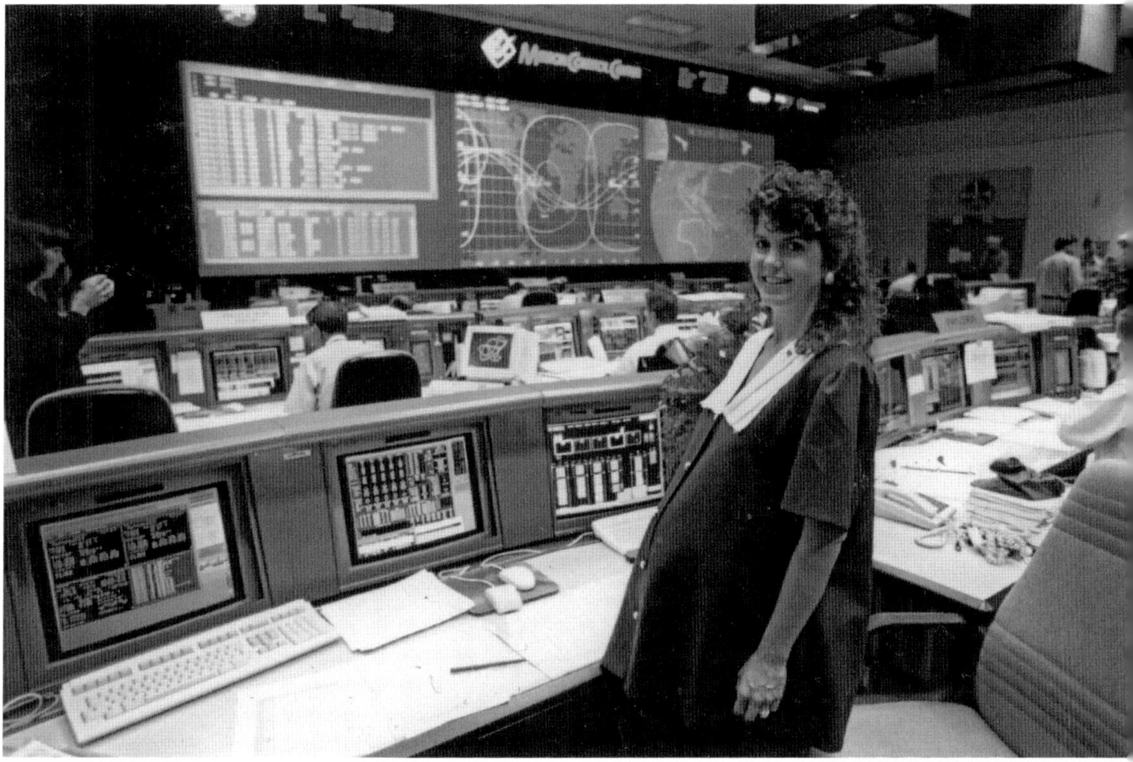

NASA Space Shuttle Flight Controller
Michelle LaFleur MacFadyen worked from 1988 to 1990 at Unisys Corporation, where she wrote software for simulating external environment to test space shuttle software. For eight years, she worked for the National Aeronautics and Space Administration (NASA) where she was space shuttle flight controller responsible for all crew procedures related to the onboard computers and display systems. She also was responsible for monitoring flight data and troubleshooting failures during space shuttle flights. Simply, her job was to take care of the five computers (during the flight) that flew and controlled the space shuttle. In preparation for flights, MacFadyen logged thousands of hours on simulation flights, which meant that the astronauts were in their mock-up vehicle and she was in Mission Control. She practiced and practiced working through failures with the astronauts so that none of them would flinch if a computer failed especially during critical and stressful events like launch and landing. One situation stands out in MacFadyen's memory. The key players portrayed in the 1995 movie, *Apollo 13*, were in management in MacFadyen's division. She asked her boss, Jack Knight, how he felt about the movie. With tears streaming down his face, he told her that the movie was so accurate that it brought it all back to him—the stress, the emotions, the fatigue. MacFadyen explained that for the first time, she glimpsed the dedication of the men who forged the way through the Apollo years, sometimes flying by the seat of their pants. During MacFadyen's last space shuttle flight, STS-95, in 1998, John Glenn was scheduled to make his second flight. She was 8.5 months pregnant when she visited with Glenn after his return to Earth. As her farewell gift, Glenn signed a photograph of himself "in great expectation" for her first child. Though in a male-dominated career field, MacFadyen felt there was no gender bias. If there was any bias, it was age discrimination from those who believed she was an intern, so she was careful to maintain a professional appearance to be taken seriously. The crew of the 1998 flight called down to specifically tell her farewell and to mention that they would miss her Cajun cooking. MacFadyen is the daughter of Dr. Gary and Amanda Rozas Lafleur. She is a graduate of St. Edmund High School and the University of Louisiana. (Courtesy of Michelle Lafleur MacFadyen.)

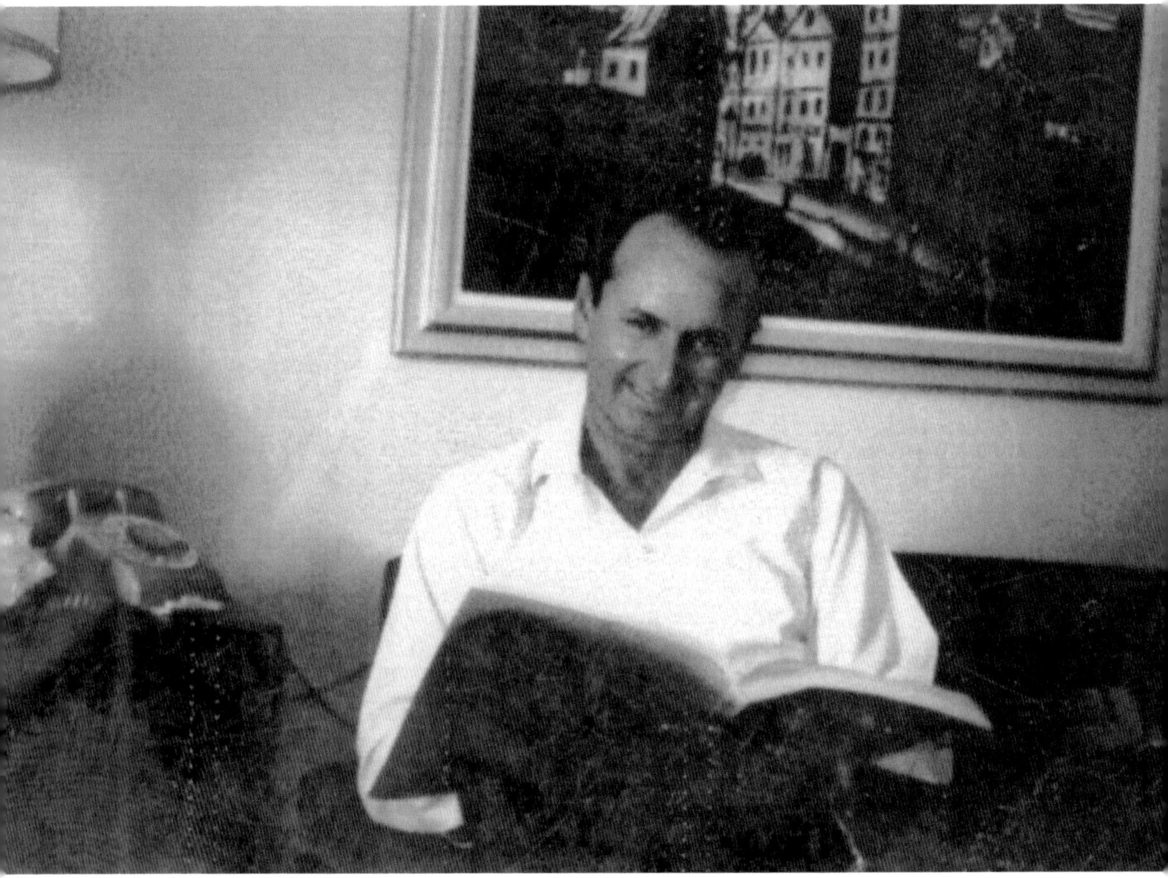

Investigated JFK's Assassination

Lt. Francis Frugé, son of Dorcenus and Maya Frugé of Basile, was with the Louisiana State Police for over 20 years. He specialized in narcotics cases, but the drug user he was called to transport from the Eunice hospital to the city jail on the night of November 20, 1963, was anything but a usual case. She turned out to be a prostitute and habitual criminal. Frugé's fate suddenly became entwined with a woman who tried to warn officials that the president would be killed. She had been ejected from a fast-moving car somewhere west of Eunice on Highway 190. But, even that action wasn't uncommon for drug users. What was unusual was her farfetched story. Dr. F.J. Derouen committed the woman, Rose Cheramie, to the state mental hospital at Jackson, Louisiana. Again, Frugé was called to transport her there. Frugé later testified to the House Select Committee on Assassinations that he thought she was lucid when she told him the fantastic story about two men who threw her from the speeding automobile and how they were going to Dallas to kill Pres. John F. Kennedy. Cheramie identified the men as Lee Harvey Oswald and his friend. No one at the hospital paid attention to her story of the impending assassination. Frugé called the FBI, who told him that they had the killer and the case was closed. However, Frugé was encouraged by his boss to follow up on leads regardless of Oswald's arrest. Along with Louisiana state trooper Wayne Morein of Ville Platte, Frugé became part of the first nonpublicized investigation into the murder of President Kennedy. Working with D. A. Jim Garrison of New Orleans, Frugé conducted his investigation of Lee Harvey Oswald's connection to Louisiana, and his possible involvement with Clay Shaw, a New Orleans resident who witnesses claimed entertained Oswald at his home. Before he was called to testify, Frugé learned that Rose Cheramie was found dead along a roadside in Texas. (Courtesy of Dr. Ned Frugé.)

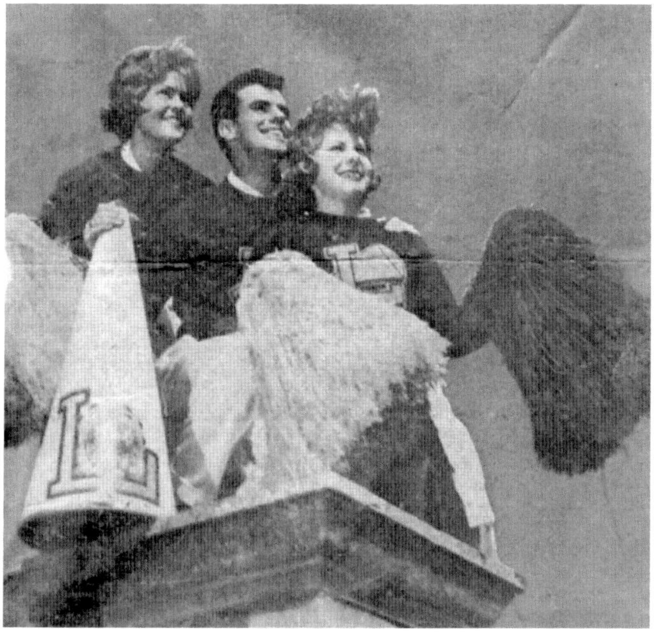

LSU Cheerleader
Frankie LaFleur, center, was pictured atop the LSU Campus Gates with Gay Sneider, left, and Carolyn Cherry, right, in 1961. LaFleur was practicing with the gymnastic team when the cheerleaders asked him for help with their stunts, then encouraged him to audition for cheerleader. Chosen over 100 hopefuls, LaFleur was an LSU cheerleader from 1961 to 1963. Today he is a successful businessman. (Courtesy of Frankie LaFleur.)

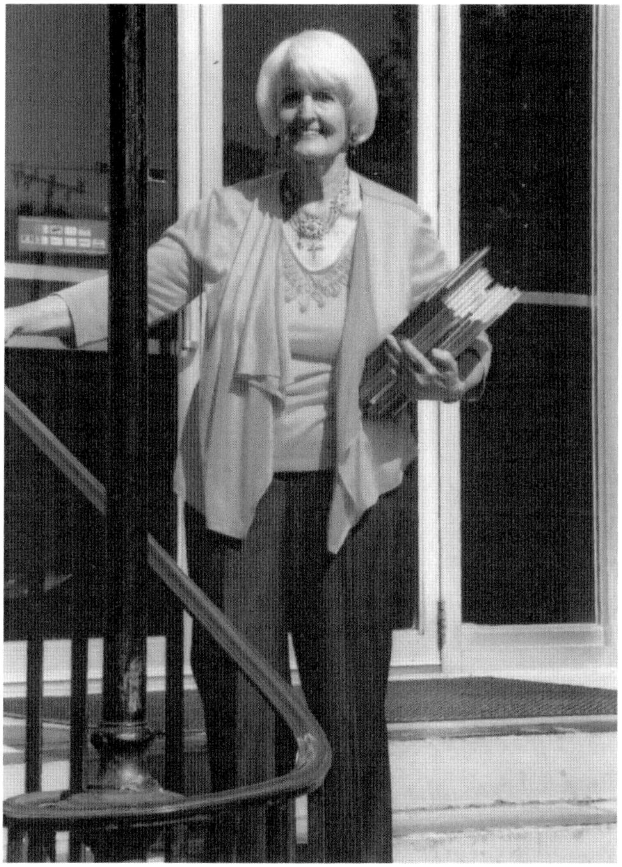

Fighter for Literacy
Jean McCormick McManus succeeded in bringing the Dolly Parton Imagination Library to Eunice, the first community in the state to have one. McManus received numerous awards for her efforts including Rotary Club Citizen of the Year in 2008 and a statewide grant of $20,000 for literacy. (Courtesy of Jean McCormick McManus.)

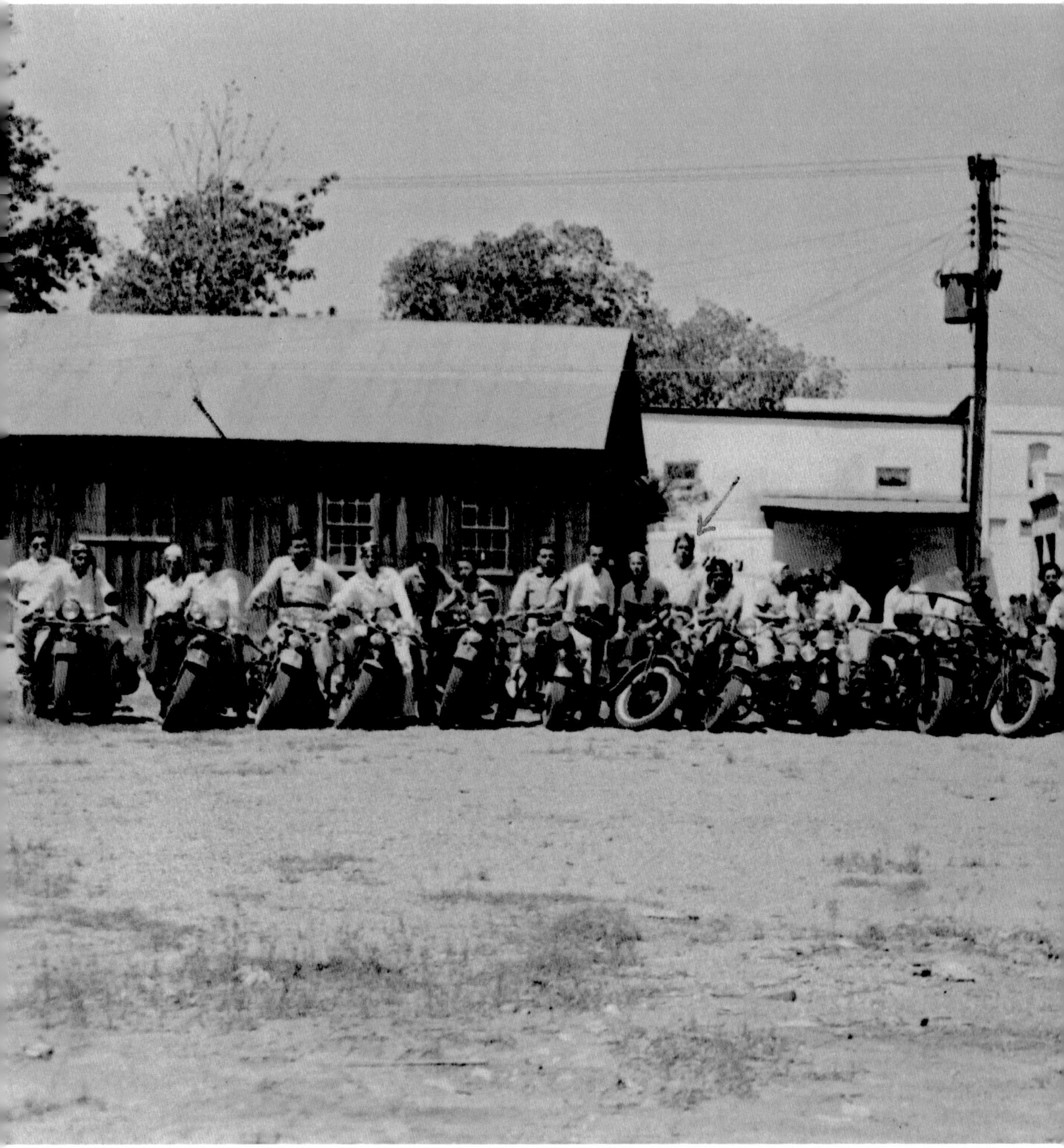

Motorcycle Club

White Hawk Riders was a group composed of members whose primary interests and activities involved motorcycles. Members joined for camaraderie, rider training, and socialization and their programs stressed safety and rider skills in their meetings. In the 1950s, the group was a highlight of local parades in which they performed precision motorcycle-riding maneuvers. Members attended several national motorcycle rallies. Some of the riding club members pictured are, in no order, Garnet Milner Jr., president and road captain, Durwood Young, Percy McGee, Etienne Feucht, Wilbur Miller, William O. Milner, Theo Soileau, and Gordon Milner. (Courtesy of Audrey Clayton Milner.)

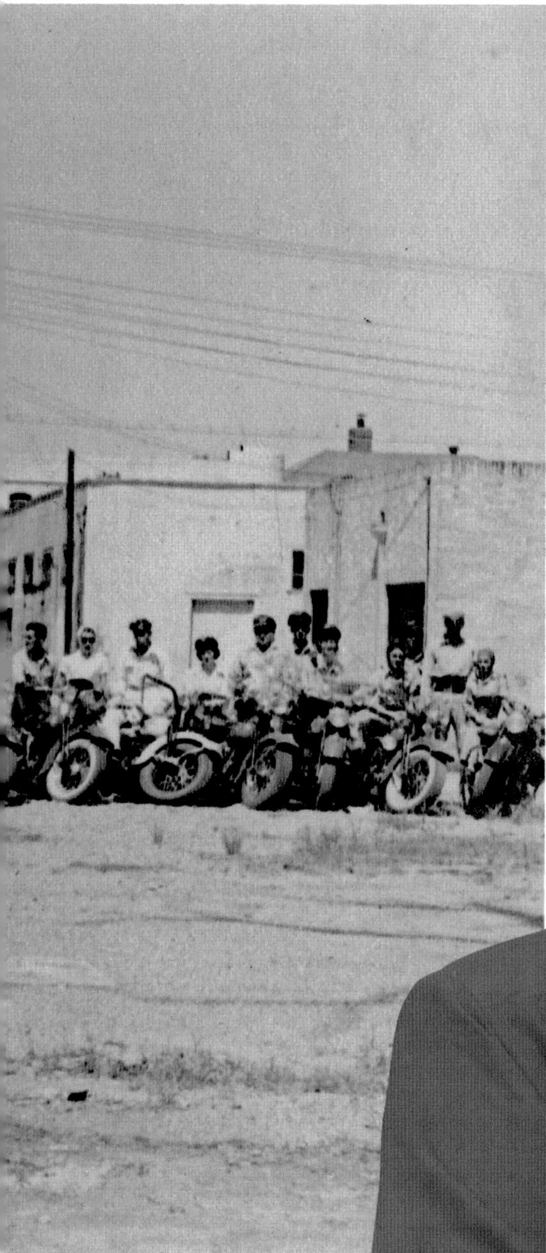

Faithful Foster Mom

Willie Mae Fuselier, daughter of a city pioneer, Saven Fuselier, and the former Azeline Frugé, married Cagey C. Fuselier, and when widowed, Clyde E. Nelson. Her children are former Eunice chief of police Tony Fuselier, Denise Nelson, Michelle Nelson Andrus, and two foster children. Fuselier was bookkeeper at Moosa Pontiac for over 20 years. An avid St. Edmund School Booster Club member and attendee at both St. Anthony and St. Thomas More Catholic Churches, Fuselier was proud of rearing all her children including the two foster children in Catholic schools and churches. (Courtesy of Tony Fuselier.)

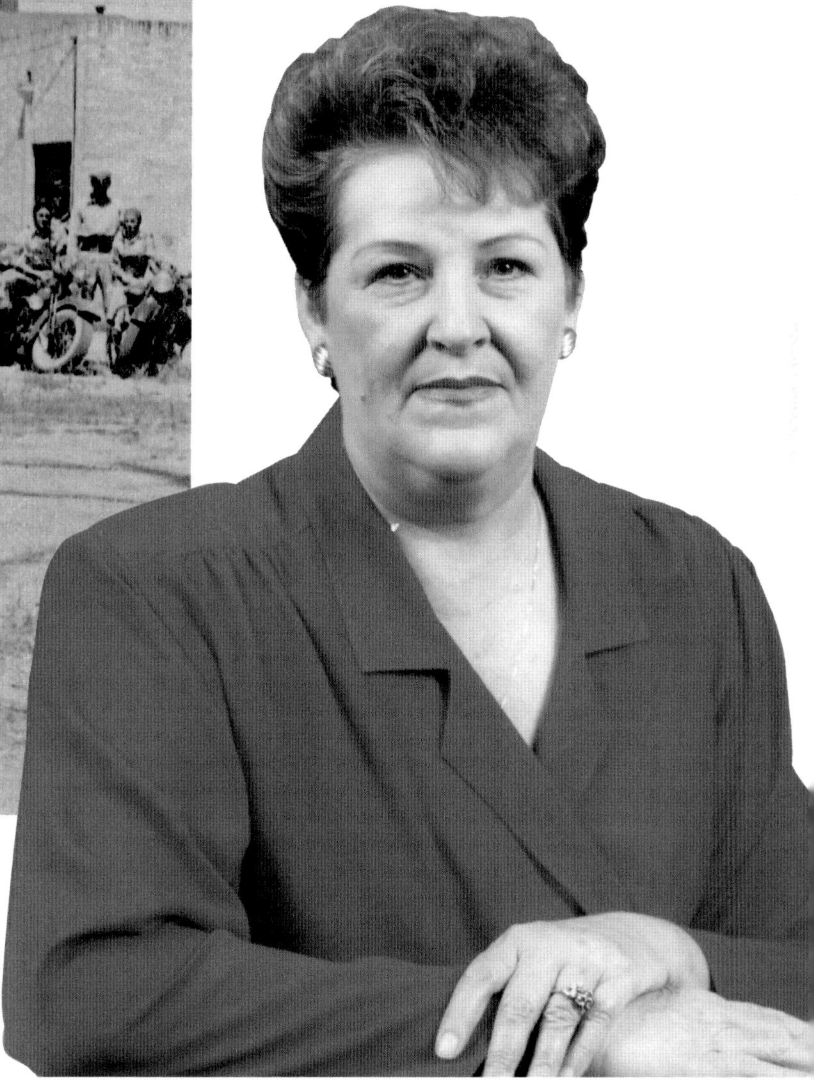

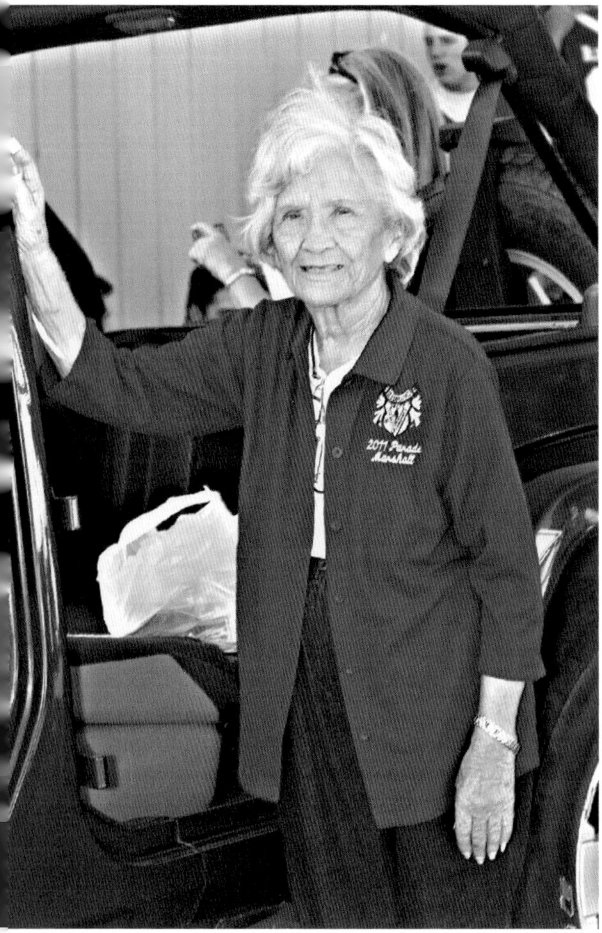

Venerable Teacher

Jackie Trichell Sanders was born in Norphelet, Arkansas. Her father was a "wildcatter," searching for oil, which necessitated her family's many moves. Finally he bought a Eunice company, and the family settled here. A 1949 LSU graduate, Sanders was "pushed" into teaching by Dr. Gladys Peck and has been happy teaching since 1954. She was pictured in 2011 as parade marshal at St. Edmund's Homecoming. (Courtesy of Trosclair Photography.)

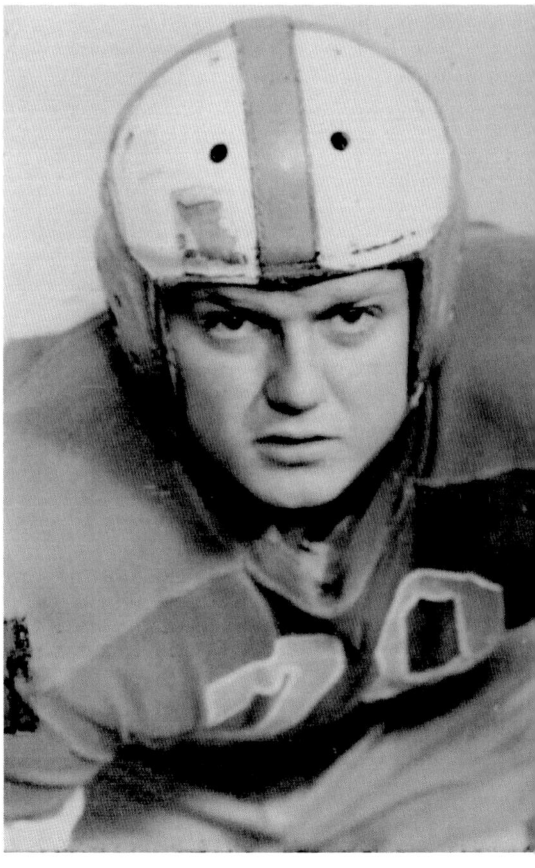

Teacher and Coach

Allen Horton Jr. was born to F.A. and Lillie Mae Wyble Horton in 1933. At Eunice High School, he lettered in football and played on the state championship Woodmen of the World baseball team. Horton coached under Faize Mahfouz at Eunice High after graduating from Northwestern State College. He obtained an Educational Specialist degree in school counseling, and completed rewarding careers as a teacher, coach, administrator, and salesman in New Iberia. Married to Betty Millspaugh of Natchitoches, he is the father of two sons, Allen III and Steven. (Courtesy of Allen Horton Jr.)

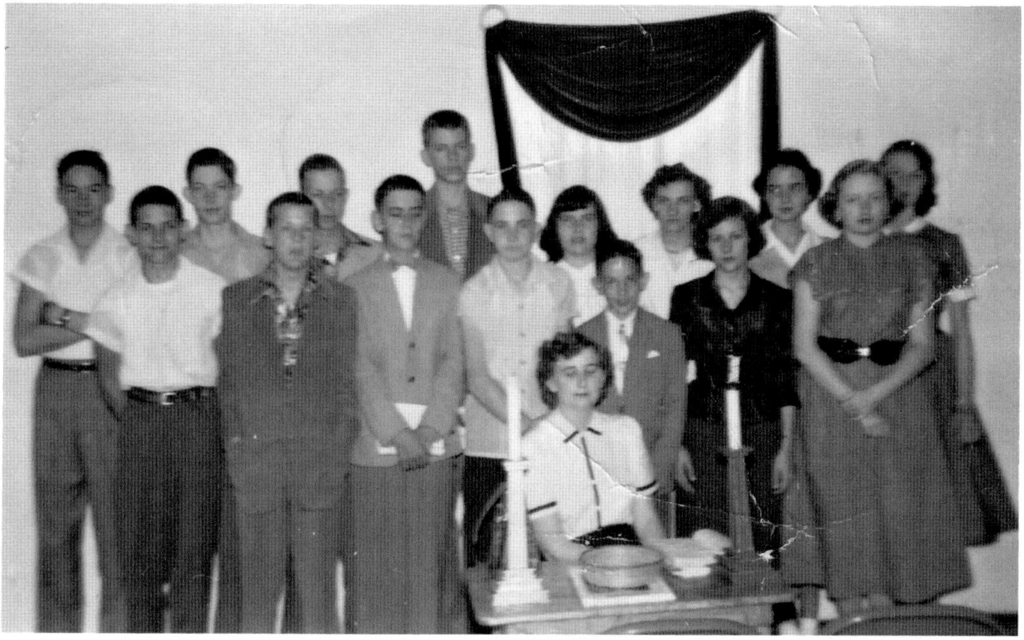

Sunday School Teacher
Helen Allen Mahfouz, wife of Coach Faize Mahfouz, was born in Kentwood, Louisiana, in 1918. She met her future husband at Louisiana Normal in Natchitoches. They both came to teach in Eunice, eloping during the Christmas holidays in 1940. She was active in the Methodist Church as a Sunday school teacher and in Camp Fire activities with her daughter, Claire. Mahfouz is shown seated in the 1950s with her Sunday school class. Pictured from left to right are (back row) Billy Haristy, Bob Butler, Carol Young, Ron Harris, Geraldean Goldman, Bessie Hackler, Deanna Thompson, and Martha Hayes; (first row) Don Horton, Billy Lee, Deen Thompson, Randy Simmons, Leland Wade, unidentified, and Lucille Stroud. (Courtesy of Deen Thompson.)

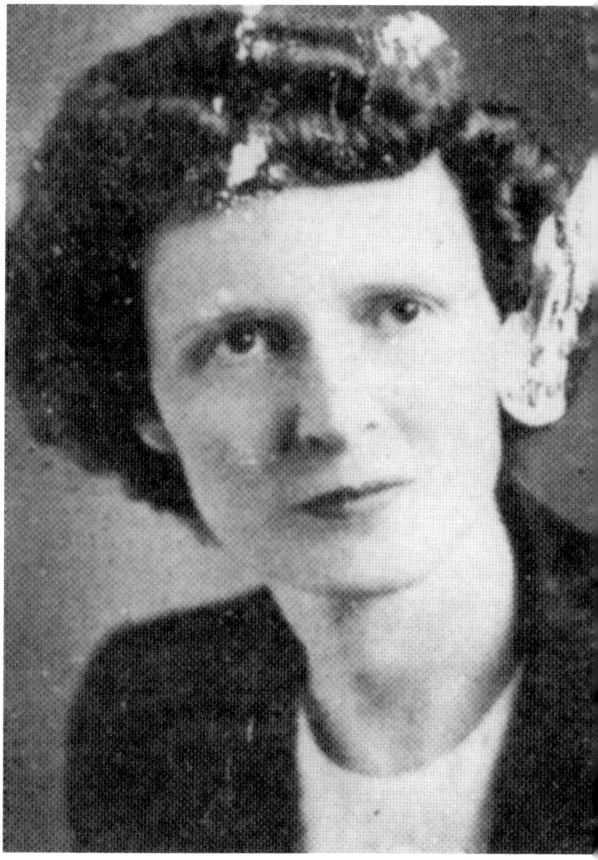

Oldest Active Nursing Home Administrator
Wilma Buffington Bedell Ball came from Missouri during the Great Depression when her husband found dragline work with B. Lewis Contractors. She worked as secretary of the Tri-Parish Fair and the Southwestern Louisiana Fair. In 2011, she was honored by the US Congress and Missouri Legislature as the nation's oldest active nursing home administrator at age 94. (Courtesy of Allen Bedell.)

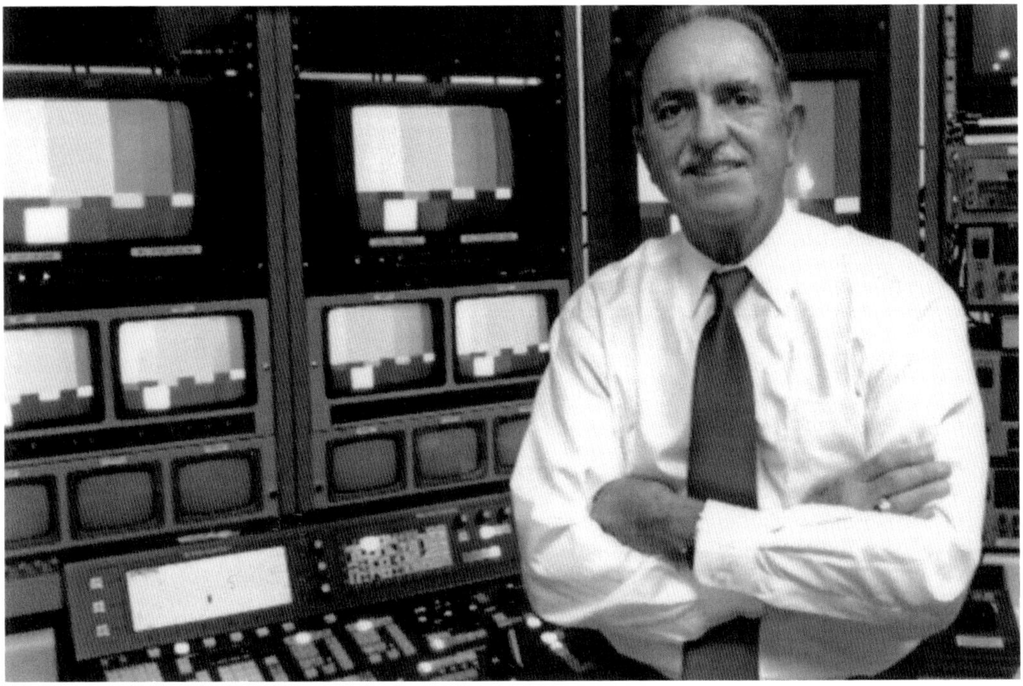

Broadcasting for Half a Century
Tom Voinche has been in broadcasting since 1961. He is the morning news co-anchor on KATC TV 3 in Lafayette, host of a weekly radio show on KBON FM 101.0 in Eunice, and an adjunct instructor at the University of Louisiana at Lafayette. A member of various civic clubs, Voinche was named the Eunice Rotary Club's Citizen of the Year in 1985. (Courtesy of Thomas Voinche.)

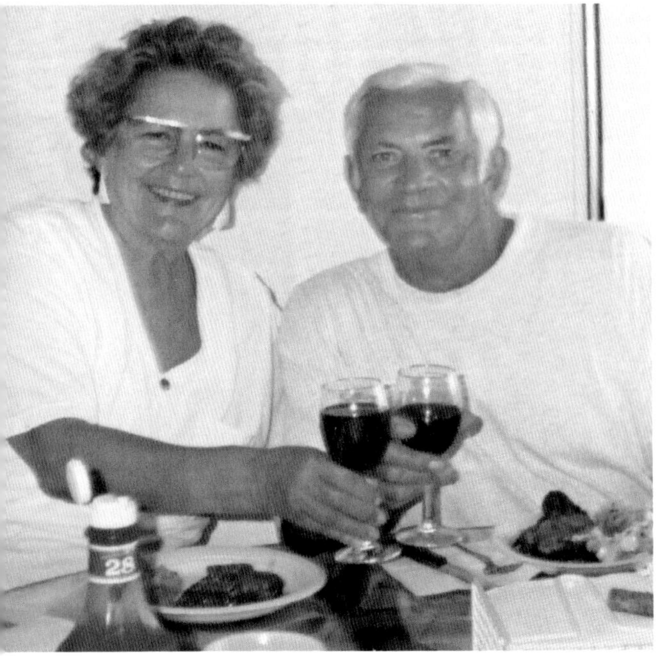

Colorful Couple
If life experiences had colors, Adam "Brother" and Pat Leonards Johnson's lives would be vivid. This unusual couple has acted as ambassadors for their hometown on each cruise they have taken—all 40 of them! After working a variety of jobs—mortician, deputy sheriff, pipeliner in Africa and the Middle East, superintendent on the Alaskan pipeline, and an abortive effort to work in Communist Russia in 1977— "Brother" opened a family business. Johnson's Eunice Lock & Leave It Self Storage was the first self-storage facility in town. Pat is well known as one of the initial Eunice Crawfish étouffée Cookoff chefs, winning nine trophies, serving as a judge one year, and winning cooking contests at the International Rice Festival in Crowley. Retired now, the couple enjoys traveling in their golden years. (Courtesy of Adam Johnson.)

CHAPTER FOUR

The Business Community

C.C. Duson's real estate venture, Eunice, built its economy on timber, the railroad, and rice production. In the late 1920s and the early to mid-1930s, the early economic downturn flattened the young community's economy. Some of the old business firms such as Ardoin's Clothiers, and Picou's Drug Store managed to survive, but others were hard hit. One Cajun was heard to say, "A depression? We had one? I didn't notice. We've been so poor for so long, it didn't make a difference." In the mid-1930s, the town gradually recovered from the downturn, but some hard times remained until a new oil deposit brought in businesses. The Tepetate oil field gushers blew in new fortunes, drew in speculators and "wildcatters," including George Bradley and Mordello Vincent, and provided employment when oil field service companies, including Ashy's Construction and B. Lewis Construction, began hiring workers. With the opening of the Tepetate field, Eunice was saved from the worst effects of the Depression. The construction of Highway 190 created more jobs and better access to Eunice merchants. By 1941, the Louisiana Maneuvers war games brought in 1,200 troops requiring 100 train carloads of food daily. The POW camp also purchased food from Eunice merchants. By 1950, the population was up to 8,184 and business was a little better, but the town made it through the decade mostly on hope and ambition. The 1960s saw Eunice go from town to city and times were good. Several substantial industries moved into town as did a two-year branch of Louisiana State University. The efforts of Mayor Curtis Joubert and US senator Bennett Johnston turned the area's cultural heritage into a marketable commodity during the late 1980s when the renovated Liberty Theater began hosting the *Live Cajun Radio Show* and Mardi Gras participants were invited to parade through the downtown. The Jean Lafitte Acadian Cultural Center, a national park, was a magnet for tourists and their money. The cultural heritage activities, LSU Eunice, the oil industry and the mom-and-pop businesses have provided the backbone for Eunice's economy to this day. Although Eunice's economy fluctuates, there is a sense of civic pride and desire for progress.

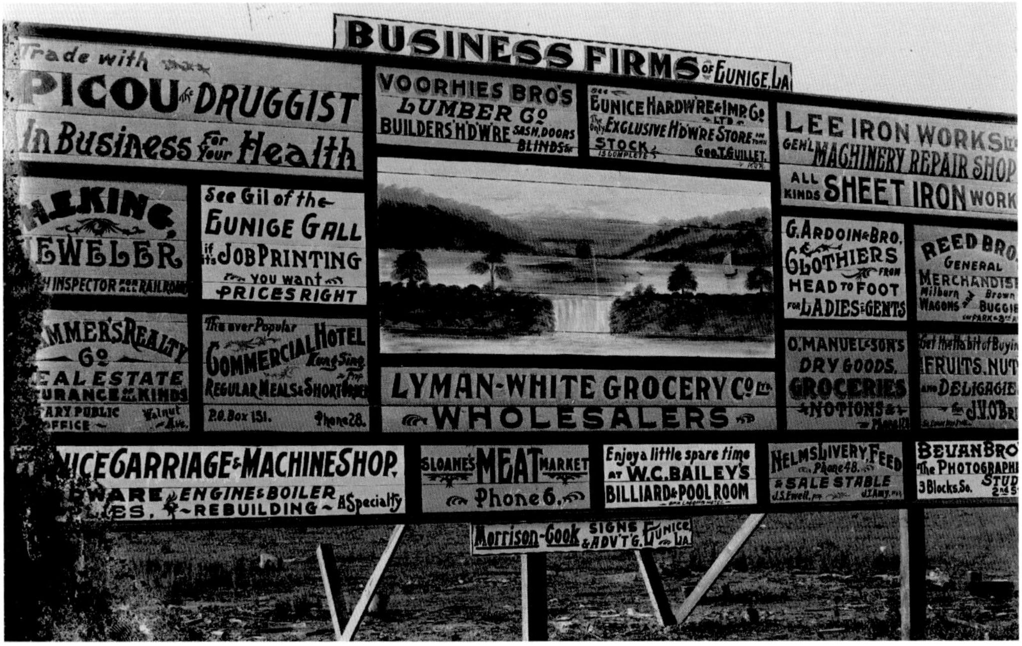

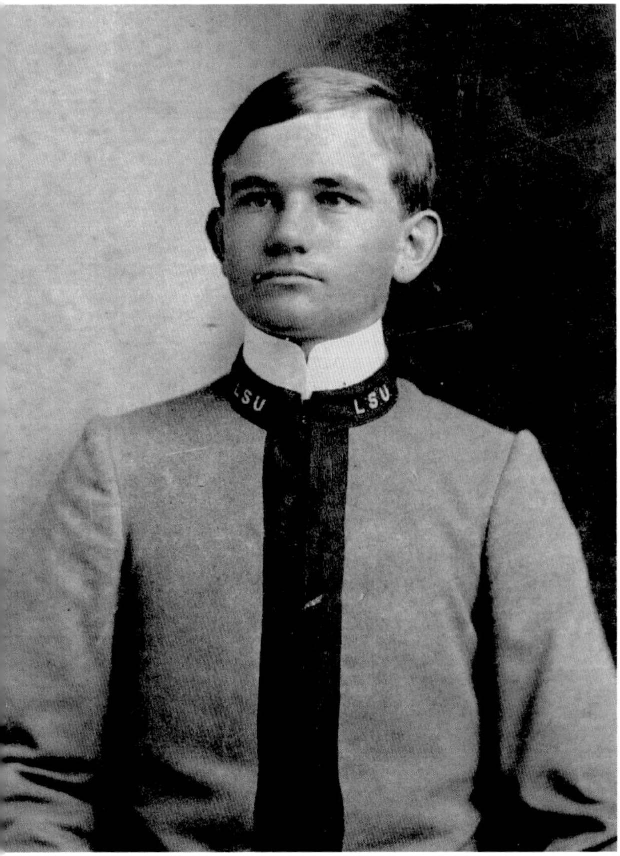

Advertised Businesses
This early sign was entitled "Business Firms of Eunice," and served as a homemade billboard advertising Eunice's businesses. The sign was likely erected between 1907, the year the Bevan Brothers photographers arrived in town, and 1919 when the *Eunice Gall* merged with the *New Era* newspaper. The *Gall* was listed on this sign. Eunice merchants were progressive and open to new methods of advertising their products and services. (Courtesy of BBHC.)

He Wore Many Hats
Dr. Harry Jenkins's parents were William and Clara Jenkins. Attending LSU, he was pictured in a cadet's uniform. Jenkins practiced medicine for 61 years. His first wife, Ethel Diana Nicholson, died in 1931. He married Catherine Leona Bonvillain, a nurse and native of Erath, Louisiana. They had six children. Jenkins was a charter member of the Eunice Rotary Club, a founder of Tri-Parish Bank, a farmer, a city councilman, and an assistant coroner. The doctor was awarded Rotary Club's first Citizen of the Year award in 1942. He died in 1970 at the age of 86. (Courtesy of Kakie McGee Manuel.)

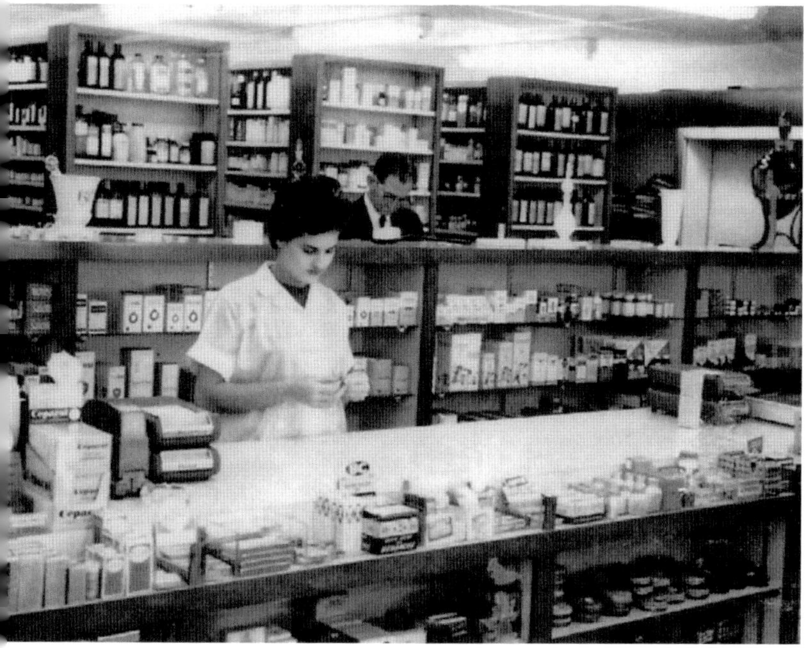

Pharmacist and Civic Leader
Chester Derbes worked for other druggists until he opened his store in the Liberty Theater Building in 1936. Derbes moved to Second Street and served the public for 22 years. In 1961, he built a modern store, where he is pictured, right, with employee Leanna Balfour. Derbes, a moving force in Eunice's progress, served on the city council and was mayor in 1945. (Courtesy of Leanna Balfour.)

Italian Businessman
Phillip Montelaro, right, a son of Carlo Montelaro and Frances Siggio both natives of Lucca, Sicily, owned and managed the Mayer Hotel. Montelaro also owned the Crystal Bakery in the 1940s. Pictured with two unidentified employees, his wife, Annie Ferruggia Montelaro, is third from the left. (Courtesy of Frances Montelaro Frugé and Mary Margaret Montelaro.)

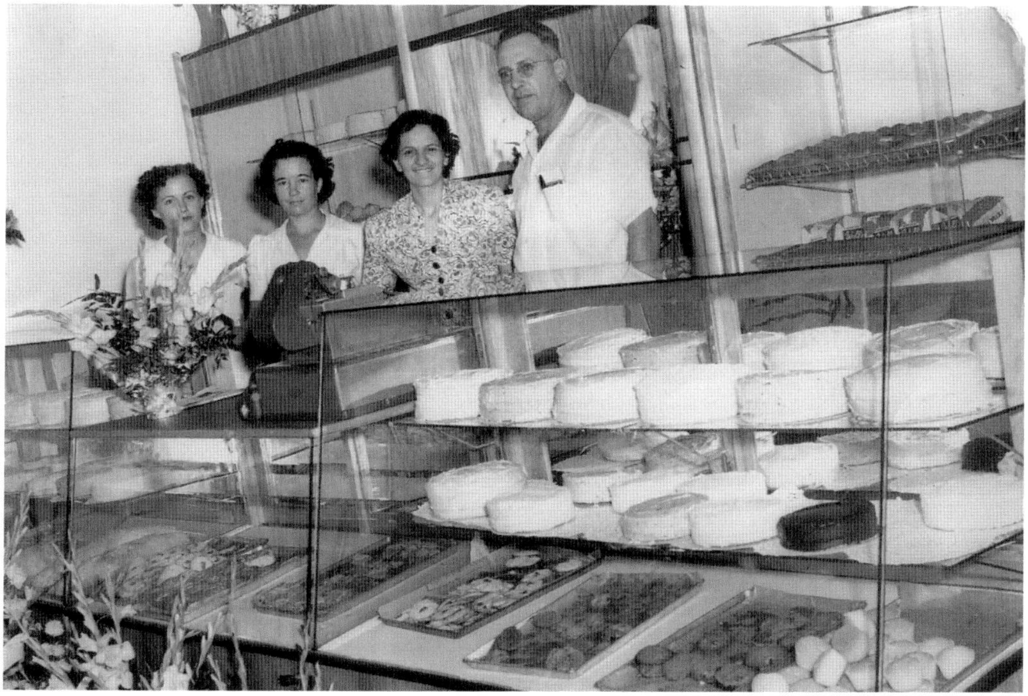

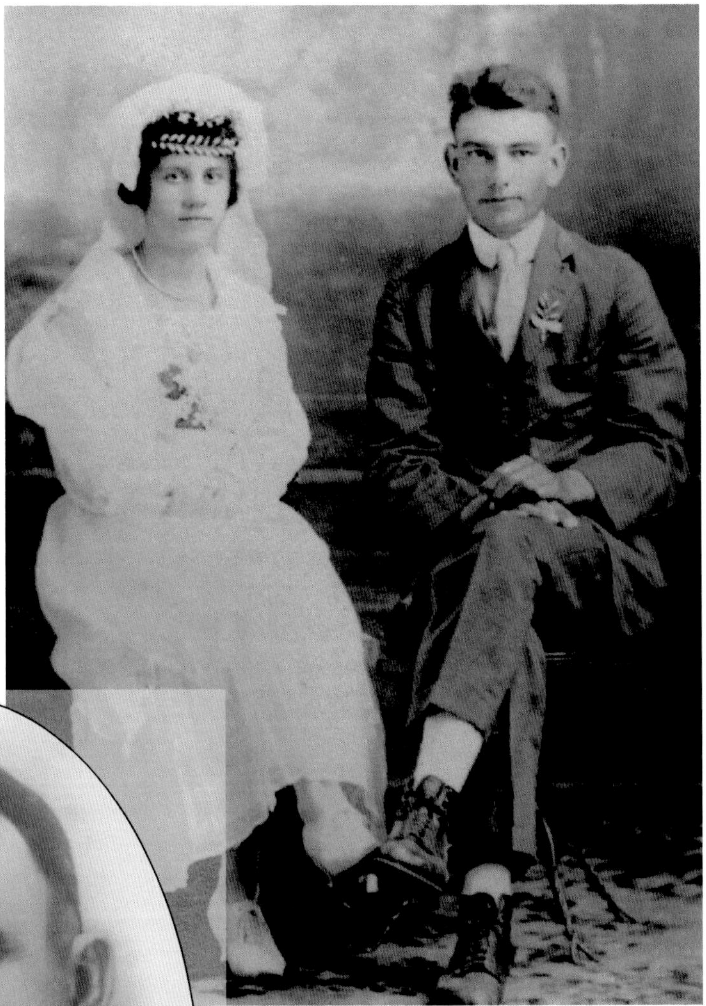

Post Office Café
Enos and Gertrude McGee Fontenot operated the popular Post Office Café located across Laurel Avenue from the US Post Office from 1955 until the 1980s. They were photographed at their wedding in 1921. He was a son of Theogene and Aimee Miller Fontenot, and Gertrude's parents were Theodore and Doris Marie Fontenot McGee. Enos also descended from the famous Cajun leader, Beausoleil Broussard. (Courtesy of Dr. Jack D. Miller Jr.)

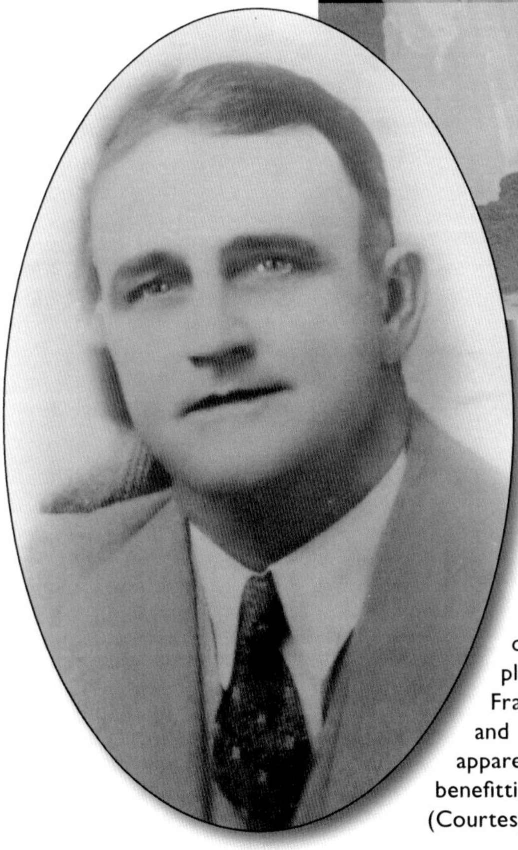

A Wildcatter
George Bradley, of Irish extraction, was born in Nodoway, Iowa, in 1886. His parents, Cornelius Thompkins and Mary Elizabeth Grover Bradley, were native New Yorkers who arrived here in a covered wagon from their home in Oklahoma. George, one of the first "wildcatters" to drill for oil in the Evangeline oil fields, owned Camellia plantation south of Eunice. He married Theresa Francois, who was the mother of Raymond, Isabelle, and Edith. Bradley's successes in oil speculation apparently were well planned, since his descendants are benefitting from his hard work and expertise to this day. (Courtesy of Pam Parrott Quirk.)

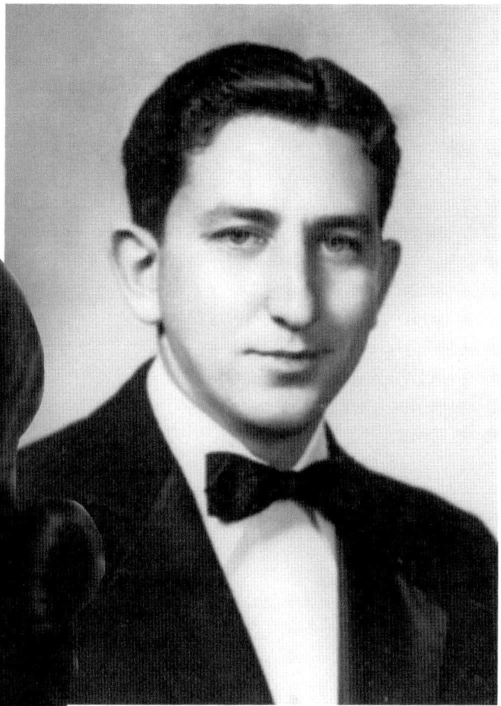

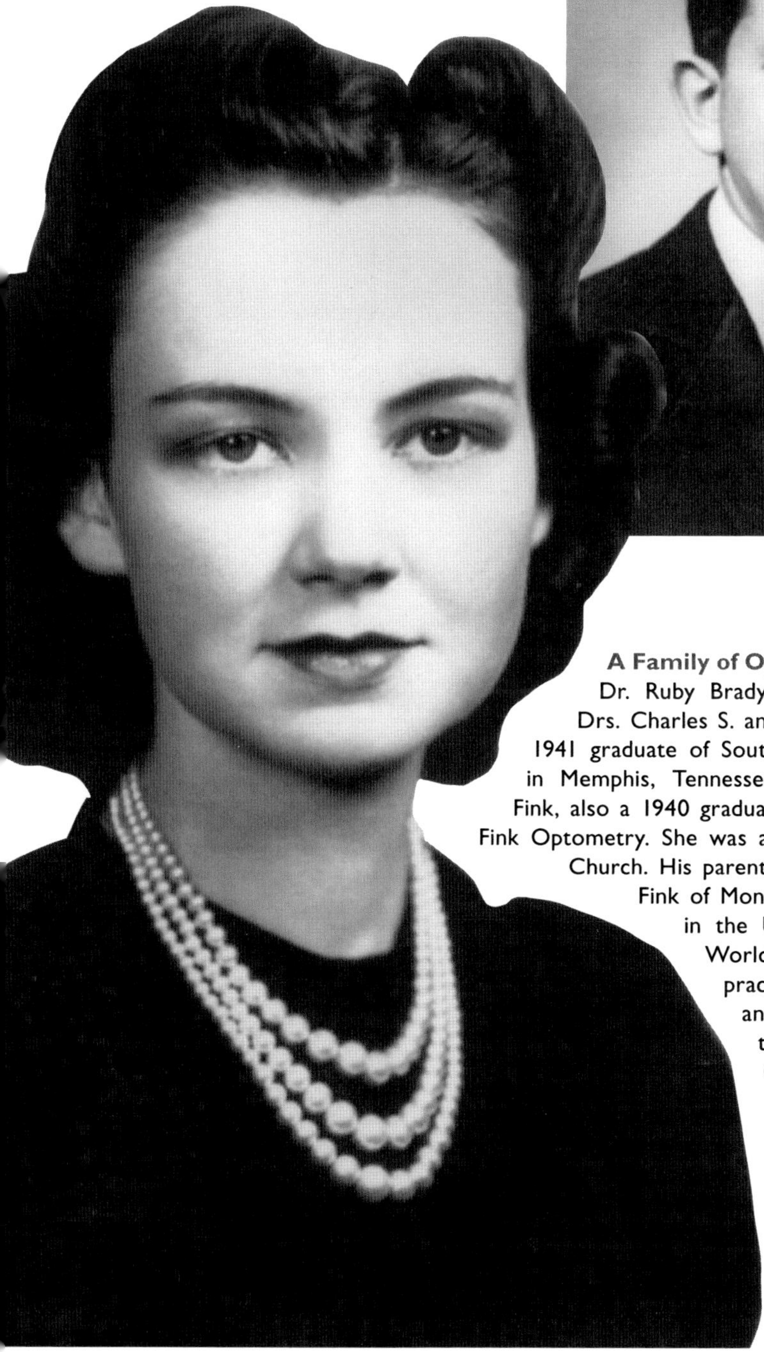

A Family of Optometrists

Dr. Ruby Brady Fink was the daughter of Drs. Charles S. and Martha Franques Brady. A 1941 graduate of Southern College of Optometry in Memphis, Tennessee, she married Dr. Roland Fink, also a 1940 graduate, and they founded Brady-Fink Optometry. She was active in the First Methodist Church. His parents were Max and Julia Jacobs Fink of Monroe, Louisiana. After serving in the US Army Medical Corps in World War II, he joined his wife practicing optometry in Eunice and Ville Platte. Fink served on the Louisiana State Board of Optometric Examiners from 1949 to 1954, and practiced for 60 years. A pioneer in local broadcasting, he was one of the owners of KLFY TV 10, KEUN radio, and KVPI radio. Fink was a Mason and a sportsman. (Courtesy of Dr. Rhonda Fink Pucheu.)

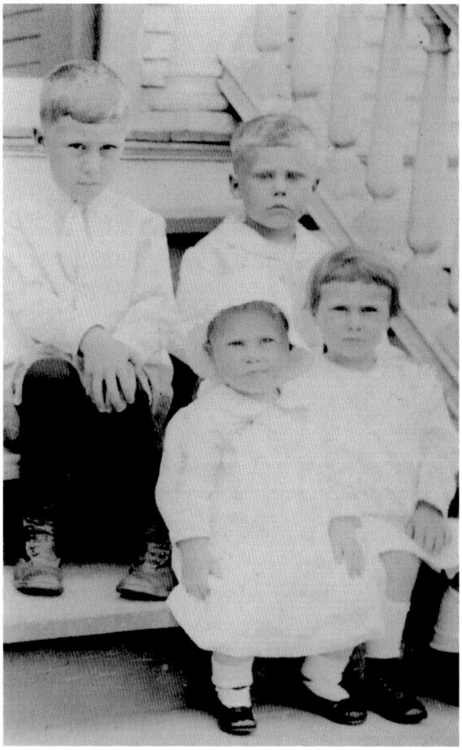

The Duplechin Brothers

Dr. Gerald "Boo" Duplechin, one of Eunice's more popular dentists, and his brothers, businessmen Jake and Aquilla, were sons of pioneer Eunice dentist and his wife, Dr. Agamer and Josephine Miller Duplechin. In 1950, the brothers purchased the Horace Guillory farm northwest of town and converted it to the "Diamond D Ranch." The Duplechin brothers posed with their sister at their family home on South Second Street in the early 1900s. They were left to right (seated in front) Jake and Valverta; (seated in back) Aquilla and Gerald "Boo" Duplechin. (Courtesy of Ruth Ellen Dupre Duplechin.)

Rice Farmer

Anthony "Tony" Bollich Sr., center, born in Nebraska in 1870, was photographed playing dominoes with local barber, Avit Bordelon, left, and Bollich's son, Henry Bollich, right. Bollich Sr. was a son of Peter and Katherina Kittle Bollich, both German immigrants. He was first married to Madeline Dischler and secondly to Edna Boudreaux. He purchased property south of Eunice, building a prosperous rice farm that his descendants still operate. (Courtesy of Hilda Bollich.)

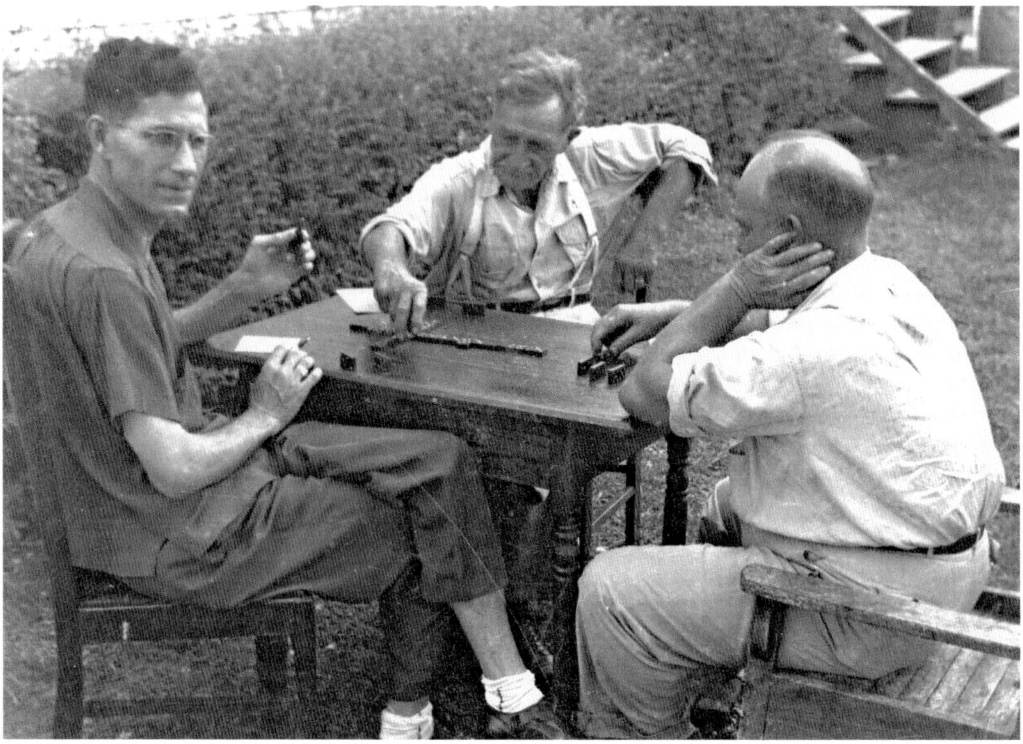

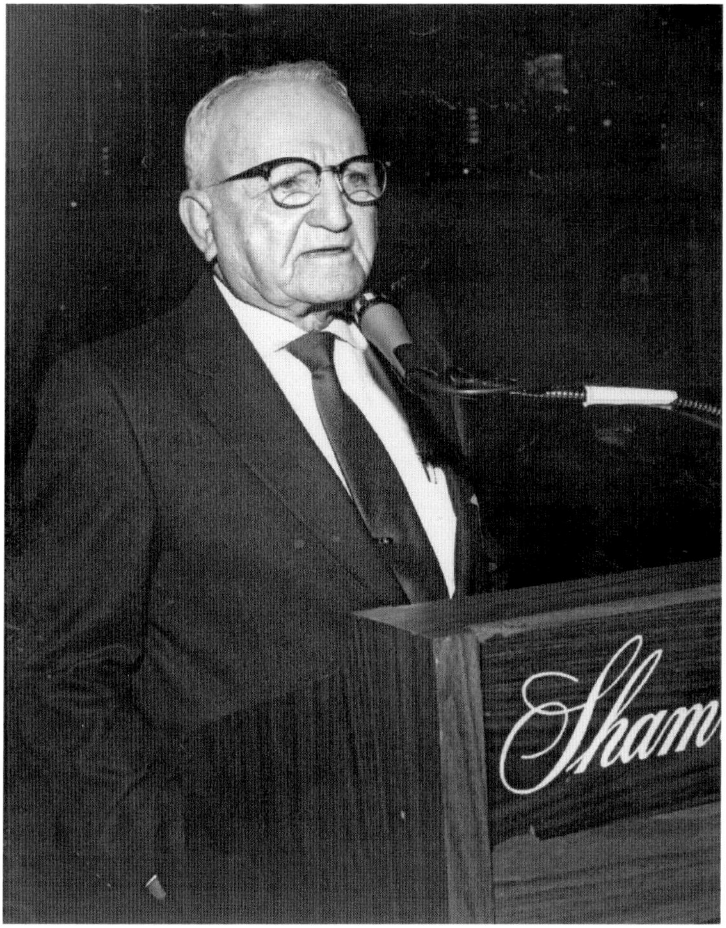

From Alabama to Mowata

Born to Thomas Taylor and Elizabeth McAlpine Atteberry in 1900, Winston "Skeet" Atteberry moved in 1902 with his family from Utaw, Alabama, to the prairie south of Eunice in the Mowata area. His father was sent to manage a large rice farm. Atteberry was a graduate of Staunton Military Academy in Virginia, attended several colleges, and received a degree in civil engineering from the University of Virginia. After many years building highway projects in Louisiana and through the jungles of Nicaragua, he returned to Mowata in 1929. Atteberry then began a career as a farmer, cattleman, and businessman. He was instrumental in organizing farm groups with the purpose of helping farmers promote and market their products. He was a leader in the organization of the Crowley Rice Drier Cooperative, a rice mill, and a livestock commission company. He served on the board of directors of the National Rice Council for Market Development and the American Rice Growers Association. In addition, he developed one of the finest herds of crossbred cattle in Acadia Parish and became actively involved in organizing the Acadia Livestock Commission Company. Atteberry served on various agricultural boards and governmental committees. A plethora of awards and offices were bestowed on him including the International Rice Festival's Rice Farmer of the Year in 1955 and the Lions Club Farmer of the Year award in 1962. He was also an active Shriner, president of the Acadia Parish School Board, and member of the Vestry of Trinity Episcopal Church. Atteberry and Carrie D Townsend were married in 1935. They had three children, Carrilyn, Winston Jr., and William "Mac." He died at age 82 in 1983. (Courtesy of William "Mac" Atteberry.)

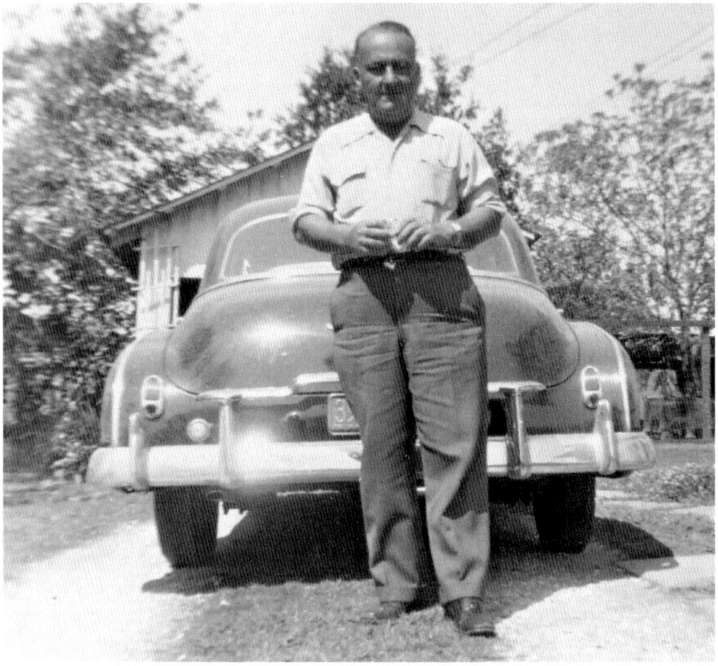

Easter Chicks

Damond Ardoin, son of Zenon Ardoin, was a well-known businessman. His feed store on North Second Street is remembered for the pastel chicks and bunnies that magically appeared in the building's show window every Easter. Ardoin married Agnes Reed and they adopted a daughter. (Courtesy of Dr. Rodney T. Reed.)

Rooming House

Born Marie Wilfert to Vitus and Rosalia Haier Wilfert in 1858, Marie married Christian Ruppert, who came from Germany in 1871 on the SS *Hanover*. Ruppert farmed rice and operated his sawmill. Like so many women of the time, when widowed, Marie Ruppert had to support her eight children, so she opened Mrs. C. Ruppert's Rooming House. People in this image are not identified. (Courtesy of Dave Ruppert and BBHC.)

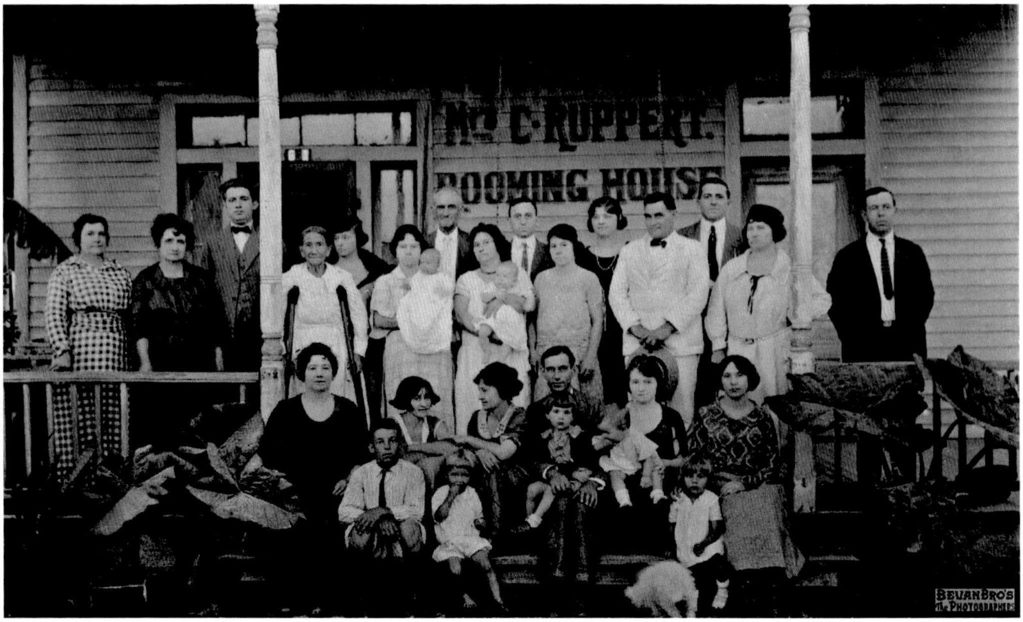

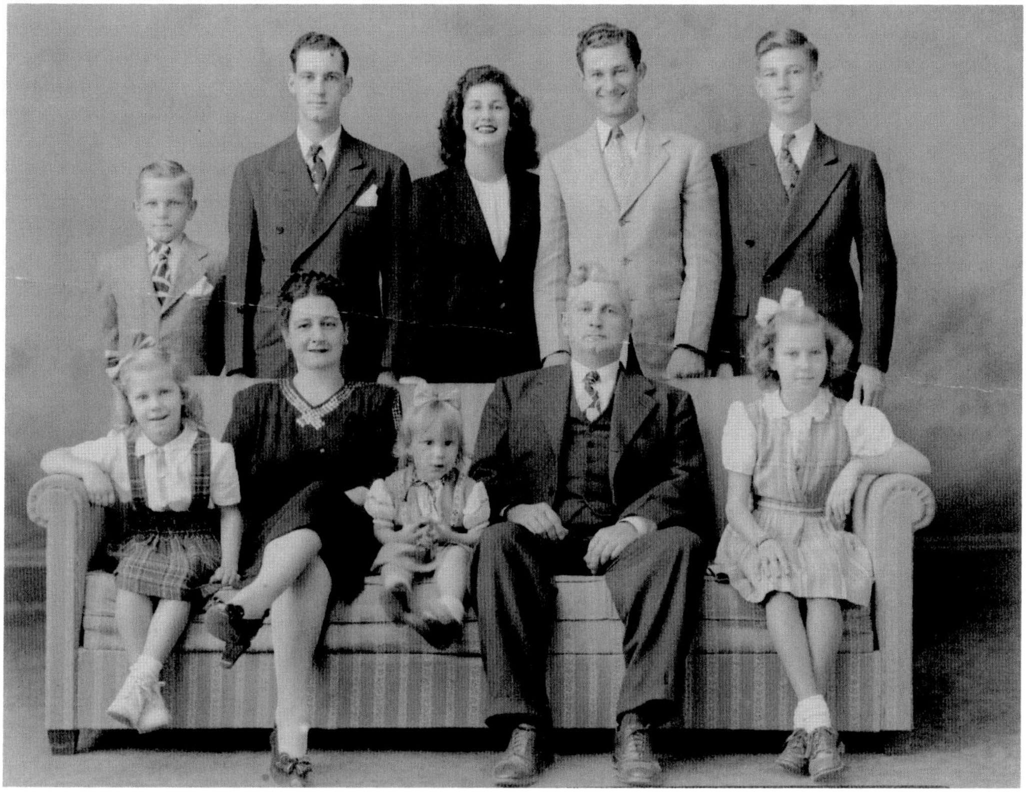

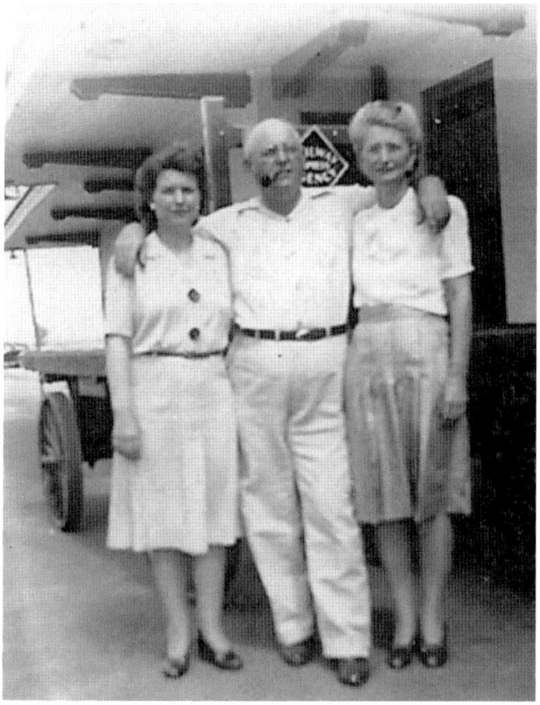

Morris Family
Samuel Jasper "Jap" Morris was the father of a large family. Left to right were (standing) Clark, Samuel Jasper Jr., Betty, Tommy, and Calvin; (seated) Bonnie, Pearl Bult Morris, Charlene, Samuel Jasper "Jap" Morris Sr., and Donna Jo. Born in 1888, Morris was appointed postmaster in 1935. A rice buyer, he purchased the old Southern Cotton Oil Company mill in the north part of town with plans to build a 1,000-barrel rice drier on part of the property. He married Pearl, daughter of Eunice pioneers, James and Rose Ruppert Bult. (Courtesy of Tommy Morris Jr.)

Railway Express Agent
Arnold E. Tyson, shown with his sisters Jewel Long, right, and Lena Curry, left, was the Railway Express agent at the Missouri-Pacific depot. Tyson married Henrietta Bordelon, who worked at Bordelon's Restaurant across the railroad tracks from the depot. (Courtesy of DeVonne Reese and Arnette Tyson Reese.)

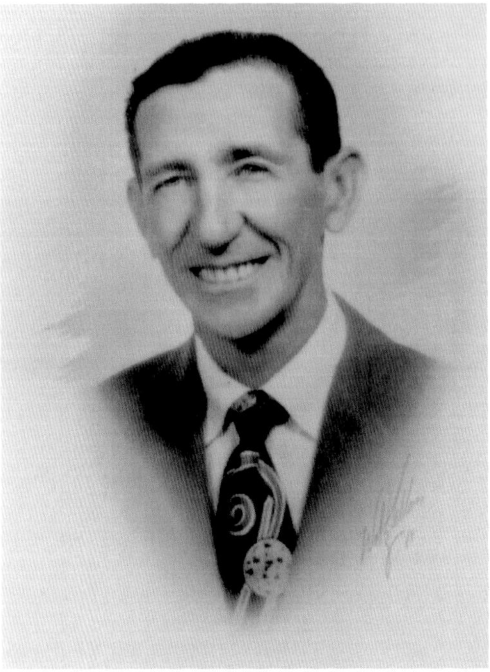

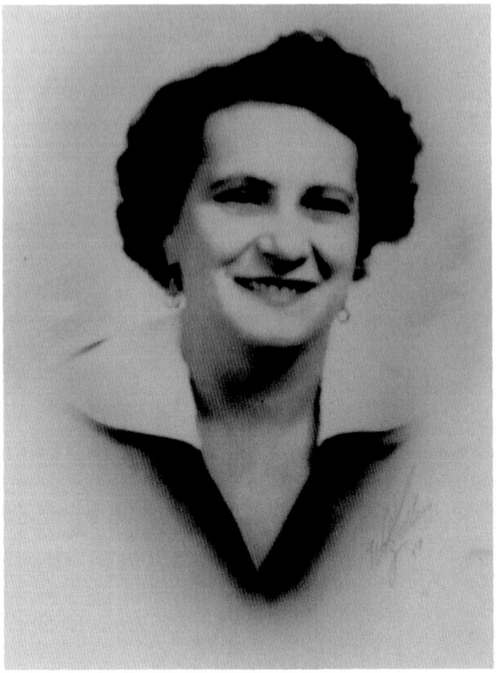

Gifts and Angola Prison

Leo Charles Ardoin, born in 1904, was educated at St. Joseph's School in Grand Coteau and at an electrician's school in Detroit, Michigan. He married Laurice Veillon, a native of Duralde in 1909, a child of Thomas and Esthelma Guillory Veillon. When he was hired as the head electrician at Angola State Prison, he moved his family into an employee's house on the prison grounds. Ardoin's house overlooked the "Red Hat" cells, which held prisoners awaiting electrocution. Later, the Ardoins moved home to open a business in the Queen Theater Building. He was in the Knights of Columbus. She co-owned Leo's Electric and Gift Shop until her daughter bought the business. From 1955 to 1957, she was grand regent of the Catholic Daughters of America. (Courtesy of Jo Ann Ardoin Amy.)

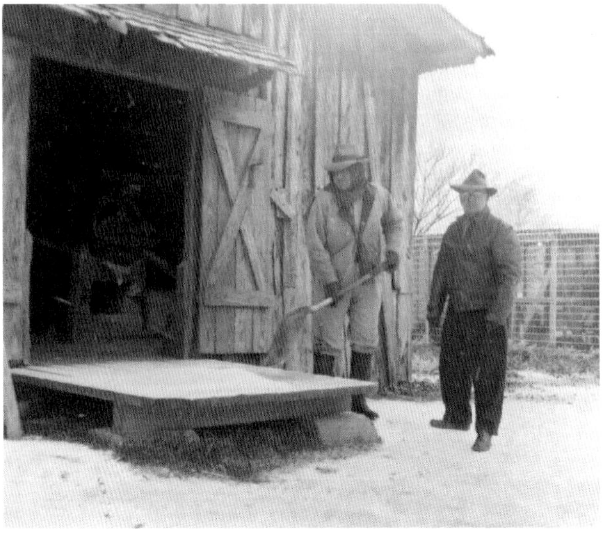

Rice Mill Owner

Sidney Courville, right, shown with his brother, Lital, owned a grocery store and small rice mill on West Maple Avenue. He married Theresa Aguillard, who with the entire family, worked in the store. Courville's mill provided rice for the POW camp at the fairgrounds during World War II. (Courtesy of Ruth Courville Karl.)

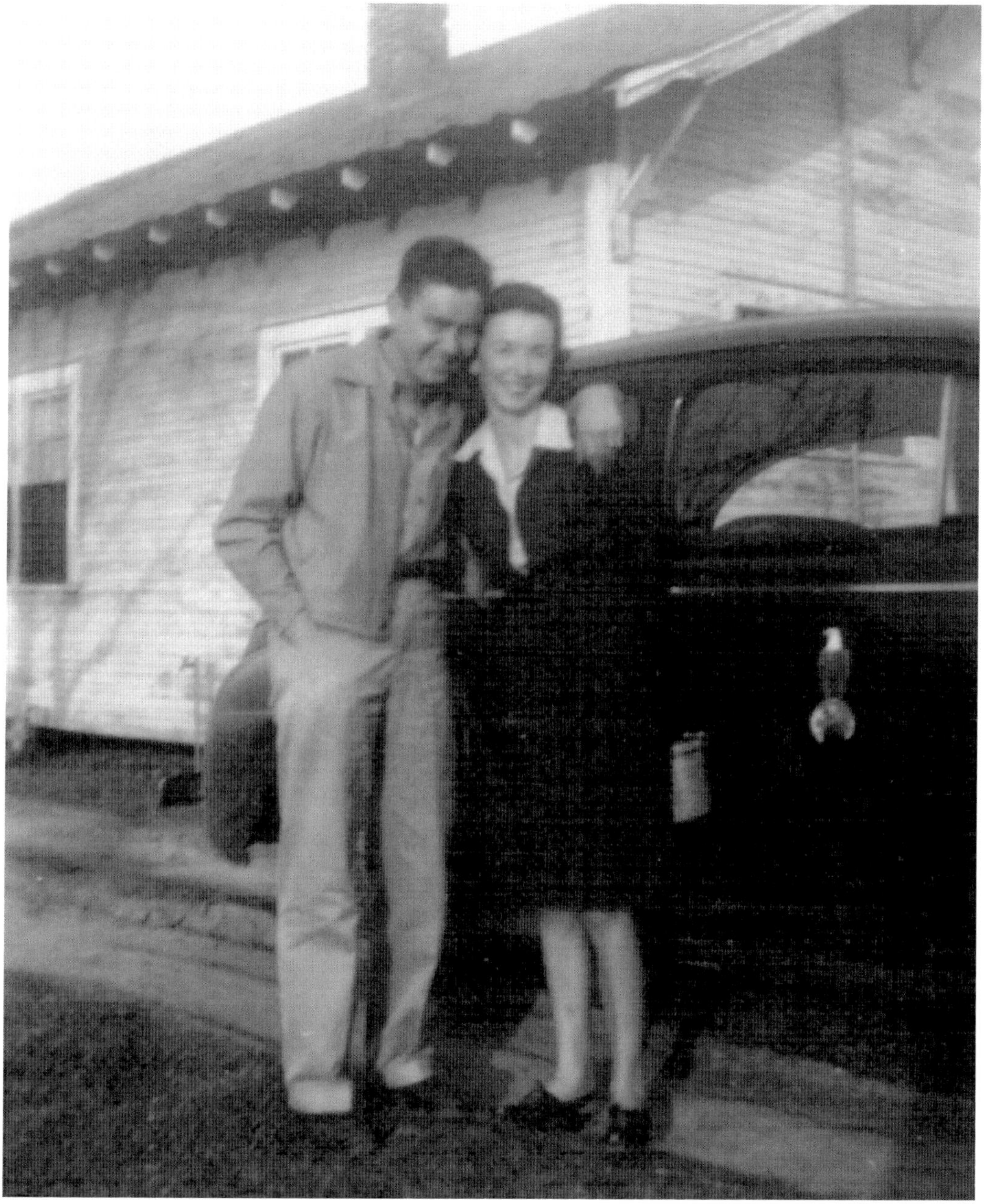

Basketball, Sales, and Chamber of Commerce

Horace G. "Andy" Jackson played semi-pro basketball and started Farmer's Supply Company in 1946 in Eunice's first prefabricated building. In 1963, he became Eunice Chamber of Commerce executive vice president where he promoted Eunice for 15 years. Jackson worked with Mayor Wilson Moosa to obtain a branch of LSU in Eunice. He was instrumental in "Operation Forethought," the renewal of downtown Second Street. He was a 30-year member of Rotary with perfect attendance, a leader at First Baptist Church, and Citizen of the Year in 1966. Jackson married Dorothy Gale "Dot" Rowland, a schoolteacher. (Courtesy of H. Rowland Jackson.)

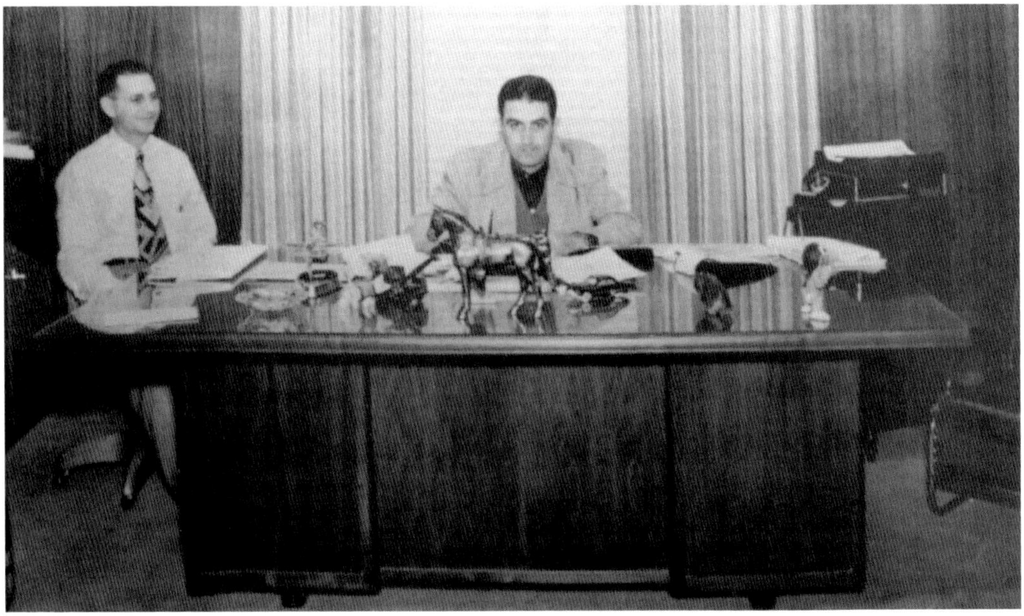

City's Largest Payroll
Mitchell Ashy, right, and Andy Cummings were photographed in Ashy's office. Ashy came to Eunice in 1934 to manage a trucking company at the Tepetate oil field. He expanded to oil field construction in Louisiana and adjoining states. In 1953, Ashy Construction had the largest payroll in the city at $47,500 monthly and employed close to 400 workers, two-thirds of whom were from Eunice. Ashy donated labor and equipment for St. Edmund High School's new athletic field, for which he was given the honor of turning on the lights to open the athletic complex. (Courtesy of Eunice Public Library.)

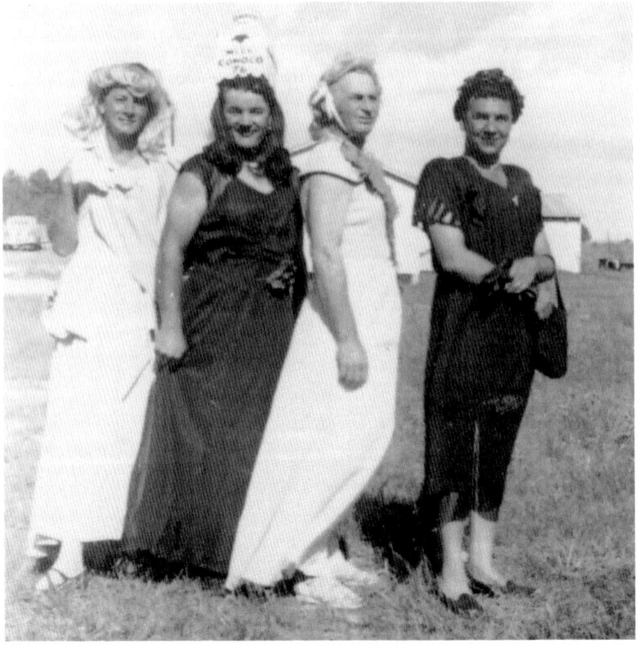

A Beauty Contest
Continental Oil Company employees at Tepetate Oil Field enjoyed company socials including the 1956 All-Male Beauty Revue. Pictured are well-known Eunice citizens who were employees of Continental and beauty contestants: left to right, Willie Parrott, Roy Eaton, Jim Spears, and John Landreneau. Eaton won the crown. (Courtesy of Lennie Parrott Buller.)

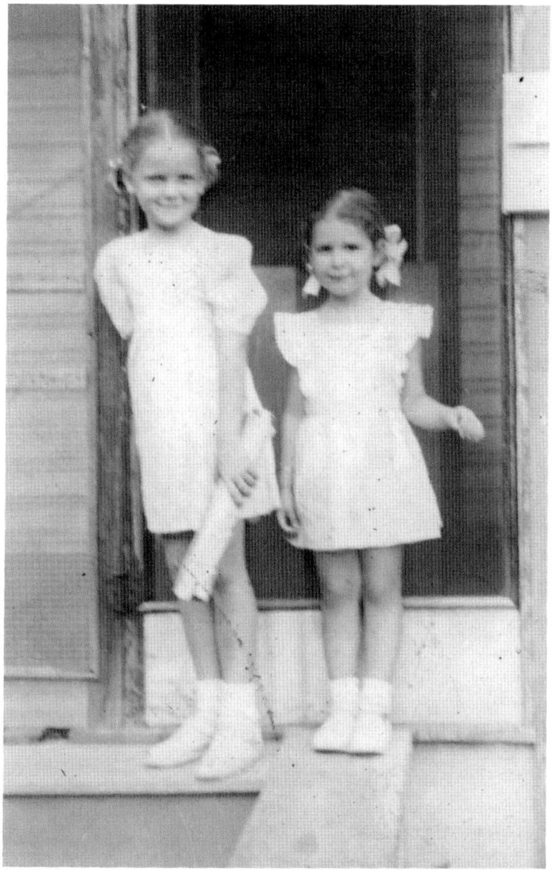

Third-Generation Merchant
Joan "Joanie" Kerstein, right, the third generation of the Wright family to operate Louis Wright Store, is shown with Mary Horton. The daughter of Irving and Sophie Wright Kerstein, Joanie served on the Opelousas-Eunice Public Library Board and was instrumental in founding Eunice Players' Theater for which she was treasurer. She loved to discuss city affairs. She is buried at Lafayette Jewish Cemetery. (Courtesy of Allen Horton.)

"Uncle Tom" Bevan
Tom Bevan was born in Wales. When his father settled in Missouri to work in the coal mines, Tom decided coal mining was not his destiny. Consequently, Bevan decided to join family in Louisiana. He traveled in this wagon that was equipped with a complete darkroom for processing photographs on the road. His brother, George, joined him later. The Bevan Brothers opened photography studios in Eunice, Elton, and Ville Platte. With their nephew, Leonard Thompson, the three men visually recorded the significant life events of area citizens. Tragically, a fire destroyed their studio. (Courtesy of BBHC.)

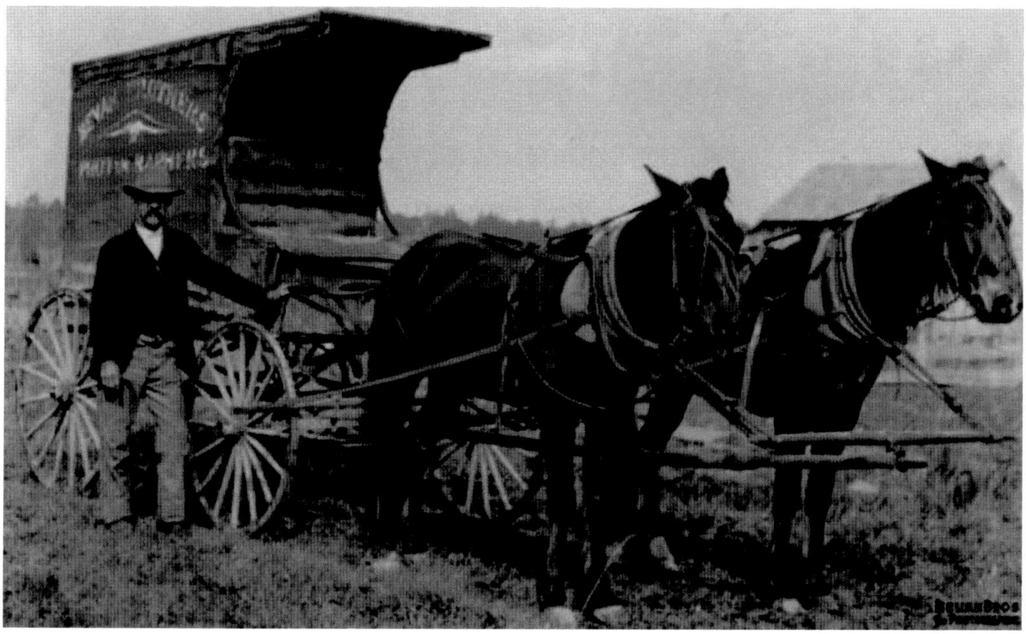

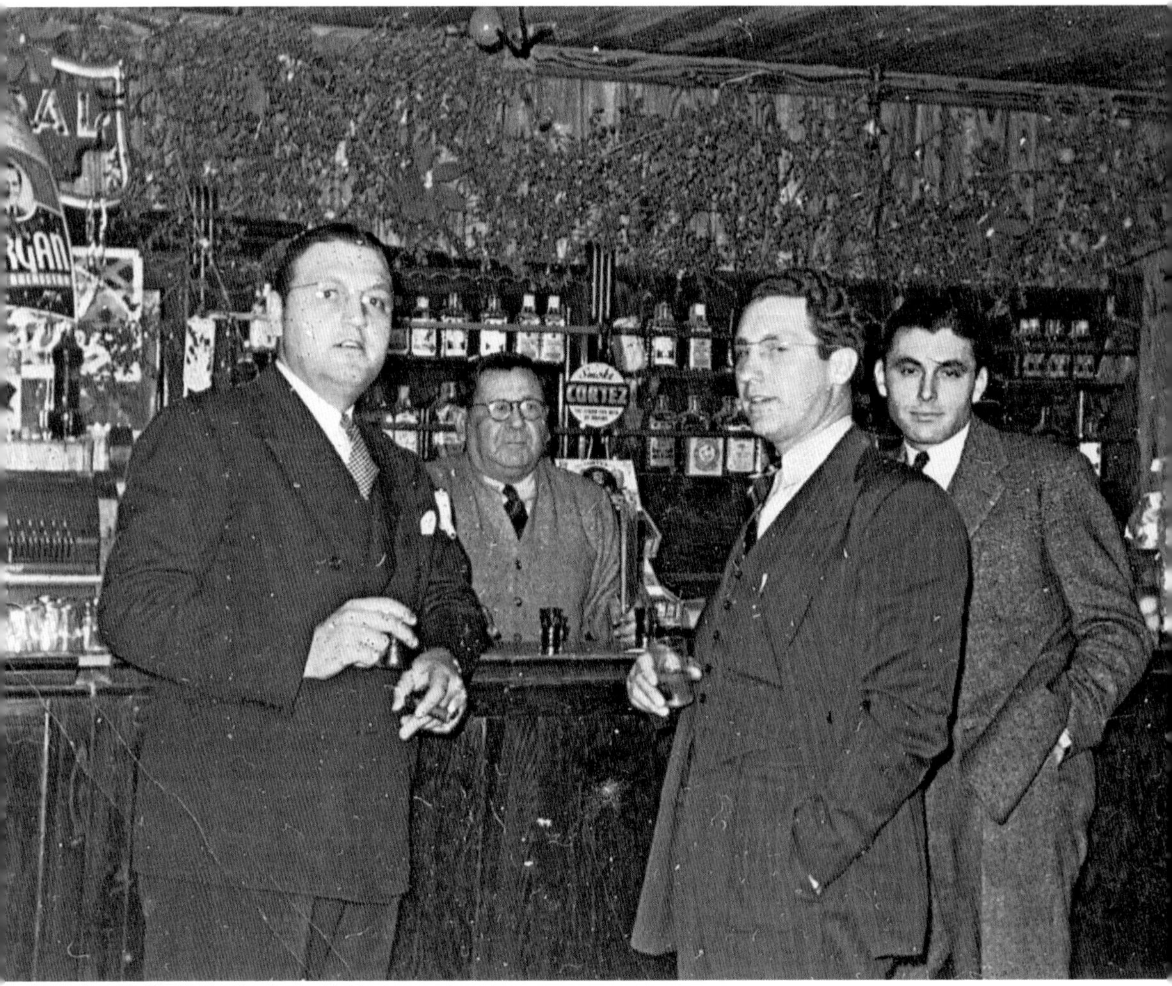

Mayor, Club Owner, Tailor

Stanislaus "Tony" Wyble, second from left, was seen with three unidentified liquor salesmen in his popular club, Tony's, which was located on Highway 13 South. Tony's Club was one of the largest providers of slot machines in the city prior to the "war on gambling" conducted by the state police. Col. Francis Grevemberg, superintendent of the Louisiana State Police, began his crusade to "close up the joints" as part of his all-out warfare on any form of gambling and vice. The colonel and his troopers worked on the eradication of the "one-armed bandits" first. Tony's had slot machines, but was not a "joint." Records of whether Wyble's club was a target of Grevemberg's troopers are not available. However, as a supper club, Tony's reputation for the delicious barbecue served on the premises has outlived the owner. Wyble wore many hats including that of mayor as he served 20 years of nonconsecutive mayoral terms. During his administration, a speed limit for vehicles in the city was enacted, city streets were paved, a clean-up campaign to improve the physical appearance of the town along with the passage of a stiff anti-littering ordinance was begun, and the city administration assisted in the promotion of a Bargain Day and Agricultural Meeting. He also owned and operated the first tailor and pressing shop where he sold custom-made clothing. In 1935, Wyble was installed as postmaster. All businesses in the city closed during the time of his funeral to show their respect. He married Anastasia Reed, daughter of pioneer settlers Theogene and Emmaize Guillory Reed, and they were parents to seven daughters and one son. (Courtesy of Allen Horton.)

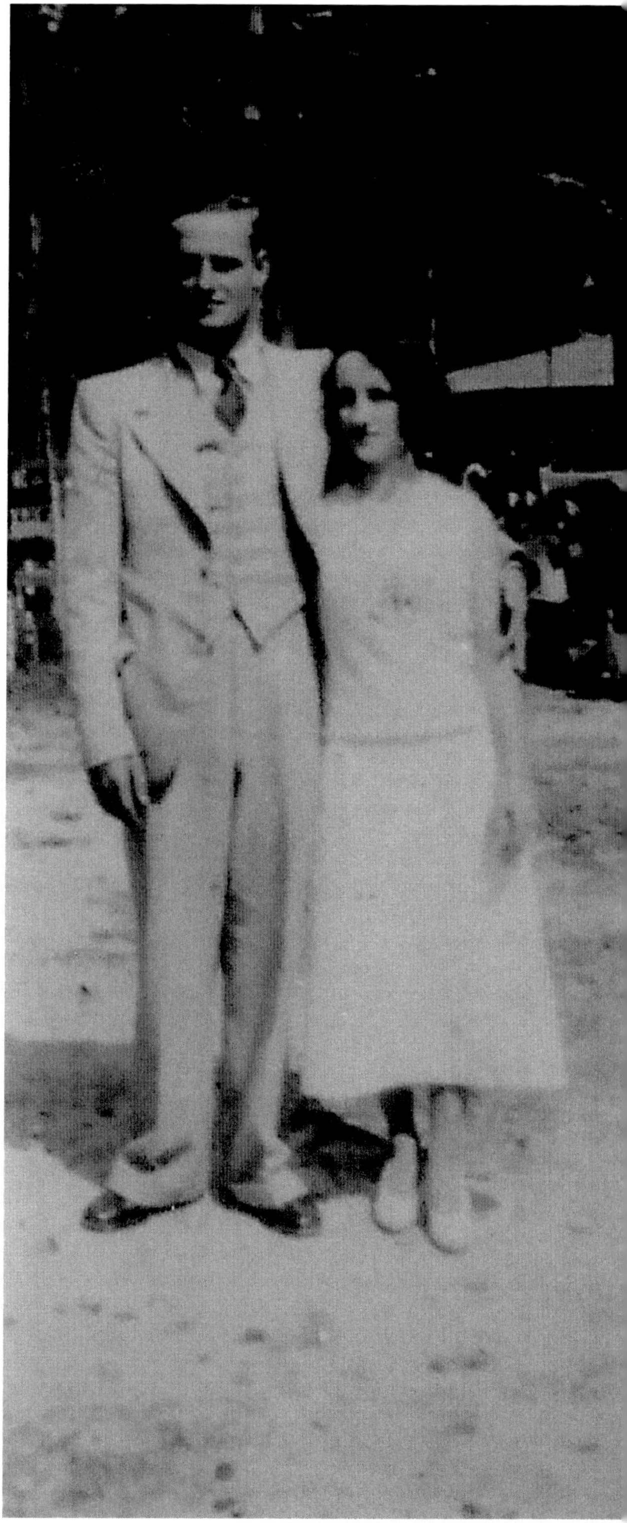

A Widow's Work
Historically, widows had to struggle to support their families or, many times, they had to remarry for survival. After World War II, thanks to the Rosie the Riveters, women tasted independence. Ena Aguillard LaFleur was such a lady. Born in 1913 in the Savoy community about five miles east of Eunice, she was the daughter of Luma and Clara Savoy Aguillard. Ena's mother died when she was very young and Ena's older sister reared her. She married a young farmer, Peter Ray LaFleur, and was the mother of five children. Her husband had a dairy farm in the same community. She was widowed at the age of 34 in 1948, when her husband, who had been milking his cows, walked out of the barn pushing a cow that was reluctant to go outside during an electrical storm. A bolt of lightning struck the cow and passed through LaFleur as his hand was on the cow's back. Apparently, the bolt of lightning was so strong that it fused his rubber boots to his feet and blackened and burned his clothing on the right side where it entered his body. Ena's brother, Roderick Aguillard, and Lester Gil moved Lafleur to a blanket on the highway and administered artificial respiration for about 30 minutes. When the ambulance arrived, he was taken to the Eunice Hospital where the fire chief, Lannie Frugé, was waiting to use the resuscitator. Other firemen who helped with the resuscitator were Dudley Frugé, Horace LeDoux, and Red Fontenot. Ena was suddenly widowed with five young children ranging in ages from four to 14 years old to support. Without hesitation, she decided to continue working the dairy to pay off the debt. Her oldest child helped with the dairy work. Years later, the widow worked at Moosa Memorial Hospital for over 20 years before retiring from that job in 1979. Even in her retirement, she was active. Ena raised a few cattle and chickens and worked as a sitter for the elderly. She lived to see all her children become successes in their chosen fields. The oldest, Janet, went into business with her husband. Gretchen, Annel, and Carolyn were all registered nurses. Aubry, the only son, became a rice farmer. Ena died in 1990 at 77 years of age, leaving a legacy of hard work and independence. (Courtesy of Ileen Weber LaFleur.)

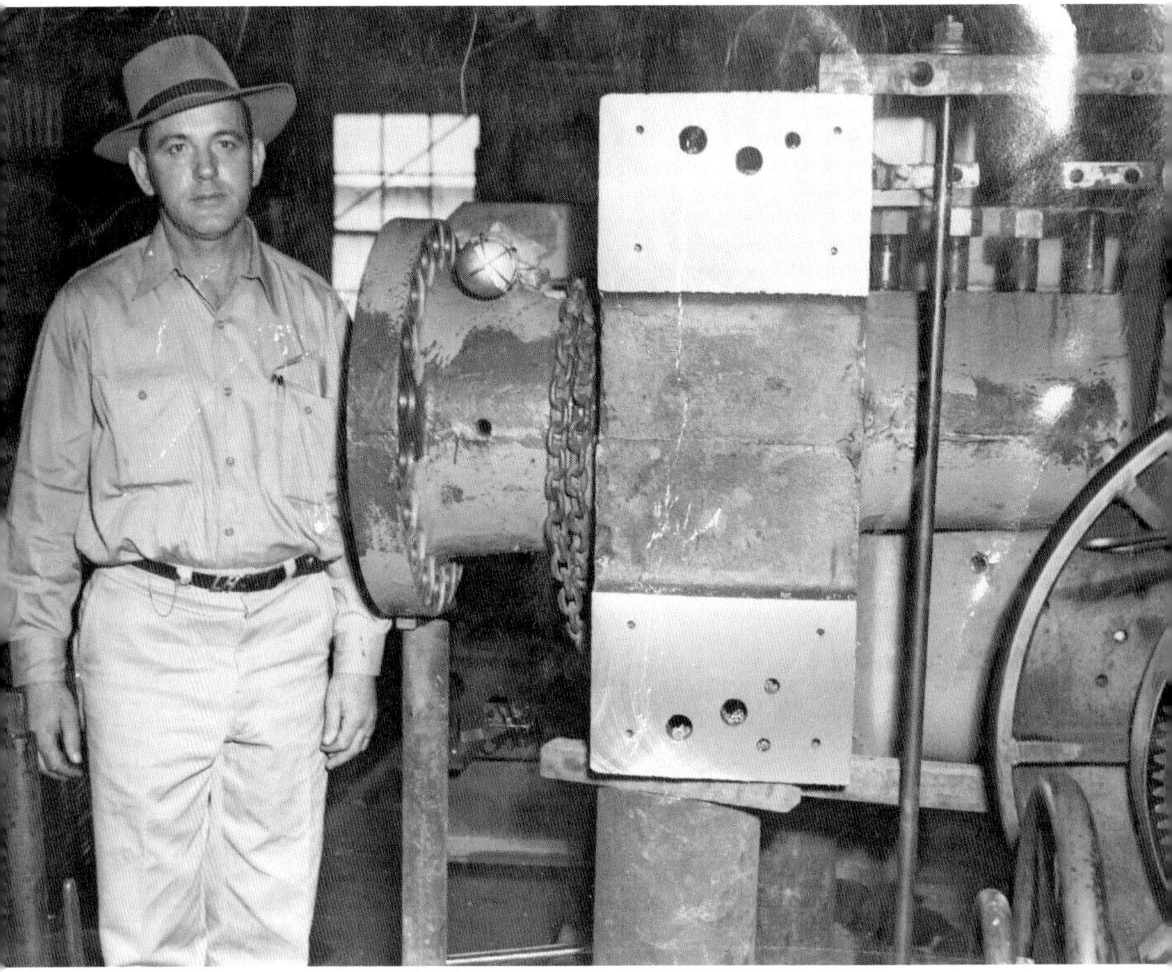

Drilled for Eunice's Water

Leo Ferdinand Heinen Sr., pictured standing near large machinery in the iron works building, was a descendant of pious German Catholic immigrants who settled in *L'Anse Robert,* or Robert's Cove. In 1932, he married Marie Catherine Hensgens, who also descended from other German Catholic settlers. They were the parents of Gwendolyn, Lowell, Brian, Janet, and Leo Ferdinand Jr. Heinen began his career as a bookkeeper, but he soon moved up to be the manager of the Eunice Iron Works. In 1952, Heinen's employees drilled a 392-feet-deep well adjacent to Vine Avenue for Cleco Electric Company. Water surged at the rate of 3,000 gallons a minute, providing the city with a higher volume of fresh water. Eunice Iron Works was responsible for drilling numerous irrigation wells for area rice farms. Interestingly, the German immigrants were the first farmers in southwest Louisiana to raise irrigated rice for market. The German farmers learned how to construct levees around their rice fields to hold the rain water. Then they improved their methods by erecting large irrigation wells to pump water into the rice ponds. Additionally, The Eunice Iron Works was a source of wonder for children. Open windows allowed children to look in and watch the workers cut and drill metal. Some jobs are so interesting that children cannot resist observing the workers. Such was the case when children walking home from the movies in the 1950s and 1960s always stopped at the Iron Works to watch the interesting iron work or to cool off with a sip of cold water from the business fountain. Heinen had a small stool built so the children could reach the cold-water spigot of the fountain. (Courtesy of Janet Heinen Martel.)

A Man of Influence

Gladney L. Manuel was born in 1916 five miles north of Eunice to Meus and Marcelite Manuel Manuel. Of Spanish and French ancestry, Manuel was descended from Louisiana colonial settlers. After graduating from high school, he joined the US Navy and served aboard a destroyer. He entered LSU in 1937. Recalled to active service, Manuel was commissioned an ensign and saw action in the North African Campaign and later in the Southwest Pacific Theater during World War II. His ability to speak fluent French led to Manuel being sent to Washington, DC, to serve as a liaison officer between the American and French Navies. In 1945, he and his brother, Edlee, founded Manuel Brothers partnership and opened the Sinclair Service Station on Laurel Avenue. The partnership was dissolved in 1957 and Gladney opened Manuel Truck and Equipment Company. Being a man of wide civic interests, he held a variety of offices in local, state, and national organizations and was awarded many accolades, including the Rotary Club's Citizen of the Year award in 1955. He held membership in many civic and religious organizations and served as Troop 9 scout master in the Boy Scouts of America. Manuel was elected president of Acadiana Bank and Trust Company in 1967 and appointed to the Louisiana Transportation Board. Manuel was honored when a building on the LSU Eunice campus, Manuel Hall, was named for him. He married Edna Mae Matthews in 1941 and they had three children—Gladney Jr., Mary Gay, and Linda. (Courtesy of Charlie and Linda Manuel Thibodeaux.)

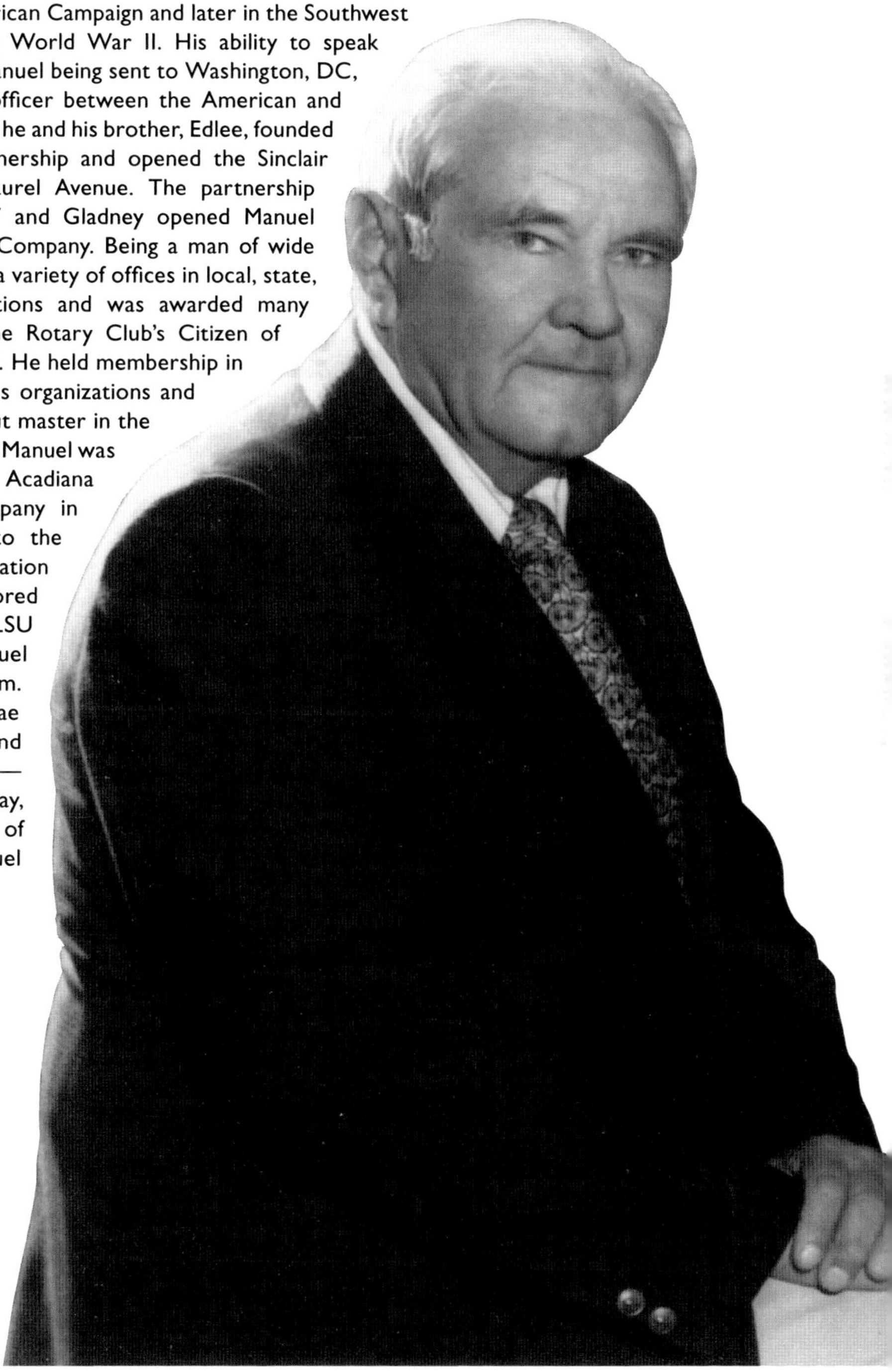

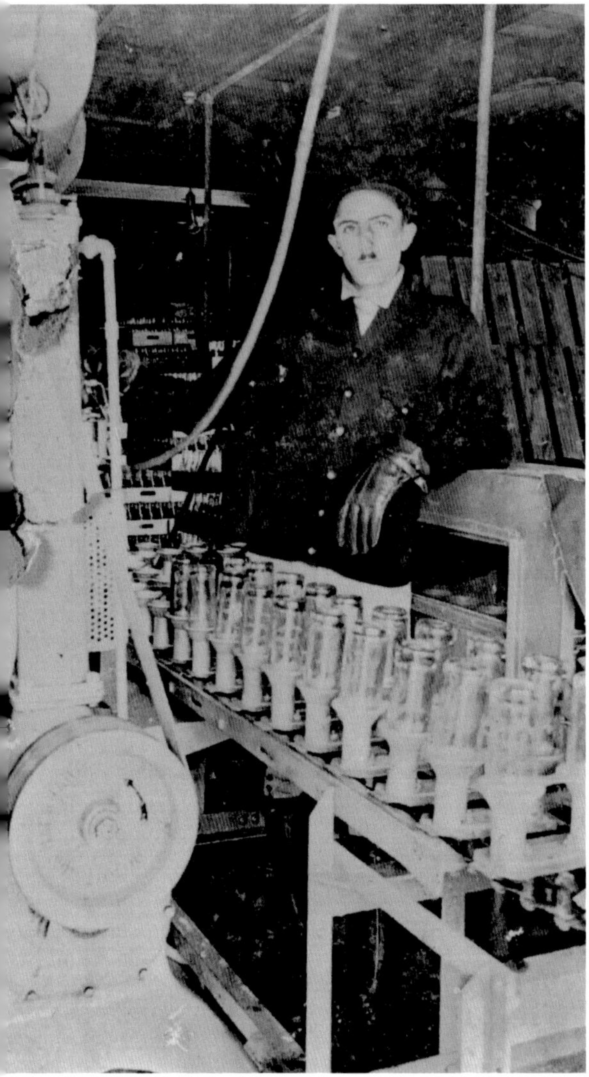

Made "U-ZO" a Household Word

Sam Lewis Uzzo's family immigrated from Italy to America with hopes for a brighter future. In search of a peaceful, country setting, Uzzo's parents moved to Eunice. Sam worked in New Orleans, but he visited his parents often. His dream was to launch his own business distributing soft drinks. His first bottling plant was located in a small building in his family's backyard. A few years later, as shown in this image, he opened a larger one, and finally, the modern plant on South First Street. Uzzo named his first business the Sanitary Bottling Company. Uzzo bottled a full line of flavored drinks bearing his private label, U-ZO Beverages. He acquired the 7-UP franchise as well as Grapette, Frostie Root Beer, and Orange Crush. The modern Uzzo plant housed full production lines with state-of-the-art equipment, a fleet of seven delivery trucks that covered five parishes, and a full line of beverage vending machines. In 1952, Uzzo installed a bottle washer and sterilizer, weighing over 18 tons, which had the capacity to sanitize 6,000 bottles per hour. Sam Uzzo served as president of the business; his son, Johnny, was vice president; and his daughter, Aneda, was secretary. Johnny Uzzo, son of Sam and Lucy Uzzo, is pictured in his automobile with his sister, Aneda, in the 1950s. Johnny attended Southwestern Louisiana Institute, now ULL, University of Colorado, and the New York School of Interior Design. Active in the initial organization of Eunice Players' Theatre and a reliable and talented actor in plays and musicals, Johnny Uzzo also was a businessman. At various times, he owned the Playbill, a bistro, and Dimensions, a jewelry and gift store. He was most recently employed at Tiffany's in New York City. (Courtesy of Aneda Uzzo Miller.)

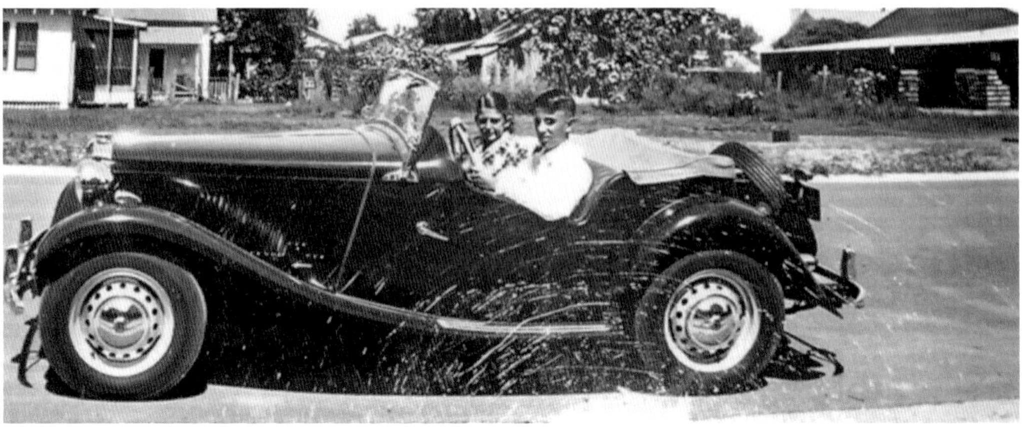

CHAPTER FIVE

The Preservationists

Southwest Louisiana, that area of the state known as Cajun Country or Acadiana, is particularly rich in traditions and folkways. It is composed of people with French heritage, mixed with any number of other national and ethnic backgrounds, but it is the Acadian folkways that predominate in the area. Since Acadian (Cajun) French culture is the dominant way of life, the lifestyles of the Eunice area have been influenced by that heritage blended with the long-held customs of rural people. It is an agricultural area infused with many African Americans whose culture had a tremendous effect on the area's lifestyle, due to the great number of those people who clung to their time-honored rituals. The melding of the distinct Acadian and African American cultures, nurtured by a rural existence and spiced with numerous other cultural folkways, gives America an incomparable culture steeped in Frenchness. It is the Cajun culture. Old ways of life, then, are cherished and revered in southwest Louisiana, especially in Eunice, which is known as "The Heart of Acadiana." The Cajun people have been described as a living repository of agrarian customs and values that have otherwise disappeared in the modern world. Eunice survives in the largest French-speaking minority area in the United States. Efforts to save the language, which has been described as a rural medieval French dialect, are ongoing. French immersion classes are taught from kindergarten in school systems. Cajun, zydeco, and la la music are varieties of homegrown folk music that resonate throughout the area on weekends. Eunice has produced many musicians from Bois Sec Ardoin to Marc Savoy, all showcased at the renovated Liberty Theater's *Live Cajun Radio Show* at one time or another. Tasty and traditional food with French names lures locals and visitors alike to the kitchens and restaurants. Being flexible and resilient, Cajuns display a reverence for old crafts including making "Ville Platte" chairs or Chinaberry tree rosaries that can be found to this day. Easter *pacque-pacques* traditionally have been held for decades after Easter masses. Festivals like Mardi Gras, which are outlets for old French traditions and a remembrance of medieval cultural traditions, abound in Eunice and the Cajun area. Thus, Eunice is an area rich in Cajun music, food, religion, language, crafts, and traditional folkways—all worth keeping.

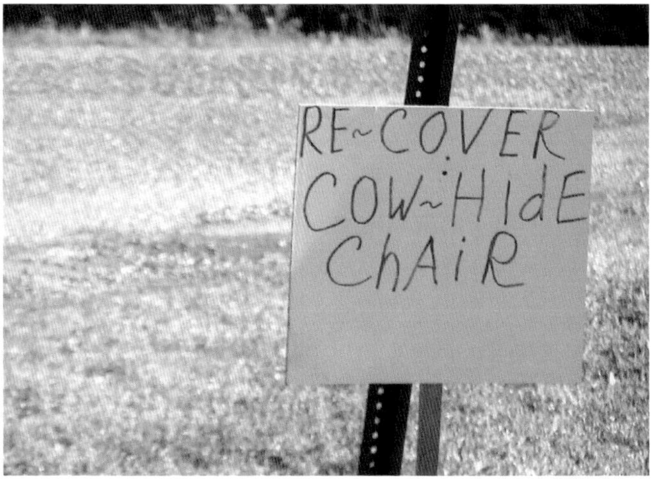

Cowhide Chair Repair Sign
Cajuns have clung tenaciously to their old customs and traditions. Strenuously resisting most encroachments from the outside, they have absorbed elements of many other cultures. Here, a sign along Highway 13 north of Eunice advertises an artisan who employs century-old techniques to repair the old fashioned "Ville Platte" or cowhide chairs. (Courtesy of authors' collection.)

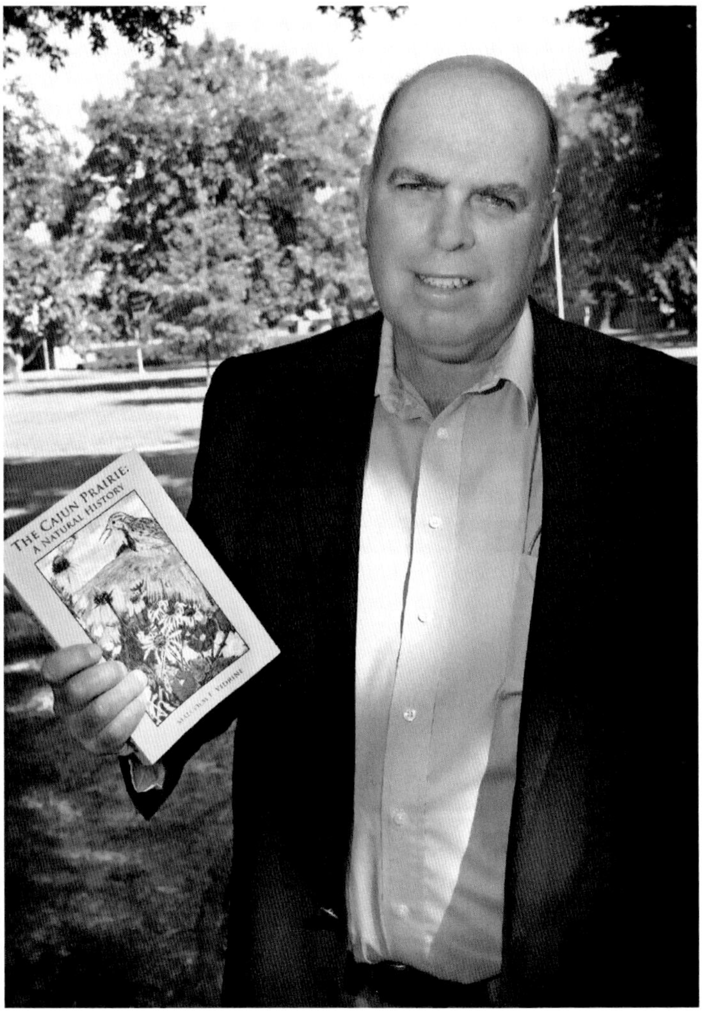

Outstanding in His Field
Dr. Malcolm F. Vidrine, son of Numa and Marie Odile Hidalgo Vidrine, is a biologist and an author of over 100 scientific papers and articles. His latest publication, *The Cajun Prairie: A Natural History*, directly addresses his passion for saving and reconstructing the remnant prairies. He has participated in the reconstruction of three prairies—the Cajun Prairie Restoration Project in Eunice, the LSU Eunice Prairie Project, and his own Cajun Prairie Gardens. Vidrine worked with the Gulf South Research Institute and is currently a professor at LSU Eunice. (Courtesy of LSU Eunice.)

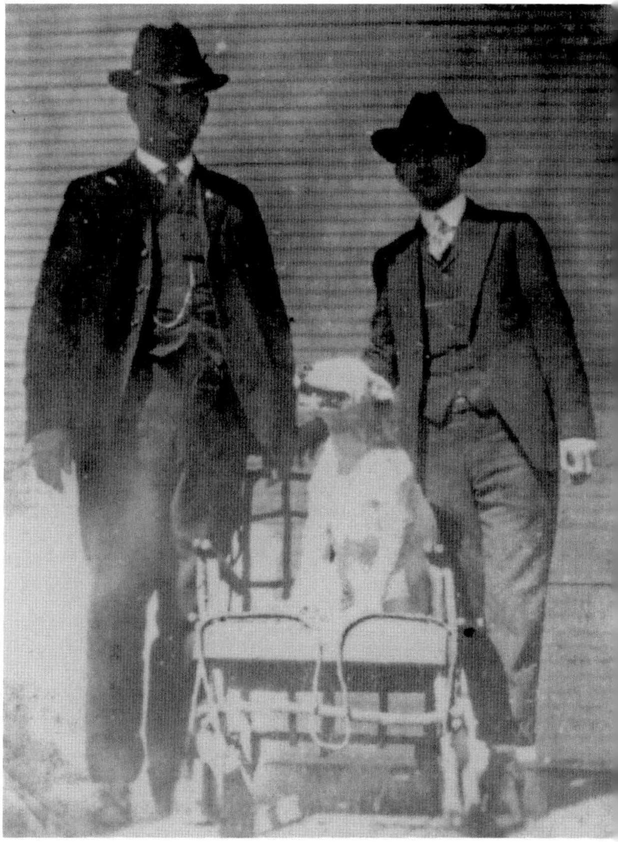

A Conservationist

Otere "O.A." LaHaye poses with his father-in-law, Oakdale, Louisiana, mayor Remi Vidrine, left, and a family dog. LaHaye, originally from Mamou, was recognized as one of Eunice's most successful businessmen as owner of an automobile dealership, LaHaye Chevrolet. He was also a Rotarian, a past commander of the American Legion, and an enthusiastic sportsman and judicious outdoorsman. However, it was as a conservationist that he is best remembered because he helped save an endangered species. In 1940, LaHaye found a wounded whooping crane in a rice field near Eunice. Named "Jo," the crane was nursed back to health and donated to the zoo at Audubon Park in New Orleans where it lived to breed numerous offspring. It was one of only 28 whooping cranes left in existence. LaHaye's rescue of the whooping crane led state officials to realize his benefit to state conservation programs. He was appointed to the Louisiana Wildlife and Fisheries Commission in 1954. While serving in that capacity, LaHaye wrote in a commission newsletter that he believed "scientific knowledge, together with common sense, would give the answers to the problems facing our fish and game species." He was honored by the Rotary Club as Eunice Citizen of the Year in 1953. LaHaye's first wife died after delivering Connie, their daughter. Eugenia and Janice LaHaye are daughters of LaHaye and his second wife, Hazel. (Courtesy of John "Randy" Vidrine and Janice LaHaye Aguillard.)

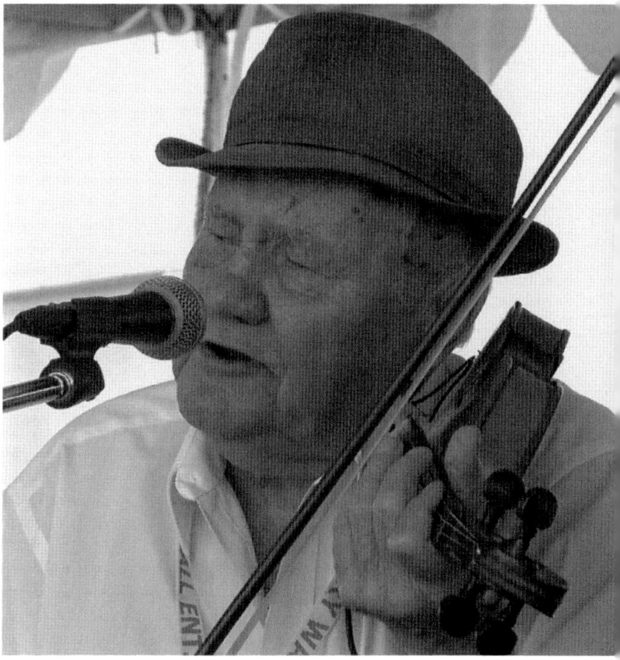

Old-Time Music

Shelton Manuel, born in Eunice in 1921, died at age 83. Rarely during his lifetime was he not playing his Cajun music. A versatile musician, he played accordion, guitar, drums, and sang in French and English. Manuel's long musical career included performing with J.B. Fuselier, Harry Choate, Chuck Guillory, Papa Cairo, Nathan Abshire, Aldus Roger, and Shirley Bergeron—all big-name performers. Despite experiencing blindness from a hunting accident, he played at all the area festivals, and he taught Cajun music workshops at the Folk Roots Festival. (Courtesy of Dr. David Simpson.)

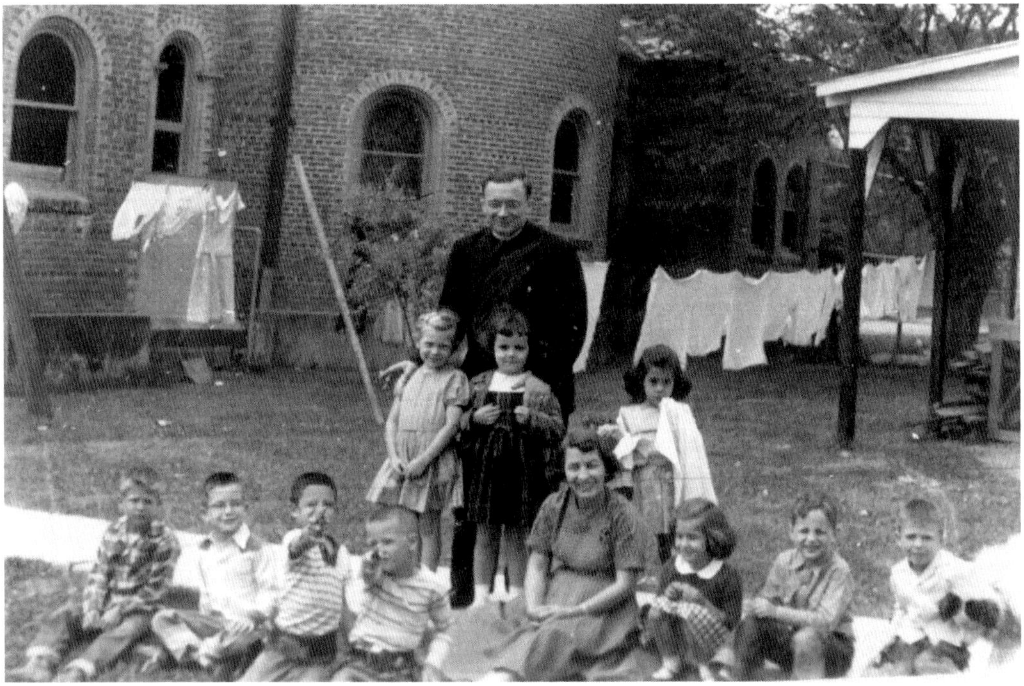

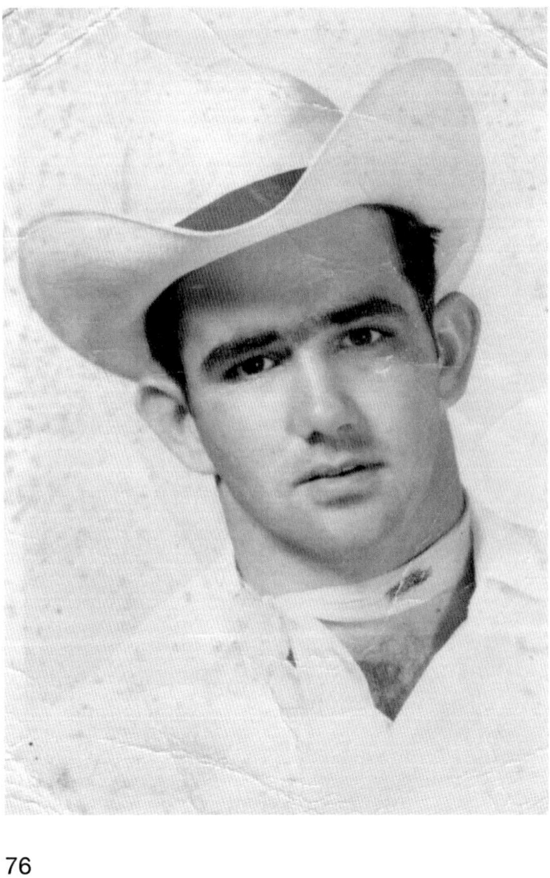

Created Clovis Crawfish
Mary Alice Fontenot (seated with unidentified children and Fr. John Engbers), author of 19 children's books about Clovis Crawfish's adventures with his bayou pals, explained that she created Clovis for her kindergarten class at St. Edmund School. "Clovis Crawfish was hatched, the result of my desperate efforts to keep 31 five-year-olds interested." Fontenot also wrote for several newspapers, published local history, and researched for author Frances Parkinson Keyes, when she was in Louisiana writing her novel, *Blue Camellia*. (Courtesy of St. Anthony's Parish.)

National Collegiate Champion
Greg "Honey Bee" Bollich was on the McNeese College Rodeo Team, the only college rodeo team to win three consecutive national championships and to bring home the National Finals trophy for three years—1957, 1958, and 1959. Bollich, pictured, is an inductee in the McNeese Cowboy Hall of Fame. He and his teammates were devoted to perpetuating historic American cowboy rodeo skills. (Courtesy of Greg and Pat Sittig Bollich.)

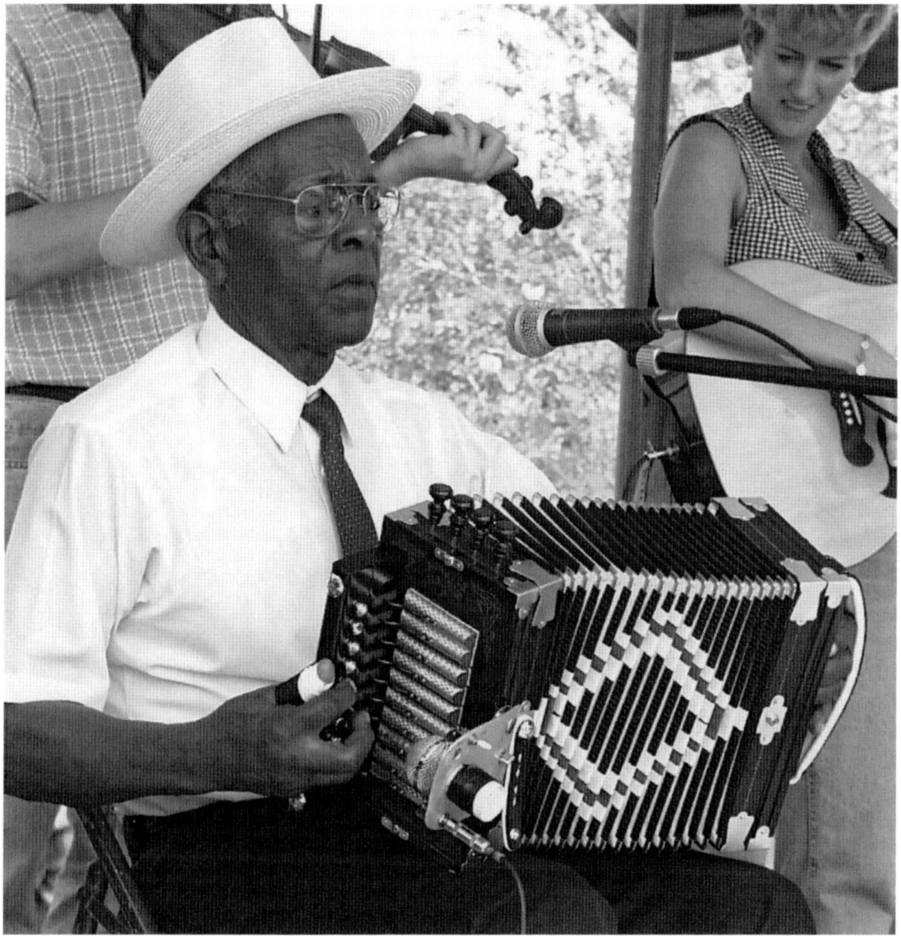

Keeper of Traditional Music

Alphonse "Bois Sec" Ardoin was a widely known and respected Creole accordion player who was born in 1915 to Gustave and Maire Cezaire Ardoin. Ardoin explained that he got his nickname, a feature common for men throughout Cajun and Creole South Louisiana, as a child. He was nicknamed "Bois Sec" ("dry wood"), because he had a reputation for being the first farm worker to seek shelter during Louisiana's heavy rain storms. Ardoin married Marscline Victorian and they made a home for their 14 children in the *L'anse Prien Noir* community north of Eunice around Duralde. He considered himself a "keeper" or "conserver" of old-time French/Creole music. Ardoin began playing at *bals de maison* (house dances), and joined fiddle-player Canray Fontenot in the early 1940s to form a band, the Duralde Ramblers, which would play in clubs. His first recording was "*Les Blues du Bayou*," on the Melodeon label. He is remembered for infusing Cajun waltzes with the blues. English speakers sometimes called the style "la la music," but it was known by its players simply as "la musique Creole." He also recorded and performed with the Cajun fiddler Dewey Balfa and later with a younger generation of Creole traditionalists, notably Balfa Toujours, led by Dewey's daughter Christine, with whom he made the 1998 album *Allons Dansera*, and with whom he was photographed here. Ardoin performed in Washington, DC, at the Newport Folk Festival, at the inauguration of President Nixon in 1969, at the New Orleans Jazz Festival, and at Carnegie Hall in the 1970s. He also played in Europe and Canada. His music preserved the unique sounds of traditional music, and in 1986, he received the highest honor the United States gives to a folk artist, the National Heritage Fellowship from the NEA. (Courtesy of Dr. David Simpson.)

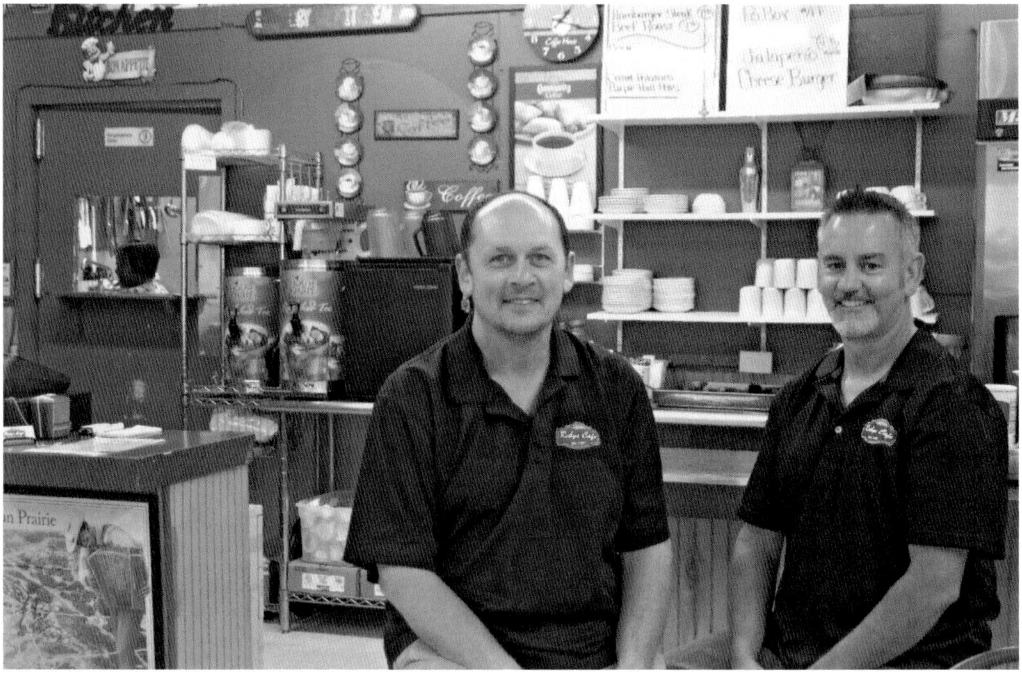

Traditional Food
Curt Fontenot, right, and Duane Vidrine own Ruby's Café, a Eunice landmark. They opened Ruby's in 2003, featuring fast service, friendly atmosphere, and traditional food. Recipes, such as *croquesignoles* (old-fashioned Cajun doughnuts), crawfish étouffée, sauce piquant, backbone stew, and filé gumbo have been handed down in their families. (Courtesy of Van Reed.)

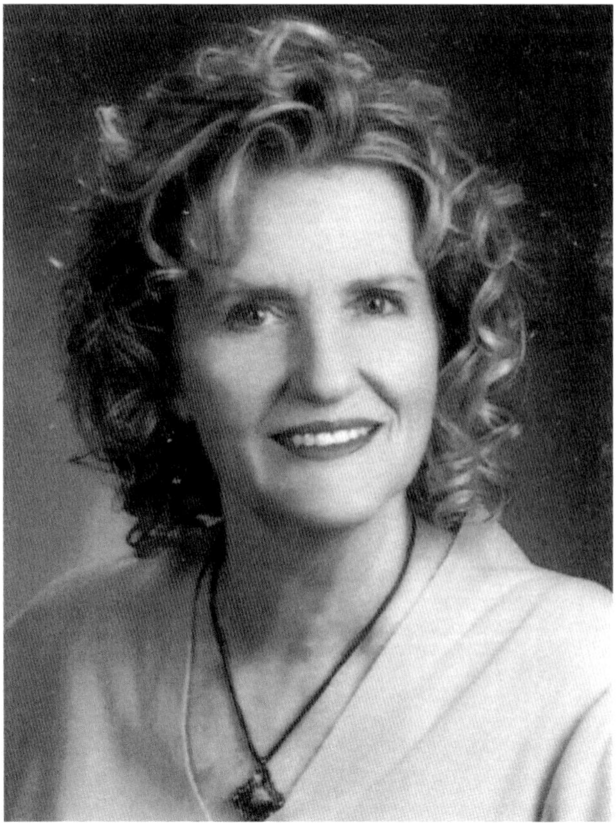

Principal and Biographer
Eugenia "Ching" Rougeau Veillon was principal of Glendale Elementary School in 1993 when *Redbook* magazine named Glendale one of America's top elementary schools. After retirement, Veillon authored a book entitled *Cajun Music Man* about the life and musical career of Alphonse "Bois Sec" Ardoin. (Courtesy of Eunice Public Library.)

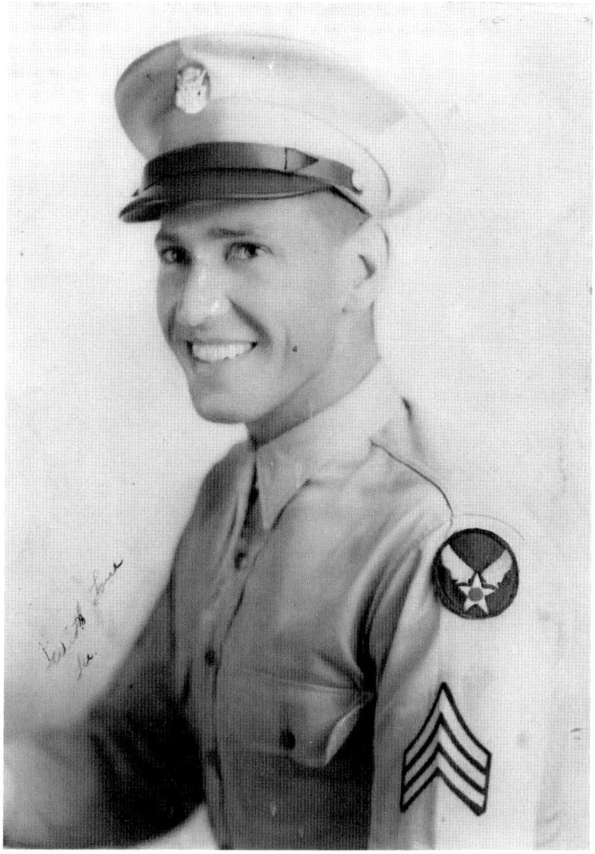

Genealogist, Author
Leland "Tiny" O'Brien, with his wife, Thoma Adams O'Brien, and Dr. James and Martha Forester, spent many days trekking through overgrown rural cemeteries to record headstone inscriptions for publication in guides for local cemeteries. O'Brien's massive genealogy of his Irish and French families, *From Shamrocks to Fleur-de-Lis*, was published posthumously. An employee of Halliburton, he held membership in First Methodist Church and Masonic Lodge. (Courtesy of Kathleen O'Brien Ebers.)

Cajun Fiddler and Horseman
Like many Cajuns, Rodney Fontenot had an unmatched talent for raising horses, such as the one pictured here. Fontenot had never traveled farther than Memphis, Tennessee, until he went with Mark Savoy's entourage to play in an "old time fiddling" festival near Seattle, Washington. It was his first airplane trip. He played tunes from the 1920s and 1930s with various Cajun bands. (Courtesy of Jesse Breaux Photography.)

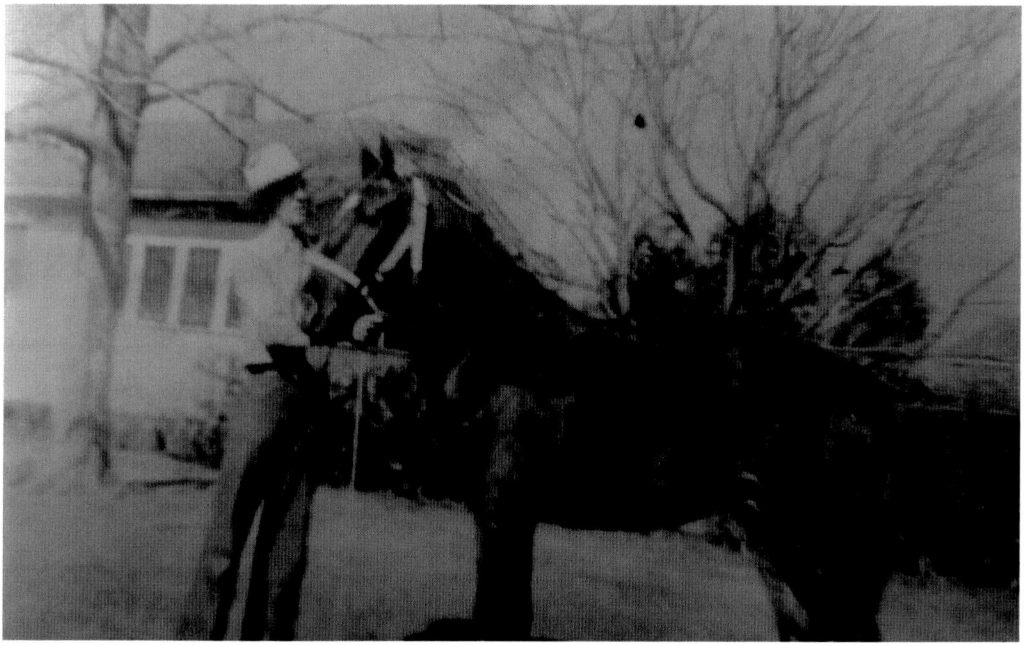

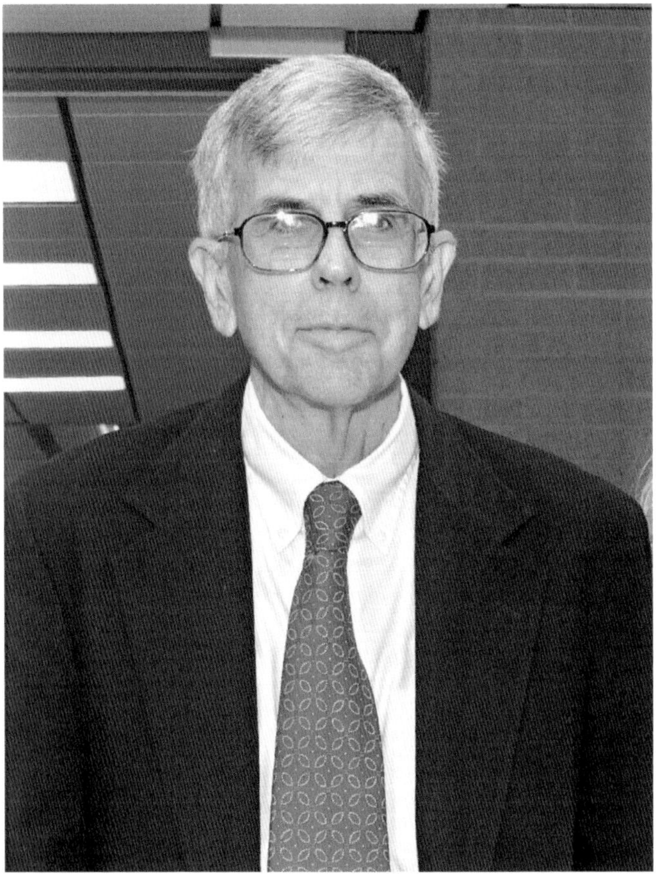

Man with His Camera
Dr. David Simpson, formerly the public relations director at LSU Eunice, has attracted tourists to Eunice with his web pages, which emphasize Cajun and zydeco musicians. Simpson posted web pages in the collection of Contemporary Louisiana Cajun, Creole and Zydeco Musicians as a public service. Eunice, the Liberty Theater, and the multitude of local musicians and festivals received free global exposure from Simpson's professional expertise. In 2006, he also added photographs of rural Mardi Gras activities. LSU Eunice's music pages became an archive of his photographs. The book *One Generation at a Time: Biography of a Cajun and Creole Music Festival*, which he co-authored, has enhanced national and international Cajun music awareness. (Courtesy of Van Reed Photography.)

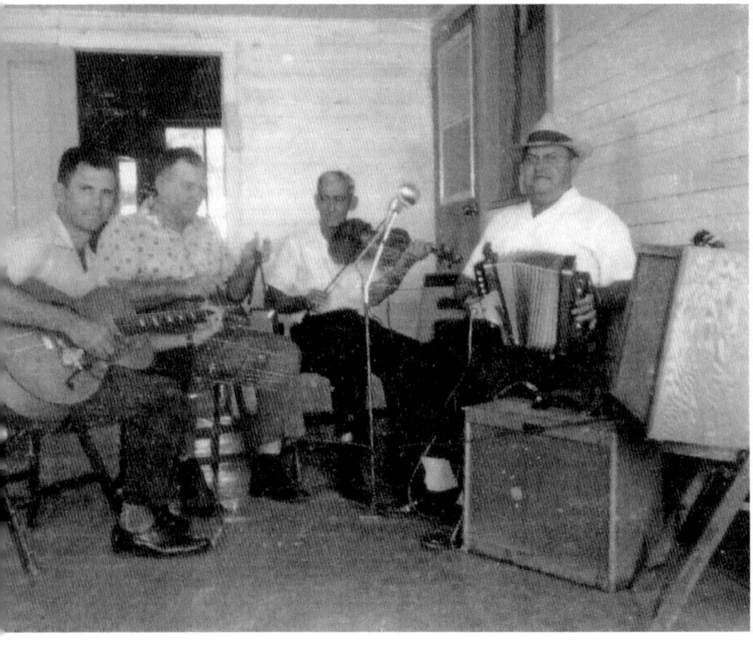

Cajun Music Man
Cyprien Landreneau, right, legendary accordionist of the *Lanse Meg* community, jammed with, left to right, Harold Landreneau, Landry Landreneau, and Isaac Soileau. Tradition dictates that any musician is allowed to "sit in" on jam sessions. Landreneau formed the Mamou Cajun Band, one of the first bands to play traditional Cajun music at the Newport Folk Festival and in Europe in the early 1960s. (Courtesy of John "Randy" Vidrine.)

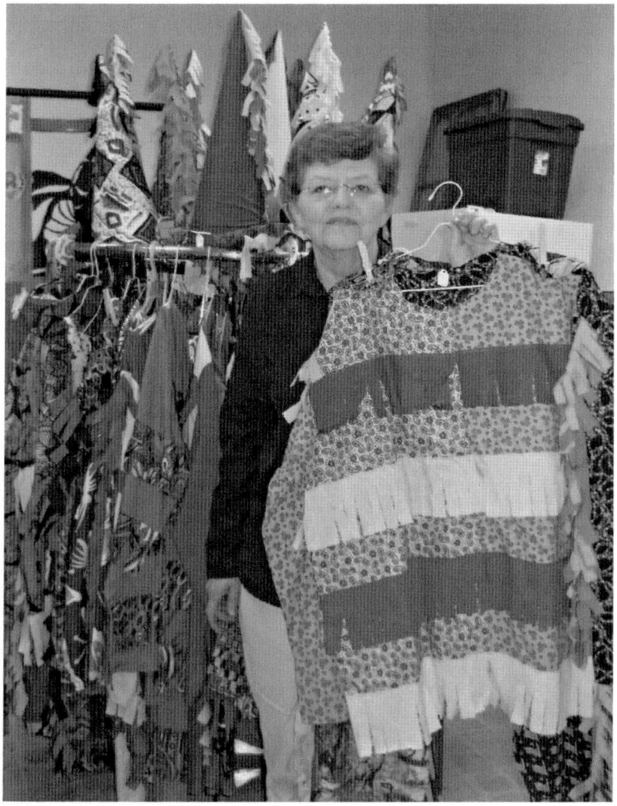

Preserves Heritage
Fred Charlie, a singer, songwriter, and acoustic guitar player of traditional Cajun dance music, recorded 84 songs of which 41 are original songs. He released a CD entitled *You Can Speak Cajun French*. A versatile man, Charlie hosts a Cajun show on KXKW 87.7 FM, and opened Eunice's first 24-track professional recording studio. The recipient of the 1991 Heritage Award, the prestigious award for Continuous Contributions to the Cajun Culture and Music at the annual "Le Cajun Awards," Charlie was also inducted into the Cajun Music Hall of Fame in 2005. Another traditionalist, Dolores "Dee" Charlie, Fred's wife, realized that locating rural Mardi Gras costumes was difficult. Thus, she makes and sells over a hundred traditional costumes annually. Charlie's cottage industry is a step in preserving traditional costuming for the Mardi Gras *courirs* (runs) as well as the Cajun heritage. (Courtesy of the authors' collection.)

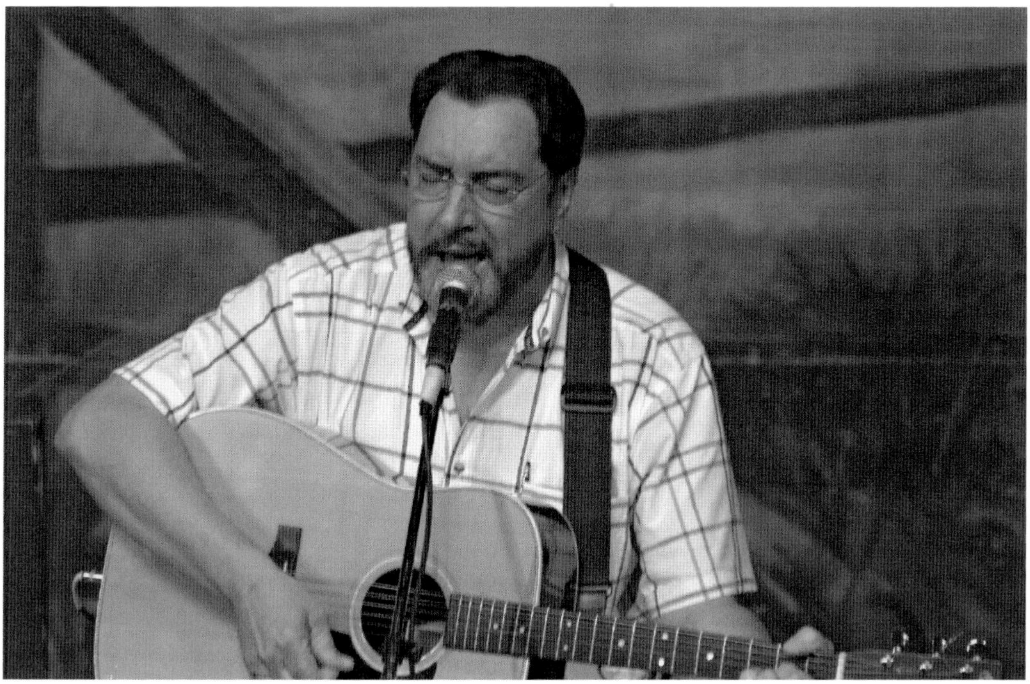

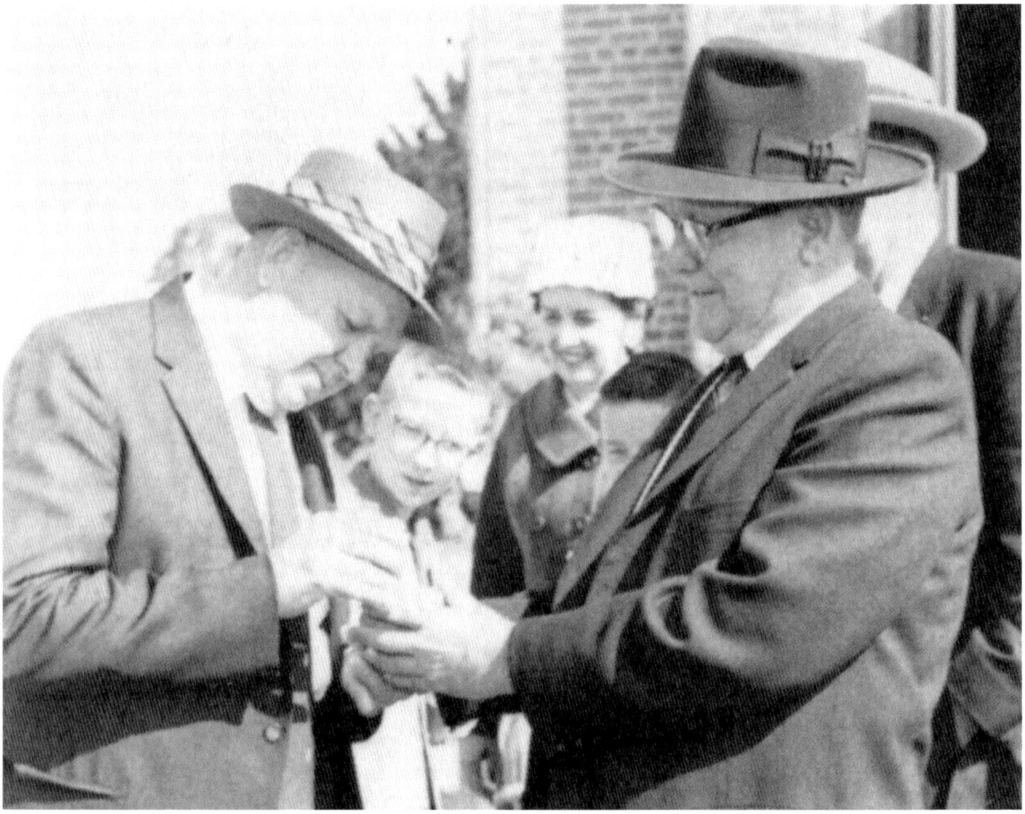

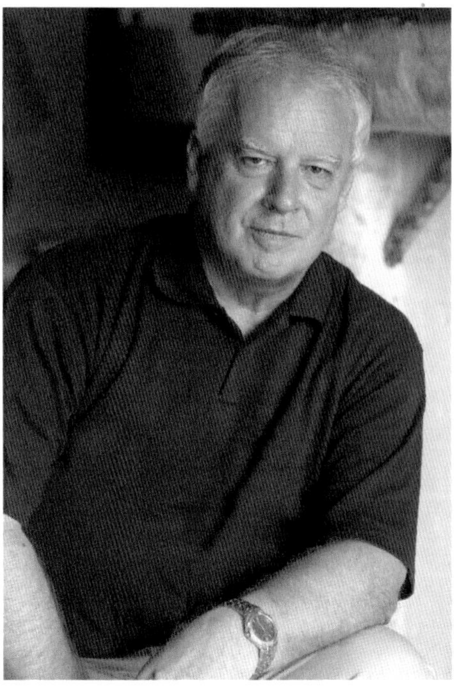

Easter Egg *Pacque-Pacque*

Best friends Stewart Rozas and Dr. Sylvan Reed carried on their 30-year French tradition of *pacque-pacquing* Easter eggs after Sunday mass. Reed is left and Rozas to the right with Ruby Reed center. Boys are unidentified. The purpose of Easter egg pocking was to strike another's egg to determine who had the unbeatable egg. Rozas worked as the manager of Kelly Weber Wholesale Company, and Reed was a dentist. (Courtesy of Dr. Sylvan Reed.)

Civil War Scholar

Known for the depth of his research, Dr. Richard Lowe, a Civil War scholar, graduated from the University of Louisiana at Lafayette, Harvard, and the University of Virginia. In various publications, Lowe documented Louisiana troops in the Red River Campaign with his portrayal of the Texas Cavalry's activities. The son of Grady and Iris McManus Lowe, he is Regents Professor of History at the University of North Texas. (Courtesy of Dr. Richard Lowe.)

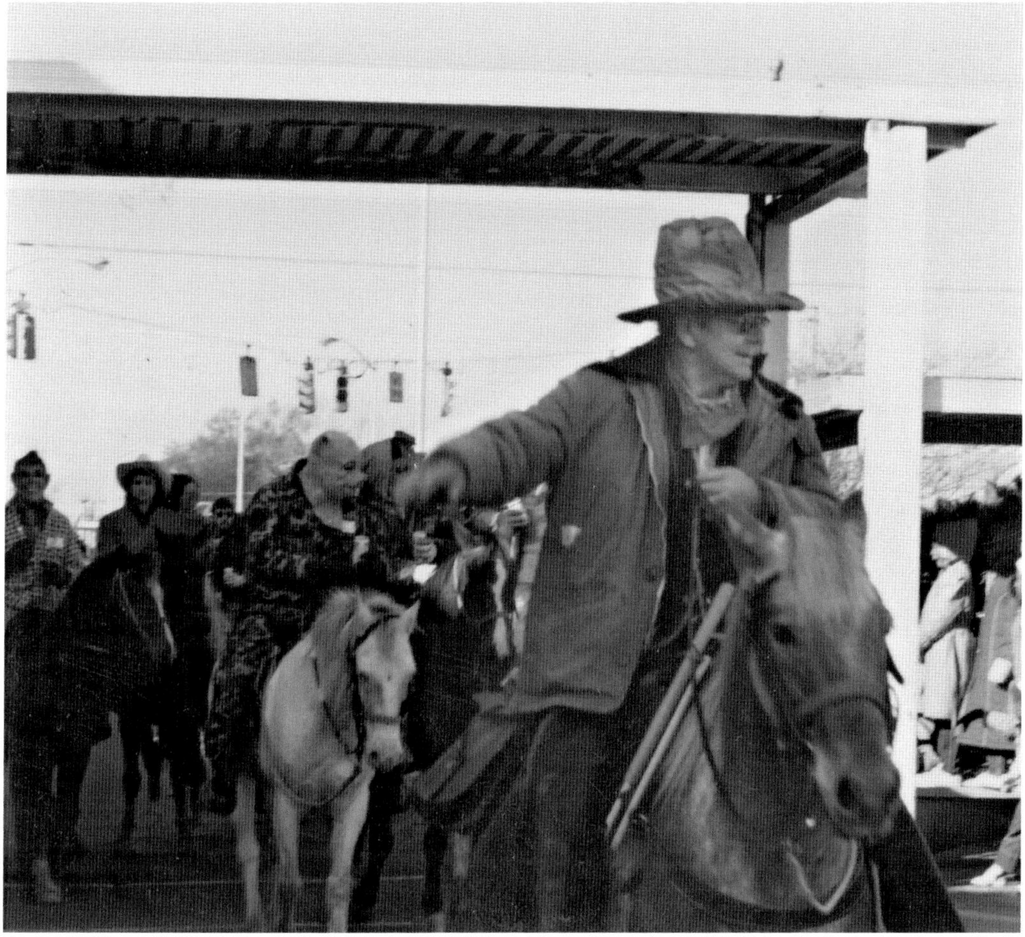

A Genuine Cowboy

J.E. "Boo" LeDoux, a self-proclaimed "swamp cowboy," is pictured riding in a 1976 Eunice Mardi Gras parade. He married Elizabeth Pricilla "Pris" Buller of Elton, had two children, Dr. Joseph E. LeDoux Jr. of New York and Bonnie Sammis of Sweet Lake, Louisiana. In his youth, in the 1930s, "Boo" worked for the huge Gray Ranch, breaking horses that were born in the wilds of the Louisiana marshes. The life of a cowboy was rife with danger. At one time, his horse fell into a rice canal, kicked him in his head, and knocked him out. When a fellow cowboy saw LeDoux floating in the canal, he pulled him out, threw LeDoux facedown on his saddle, and "rode the water out" of him. By 1946, he was making $3 a day. Soon, LeDoux was back in Eunice running the meat market that would become Boo LeDoux Meat Market. He said, "I was like a fish out of water there. I hated every day of it, but I made a living." He quit riding bulls in his 40s. But, in his 60s, LeDoux competed in bull riding at rodeos "just to prove he still could ride." He said he didn't win any money and he found the ground too hard. In 1976 for the nation's Bicentennial celebration, LeDoux was selected the wagon master for the Louisiana contingent on the historic wagon train ride to Valley Forge, Pennsylvania. Accompanied by his wife, he drove the team and they traveled almost 3,000 miles at four miles per hour, fulfilling one of LeDoux's greatest dreams. In 1983, LeDoux was inducted into the Hall of Master Folk Artists at Northwestern State College for his saddle-making skills. He also appeared at area festivals and arts and crafts shows and the Liberty Theater. The old cowboy was named Rotary's Citizen of the Year in 1976. (Courtesy of authors' collection.)

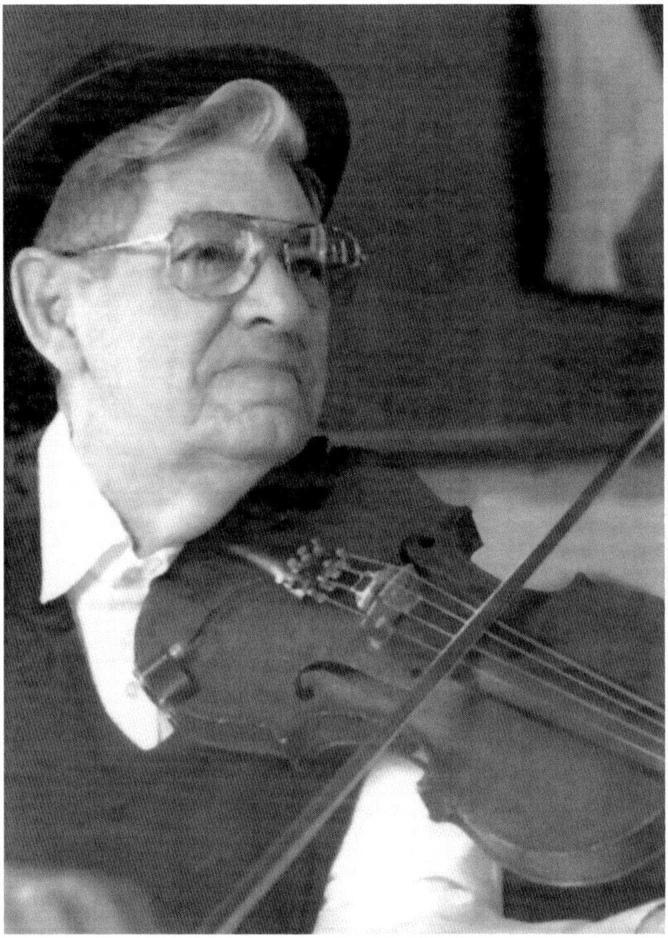

Fiddling Around

The eldest of eight children born to Enos and Gertrude Fontenot, Merlin Fontenot played a leading role in bringing Cajun music into the mainstream. He married Lillian Thibodeaux, a daughter of noted Cajun accordionist Ambrose Thibodeaux. Fontenot worked in a Navy shipyard in Orange, Texas, prior to the World War II draft. He became a .50-caliber gunner on an LTS amphibious tank in the army and served in the South Pacific. While in the Army, he played his fiddle on the *Dry Gulch* program over Armed Forces Radio for the troops. As a teen, Merlin had played in various house dances and dance halls, usually walking several miles from the family farm. In 1940, he played and recorded with Ambrose Thibodeaux. After World War II, Fontenot and his wife settled in Jacksonville, Florida, where he worked for a bread company and played with the local bands. When he was hired by the Jimmy Strickland Band, he traveled throughout the southeastern United States and played the Grand Ole Opry twice. Once the Strickland band came to Eunice and played at Enos and Gertrude Fontenot's home for all the family and neighbors. Returning to Louisiana, Fontenot has recorded and performed with Jo-El Sonnier, Ambrose Thibodeaux, the Balfa Brothers, Nathan Abshire, Rufus Thibodeaux, Sonny Landreth, and Gerry McGee. He volunteers to play his fiddle at Vermillionville, a living history and folklife park representative of villages of Cajuns and Creoles from 1765 to the 1890s, which serves to preserve early cultural resources of this unique people. Since music is one of the Cajuns' precious cultural resources, Fontenot sits in on the music jam sessions at the park and does his part to keep the old music alive. (Courtesy of Dr. Jack D. Miller Jr.)

Documentary Filmmaker

Pat Mire, born in 1953 in the rural Eunice area, is an award-winning documentary filmmaker whose cultural films have been broadcast nationally on PBS, the Discovery Channel, and TNN's *American Skyline*. His documentaries have won awards in national and international competitions, including the Margaret Mead Film Festival and the American Anthropological Film Festival, at which he won the coveted Award of Excellence. Mire and his films have been the subject of numerous articles and reviews in major magazines, newspapers, and journals. He has been called "an important artistic force at work in French Louisiana whose camera work and editing are excellent." Mire has been compared to the legendary documentary filmmaker Les Blank. His feature film, *Dirty Rice,* played to two sold-out auditoriums at the London Film Festival. Mire's passion is to correct stereotypes of his Cajun culture by presenting, in film, an insider's perspective. All of his films highlight "the good things about South Louisiana and the Cajun culture." His films showcase real people, not Hollywood stereotypes. Pat Mire was the only Louisiana filmmaker to receive a 1991 regional fellowship from the Southeast Media Fellowship Program that covered 14 states. In 1993, Mire was honored by the Louisiana Endowment for the Humanities with a Special Humanities Award for his film work. In 2000, he was given an Artist of the Year Award in Washington, DC, by Sen. Mary Landrieu. Mire directed *Against the Tide: The Story of the Cajun People*. Mire also is credited with *Forever My Love: Music from the Bayou* and, most recently, *Mon Cher Camarade*, which tells the story of the French-speaking Cajun soldiers in World War II, his father Felix Mire being one of them. Mire (center) is shown directing a documentary with Kris Kristofferson, right. (Courtesy of Pat Mire.)

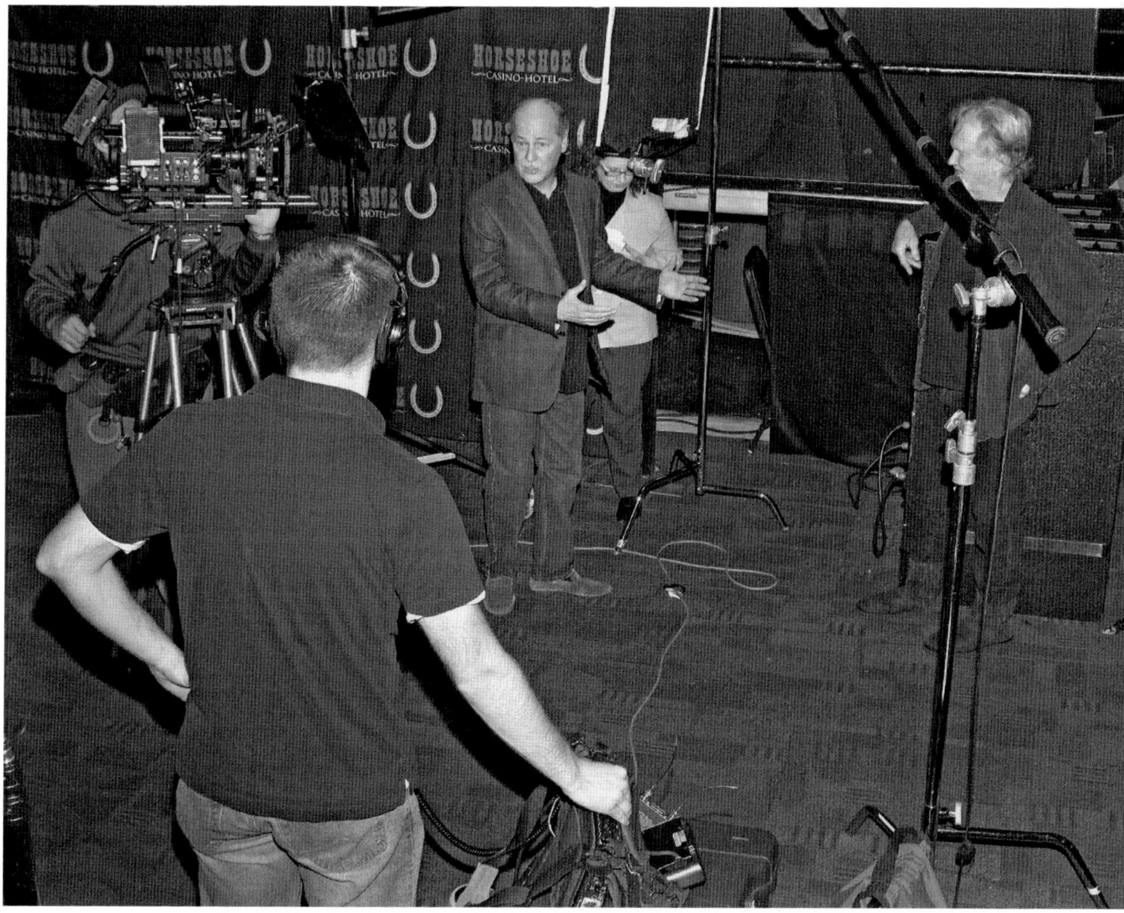

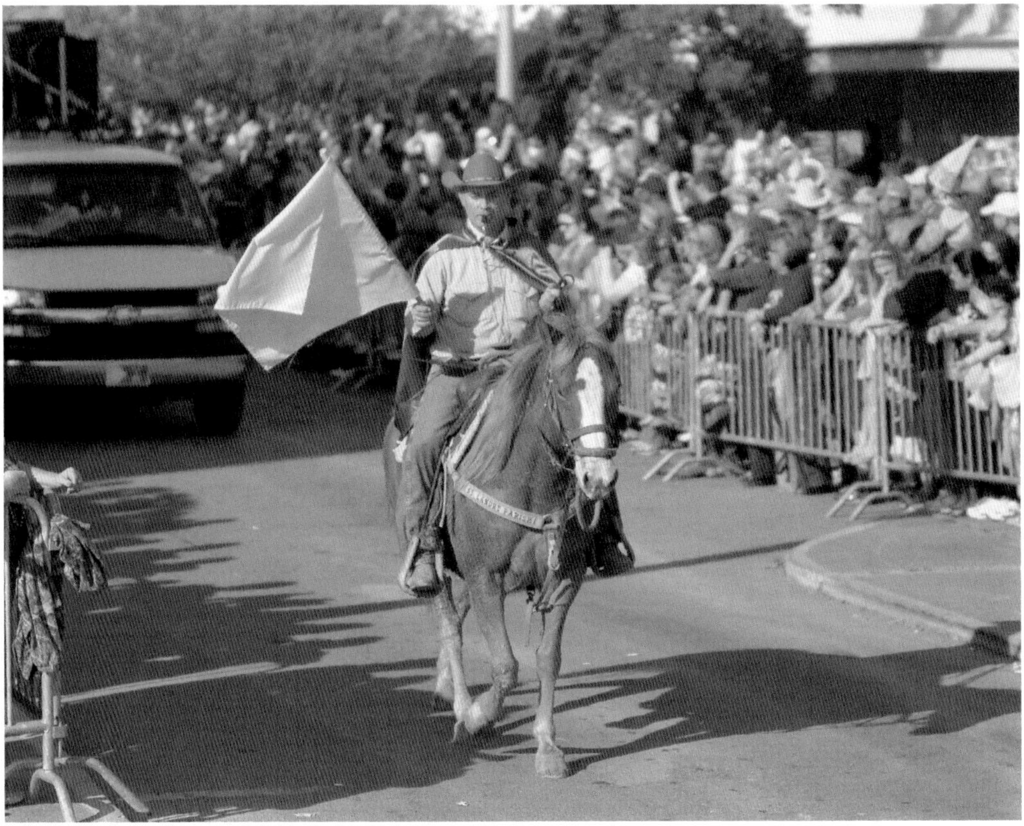

Le Capitaine

Pat Frey is devoted to preserving a very old Cajun tradition, the Mardi Gras *courir,* even though he is a son of Reginald and Joann Bollich Frey, both of German ancestry. The *courir* is the "run" where riders, dressed in traditional colorful, fringed pajama-styled costumes and wearing vividly painted screen masks and *capuchons* (tall, pointed hats), either ride on horseback or on trailers, for about 12 miles through the countryside dancing and frolicking in pursuit of chickens for a communal gumbo after the *courir.* Frey, as *le capitaine* (the leader), rides on horseback, wears a purple cape and no mask, and carries a flag. He is the first to approach a house to ask for permission for the riders to advance into their yards. There the Mardi Gras riders dance and act silly to gain a chicken. Some resort to begging for *cinq sous* (five cents) keeping up the ancient tradition regardless of today's devaluation of money. There is no doubt that *Le Capitaine* is the leader and has disciplinary powers over the riders. Frey has been a part of the annual tradition since he was 13 years old and has participated the last 22 years, first as a co-captain and the past 12 years in the leadership role. Frey's task is a serious and strenuous one. It is an all-day affair; the riders leave town about 9:00 a.m. and, after canvassing the countryside, they arrive in downtown Eunice, with their ingredients for the communal gumbo, to parade through town at 3:00 p.m. During the ride, Frey estimated that the riders consumed about 7,000 pounds of *boudin* (Cajun sausage) and hundreds of cases of beverages. Frey believes that over 1,000 locals and visitors were on hand to view the 400 or more riders in the *Courir de Mardi Gras* in 2012. The unique and colorful event promotes and preserves the Cajuns' cultural heritage. But even the most authentic cultural events must eventually bow to the changing society. Until about 30 years ago, women were not accepted in the *courir.* Prior to that time, communities held separate runs for women if they were allowed to run at all. Today both men and women may participate, but it depends on the rules of the *courir.* Some towns allow only men; others only women. Eunice allows both men and women to run. (Courtesy of Rick Nesbitt and KEUN Radio.)

CHAPTER SIX

The Heroic and Commendable

Men and women from Eunice, indeed all Cajuns, have been first in the line of duty when their homes and families were threatened. From the day Col. John Winslow barred Acadian men into the little church at Grand Pré, Acadian men have exhibited great courage. When the Acadians were expelled from Acadie, Beausoleil Broussard and his guerrilla fighters did not back down to the sheer legions of British soldiers who hunted them. During the American Revolution, Cajuns of the area were first to join General Galvez in his expedition against the British. Names like Jean Baptist LeJeune, Victor Richard, and Pierre Richard, all men whose descendants populate Eunice, show up on militia lists that saw action against the British. The same Cajuns and many others joined Gen. Andrew Jackson's forces at the Battle of New Orleans. World War I drew heavily on Eunice men. Milton and Arthur Arnold, Matthias Frugé, Loudice Verret, and Ben Miller were but a few brave souls who endured the filth and dangers of trench life during the "war to end all wars." Eunice resident Amelia Greenwald served in the American Expeditionary Force as head nurse at Verdun, France. World War II involved over 600 Eunice men and women in the military with 24 being killed in action. Some courageous men survived life in POW camps. Korea, Vietnam, and Desert Storm saw men from Eunice involved in sustaining America's freedom. Lastly, young men from the area are now called to combat in Iraq and Afghanistan. Bravery, however, is not relegated only to the military. When Riley Roy saved a young man's life in a school bus/automobile collision, he showed exceptional courage. Can one even imagine the emotions surging through Louis Nicola Pavich's mind when at 12 years old, he escaped the Communists and made his way halfway around the world to meet his parents in America? How about the example of courage that Jerry Hoffpauir left as he stepped into both the mother's and father's roles when his wife died leaving him with a special needs child to care for? When the opportunity arises, Eunice people face challenges and danger with unmitigated bravery.

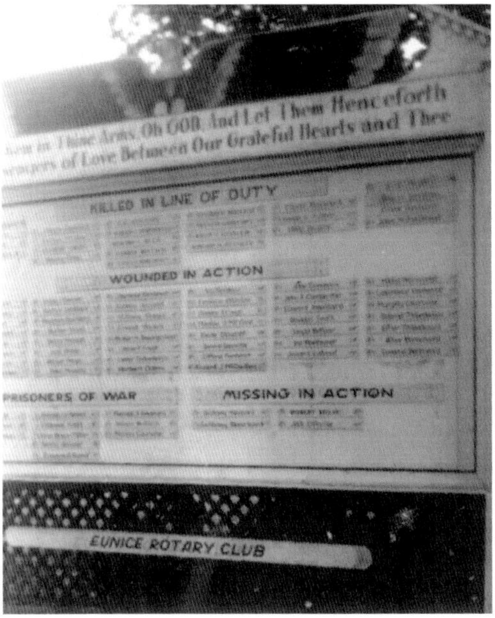

Military Memorial
In 1944, the Rotary Club erected this World War II Memorial Board on Park Avenue at Second Street to honor local military heroes, particularly the 24 killed in action. The Memorial Board included four sections: killed in action, wounded in action, prisoners of war, and missing in action. (Courtesy of Bettie Brunson Jenkins.)

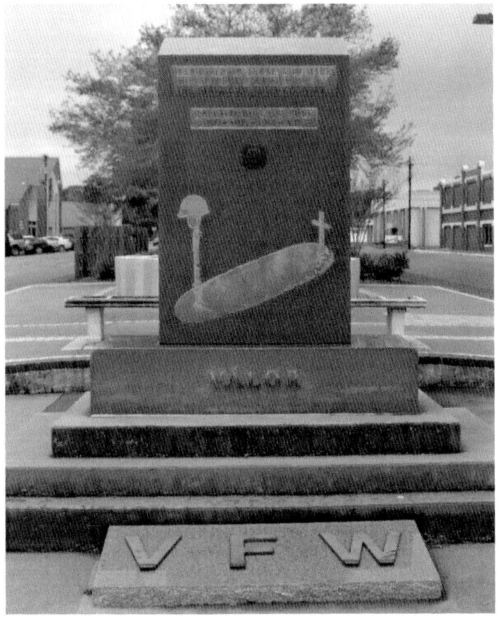

Downtown Memorial
Erected on the boulevard on Park Avenue at Second Street, in the midst of the city, this marker was dedicated in 1961 to those who made the supreme sacrifice by VFW Post #8971. It is a multi-war memorial. Gold Star Mothers routinely gather here with local veterans groups to remember Eunice's servicemen. (Courtesy of Van Reed.)

Army Master Sergeant and POW (RIGHT)
In 1930, when he was 17 years old, Raymond Reed joined the US Army. At that time, he was serving in Columbus, Georgia. Prior to the fall of the Philippines and before he was captured by the Japanese and subjected to the brutal torture and horrific starvation of the Bataan Death March, Reed wrote home sending a photograph of himself and other soldiers surrounded by Filipino children that he inscribed, "was taken while on a southern island trip . . . it was very cloudy . . . had lots of fun with kids." His mother, Mrs. Austin Reed, suffered double heartbreak when she received notice that Raymond Reed was missing in action in the Philippine Islands in July 1942. The heartbroken mother had already received devastating news that his brother, Howard Reed, was Eunice's first World War II casualty when his tanker was sunk by enemy forces in February 1942. Raymond Reed was held captive first in Manila's infamous Bilibid Prison, an old penitentiary used as a clearinghouse for all Army POWs. He was sent subsequently to Japan on the *Hokusen Maru*, a Japanese "Hell Ship," on October 1, 1944, which arrived in Formosa a month later. Little more is known about his captivity, since Reed did not talk much about his days in Japanese POW camps. Reed was liberated in September 1945 and discharged after 26 years in the military. He was married to Irene Bordelon, also of Eunice. Master Sergeant Reed is pictured on his Philippine Island trip with the Filipino children. (Courtesy of Irene Bordelon Reed.)

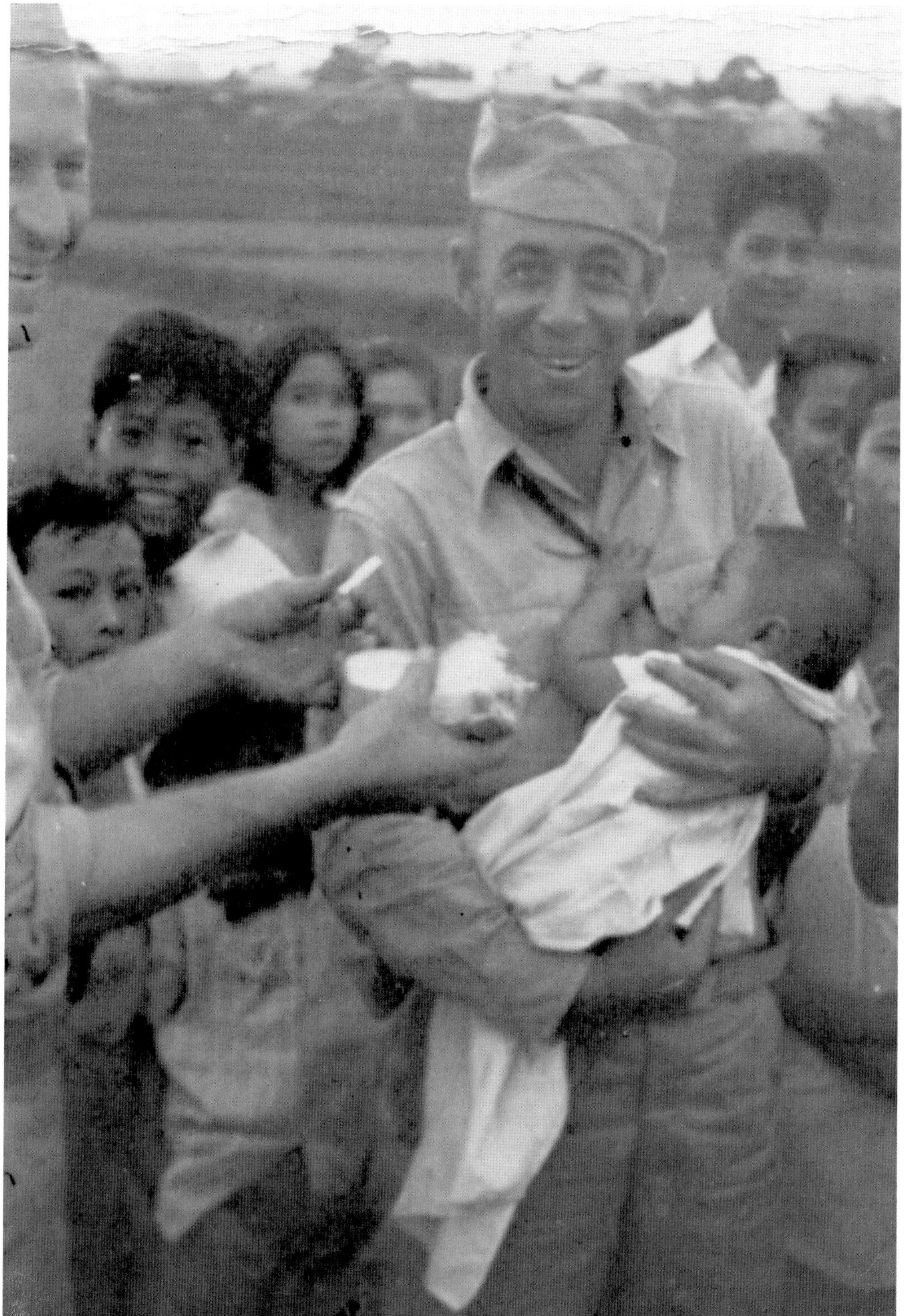

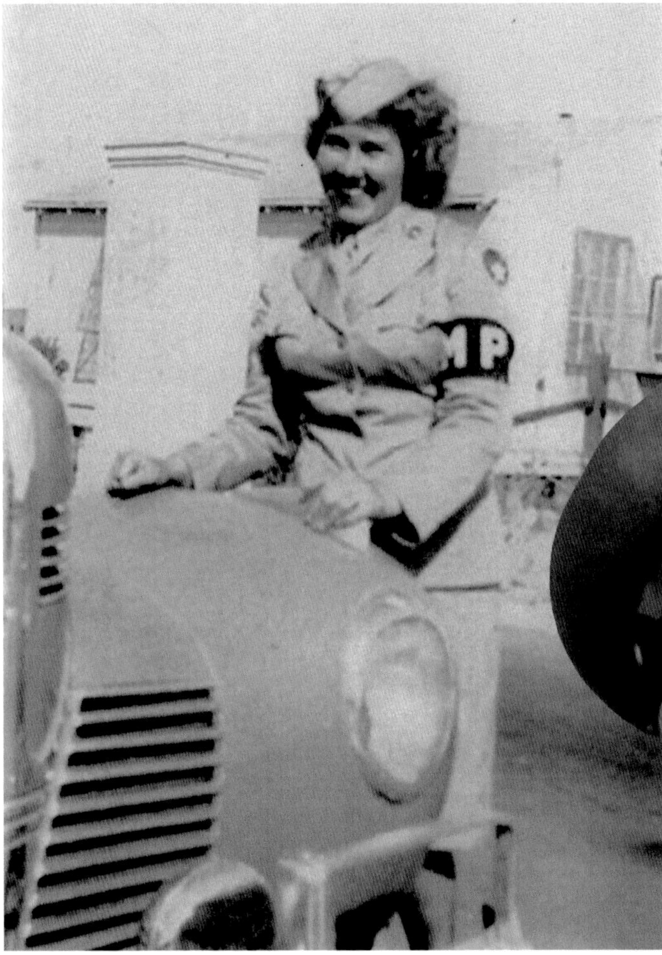

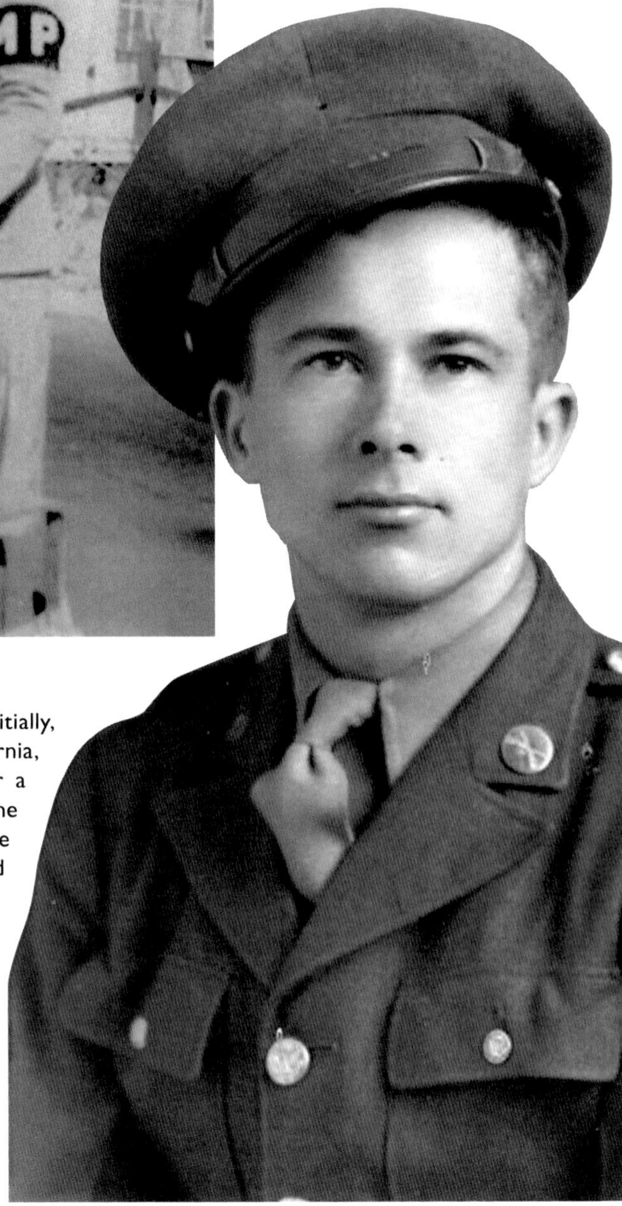

Siblings at War

Lily Brown Leaké joined the WACs in 1943. Initially, she was stationed at Camp Beal, California, where her assignments were as a clerk or a patrolman guard. She was selected for the WACs softball team. Playing on the team, she toured many states until she was discharged in 1946. Leake's brother, Eursey Joseph "E.J." Brown, was awarded a Purple Heart after he was wounded at Mindanao in the Philippine Islands during World War II. Brown, who was in the 77th Division, 306th Infantry Regiment, saw action in some of the bloodiest fighting at Saipan, Tinian, Guam, Leyte, and the Southern Philippines. He was married to Vinice Demoruelle of Ville Platte, Louisiana. (Courtesy of Chris Brown Carrier.)

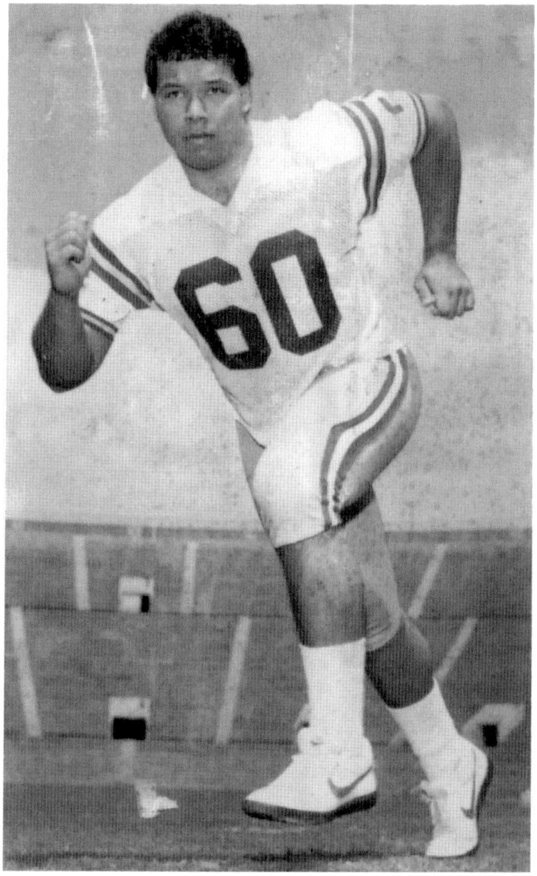

From LSU to Luby's

Described as a "natural born leader" by his employer, Todd Coutee's life has been one of leadership. He played on Eunice High School's state championship football team in 1982. He was a four-year letterman at LSU from 1985 to 1988 and captain of the team. Coutee played in the famous "Earthquake Game" in Tiger Stadium in 1988, when the LSU fans' reaction to the Tigers' win registered as an earthquake on the seismograph located in LSU's Howe-Russell Geoscience Complex. Coutee, in another leadership role, is vice president of Luby's Culinary Services in Houston, where he oversees more than 30 food service managers and more than 500 employees. Spending over 20 years in the food service industry, he has taken a few breaks for golf and fishing. (Courtesy of Ricky Coutee.)

Respected Peace Officer

Josh Alexander Reed, born to Benjamin Walter and Maria Antoinette Reed in Austin, Texas, around 1861, was a respected city marshal in Eunice's early days. He married Catrina Gillard and lived here until his death at age 73 in 1934. Reed, seated left, is shown at a local barbershop. Others are unidentified. (Courtesy of BBHC.)

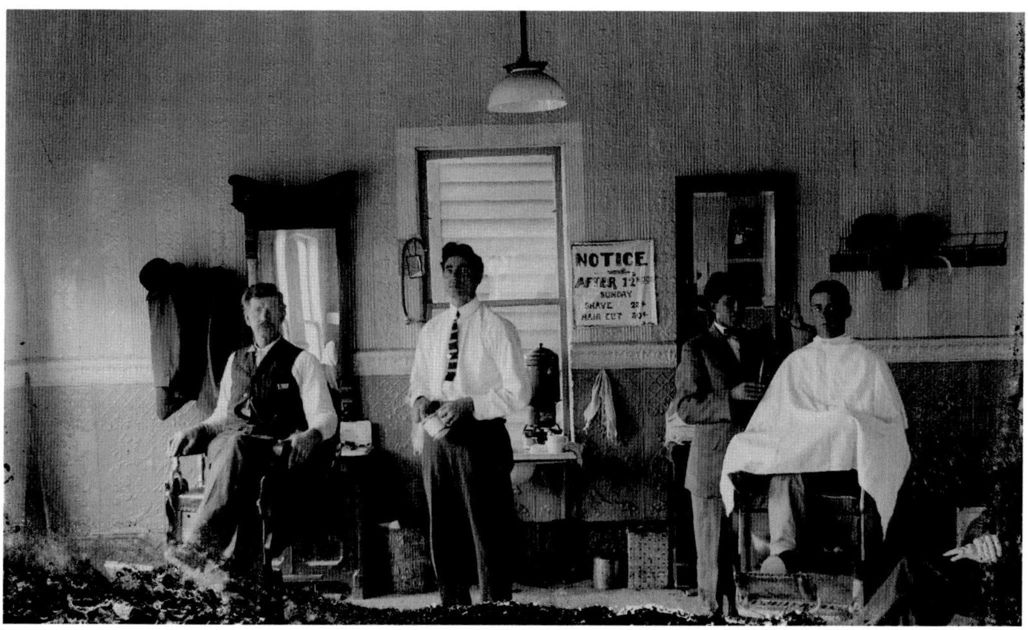

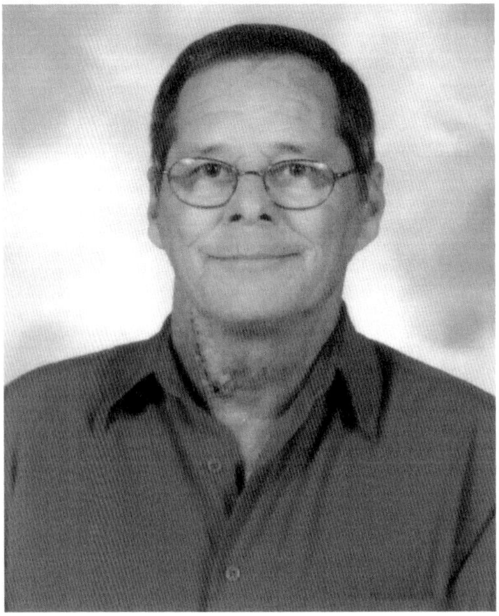

Brave Teenager
Riley Bernard Roy was a 16-year-old student who acted as a school bus flagman. Roy saved Bobby Miller Jr.'s life by pushing the younger boy out of the path of an oncoming speeding automobile. The driver had disregarded the warning signs when the bus stopped for Miller to exit. Having pushed the younger boy to safety, Roy was hit by the speeding car and received a broken leg, which required surgery and a long convalescence. Roy was hospitalized for about 19 months causing him to miss most of his sophomore year. Mayor J.J. Stagg and the St. Landry Parish Police Jury presented Roy with a citation for his heroism and bravery. (Courtesy of Jeanne Roy Rougeau.)

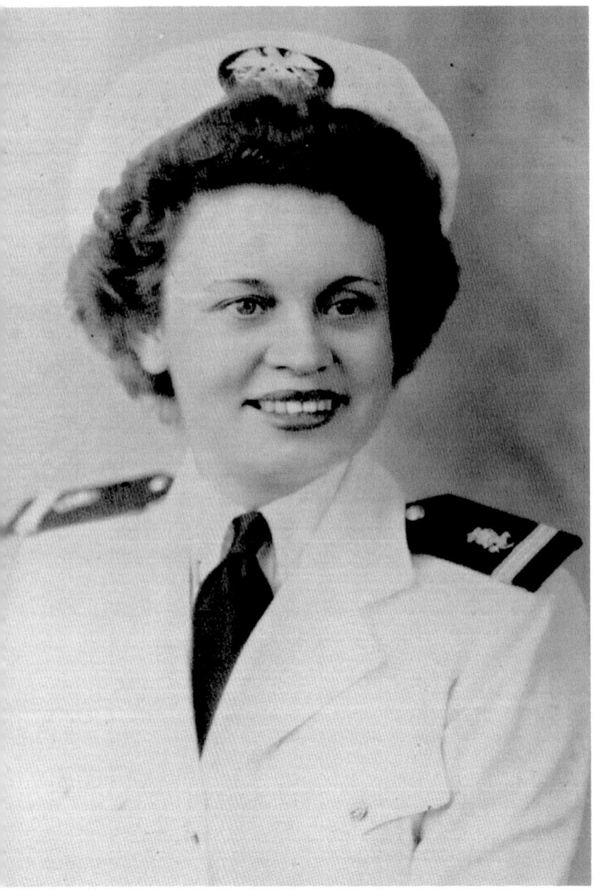

Navy Nurse (BELOW)
Luna Rose LeJeune Ardoin was born in 1920. She was a psychiatric nurse in the Navy Reserve stationed in New Orleans during World War II. Ardoin holds membership in the Catholic Daughters of America and St. Thomas More Church's Altar Society. She married Whitney Ardoin. (Courtesy of Eunice Public Library.)

ASCS National Tour Champion (RIGHT ABOVE)
Jason Johnson, a professional race car driver with 180 career victories, is called "The Cajun Sensation" by fans. Craig and Debra Johnson's son captured the Lucas Oil ASCS National Tour Championship in 2010 and again in 2011 as one of the most successful and competitive of the new generation of stars in the world of sprint car racing. (Courtesy of Tim Aylwin Photography and Jason Johnson.)

Awarded the Bronze Star (RIGHT BELOW)
Charles Seale's natural artistic skills and education have won him wide recognition and many professional awards in his specialized field of interior design. The restored 1920s-era Liberty Theater is one showcase of his talent. Seale was awarded the Bronze Star while serving in the US Air Force during the Vietnam War. (Courtesy of Charles Seale.)

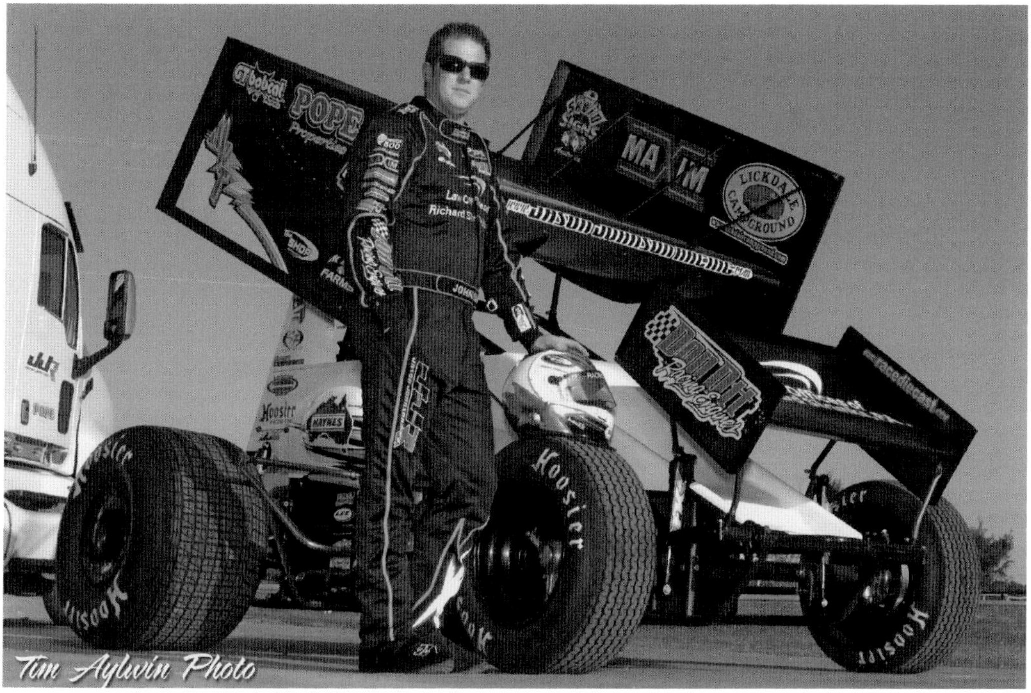
Tim Aylwin Photo
POPE
MAXIM
LICKDALE CAMPGROUND
Hoosier

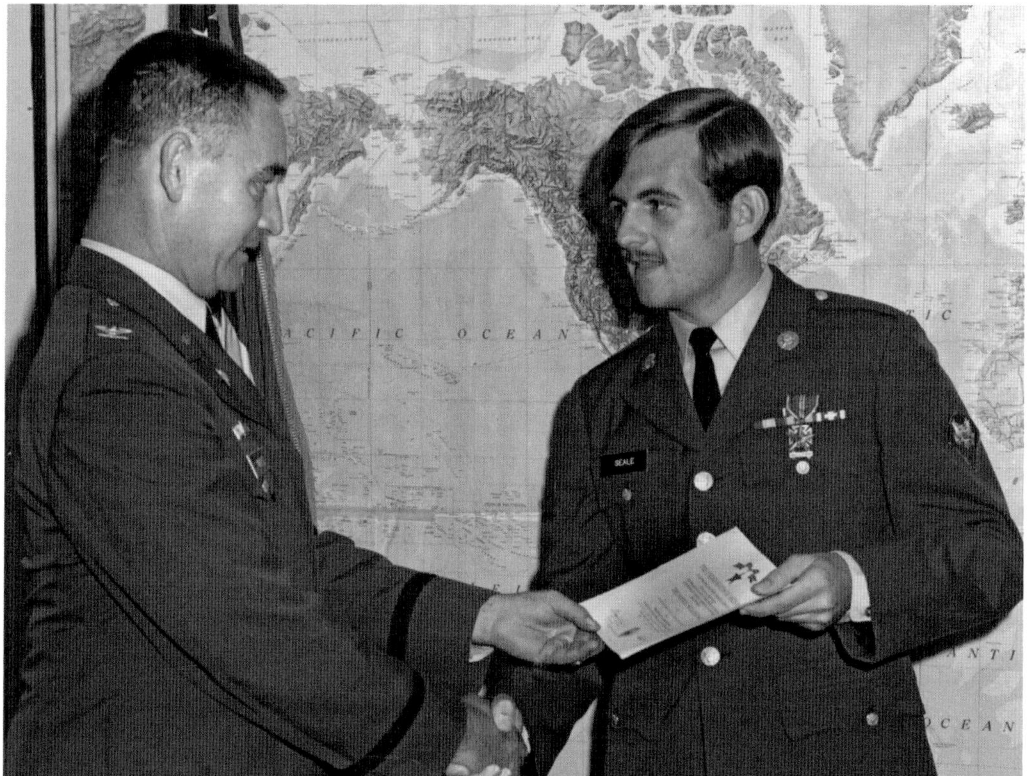
PACIFIC OCEAN
BEALE

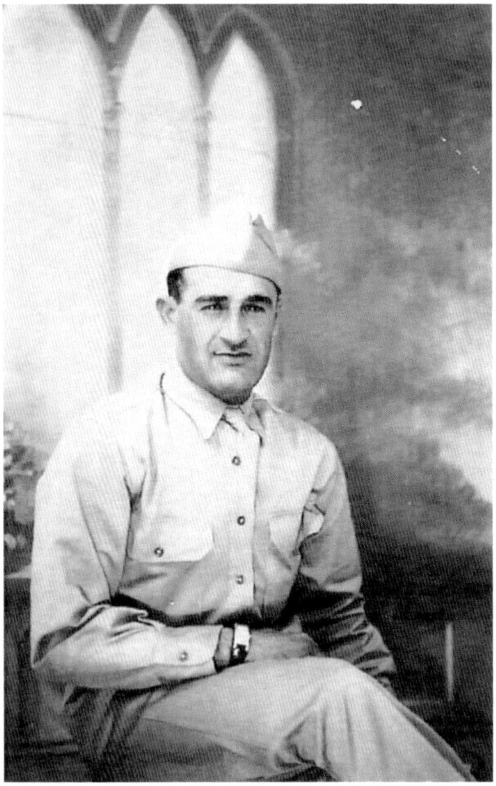

12-Year-Old Escaped from Communists

Louis Nicola Pavich and his wife, Maria Krivokucho, from Uetina, Yugoslavia, lived in the southern area of Croatia along with a large percentage of other Serbians. The Paviches, fearing for their lives, fled to the United States knowing that Yugoslavia would become dangerous to non-Communists because the new Communist government was targeting opponents who were formally educated or business owners. Educated and successful people were considered a threat to the Communist takeover. Because of the prevailing uncertainty in their country, the Paviches came to America, leaving their son, Louis Nicola "Louie" Pavich, in Yugoslavia until they could get settled in the United States. Eventually, the 12-year-old boy grew tired of waiting, so he made his way by hook or crook to England. There he stowed away on a ship bound for America where he was detained at the Ellis Island dorms for six months until a family member could claim him. His uncle, Sam Krivokucho of Chicago, went to New York, identified Louis, and returned to Chicago with the boy. Louis married Lela Mae Bertrand of Eunice, daughter of early settlers Leus and Onezia LeJeune Bertrand, and they had four children. When he left the Army, Pavich began working for the Missouri Pacific Railroad, where he remained until his retirement 45 years later. He was vocal and informed and the source of many a debate and interesting discourse, especially regarding political issues. Pavich wore his US Army uniform in this 1940s image. (Courtesy of Dr. Russell Pavich.)

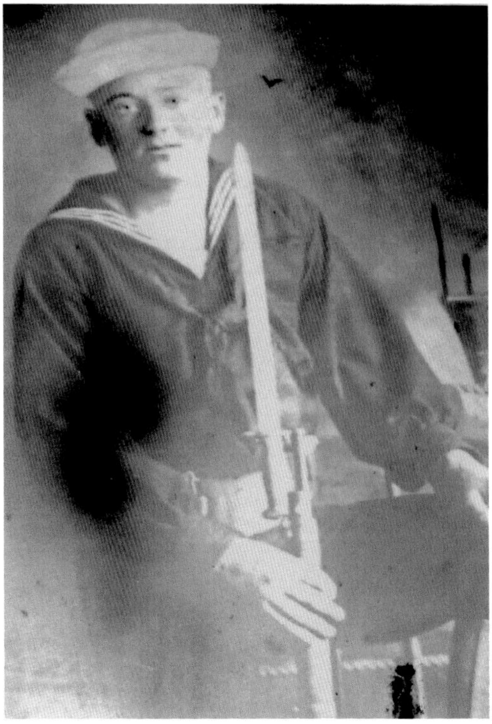

World War I Sailor

During World War I, Lital Courville was an OM 3 in the US Navy. Born in 1898, Courville was orphaned when he was five years old. He was reared by his older brother, Sidney. Courville married Hilda Landry and managed his brother's rice mill. (Courtesy of Hilda Courville Bollich.)

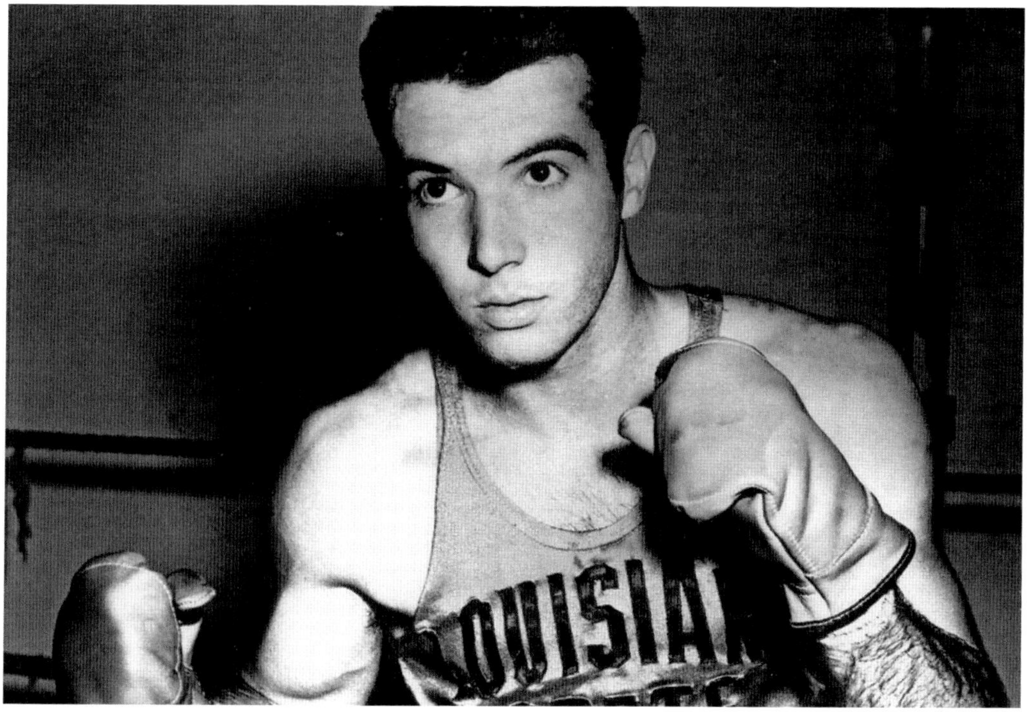

41 TKOs in 44 Fights

By his ability and training, Gilliam "Peaches" McLane made a name for himself in boxing circles in a brief period of time. The elder son of Effie Guillet, a Eunice native, and David Gilliam McLane, a machinist from North Carolina, he won state championships while a student at St. Edmund High School. Under the skilled coaching of Gerald Wyble, he was the winner of the 115-pound title in 1952, the 134-pound title in 1953, and the 145-pound class in 1954. McLane also was awarded the Brinks Trophy in 1954. He scored 41 TKOs in 44 fights and never lost a bout. LSU awarded a scholarship to McLane. While at LSU, McLane was an NCAA champion in 1956. He competed in the Olympic Trials, but lost in the semifinals. He lost his life in a waterskiing accident. In August 1957, the boxing arena at Angola State Prison was named in his honor, because he volunteered to travel there from the LSU campus to box in numerous exhibitions for prisoners. (Courtesy of *Boxing: Louisiana's Forgotten Sport.*)

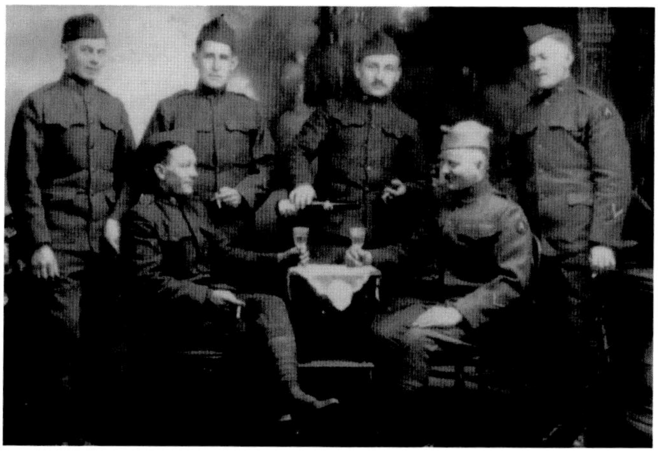

Celebrating War's End

Ben Miller, seated right, was in France with some of his fellow soldiers celebrating the end of World War I. Miller, born in Eunice in 1891, was classified as a private first class with the Evacuation Hospital 29. He died in 1941. (Courtesy of Dr. Jack D. Miller Jr.)

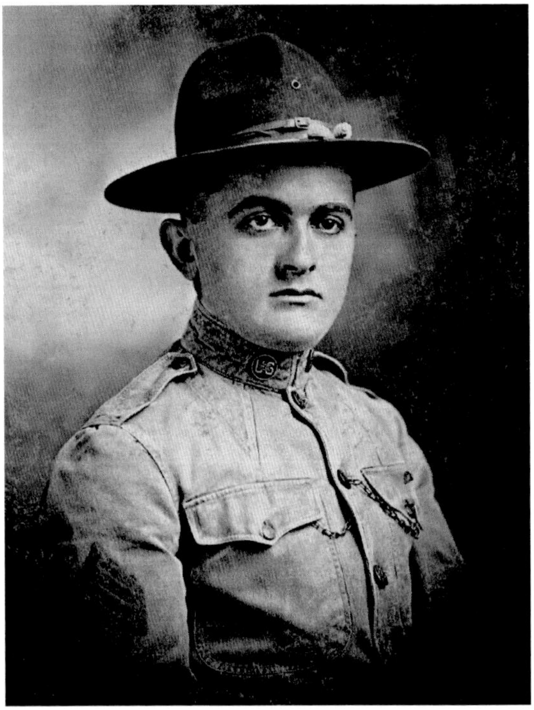

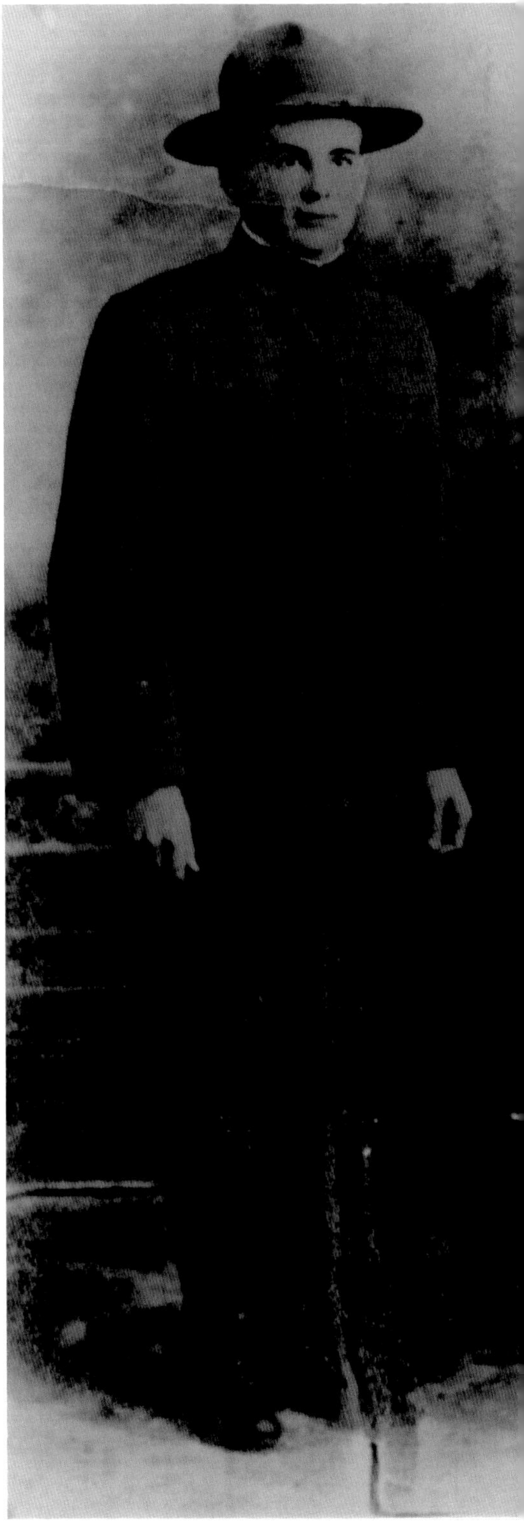

Hollywood Actor
Born in 1899, Loudice J. Verret served in World War I and was discharged as a sergeant. However, he did not return to his hometown. Instead, Verret established himself as an early movie actor in Hollywood. A handsome man, his career looked bright until the "talking" movies became popular and ended his movie career. Verret could not obtain movie roles because his Cajun accent was too pronounced. He returned to Eunice to work at the post office. A son of Achille and Mari Camelia O'Brien Verret, he married Nita Vidrine in Opelousas in 1938. (Courtesy of BBHC.)

Active Leader
Wearing his World War I uniform, Matthias J. Frugé Sr. exemplified the World War I Doughboy. Frugé was among the more notable figures of Eunice. He joined American Legion Post 129 and served numerous terms as commander. He was executive vice president of Tri-Parish Bank, member of Rotary Club, the Louisiana Civil Defense Director in 1943, and a fireman. Frugé served as Grand Knight of the Knights of Columbus from 1922 to 1924. He was named Citizen of the Year in 1960. Married to Ethel Manuel, they had two sons, M.J. Frugé Jr and Dr. Bernard Frugé. (Courtesy of Ann Frugé.)

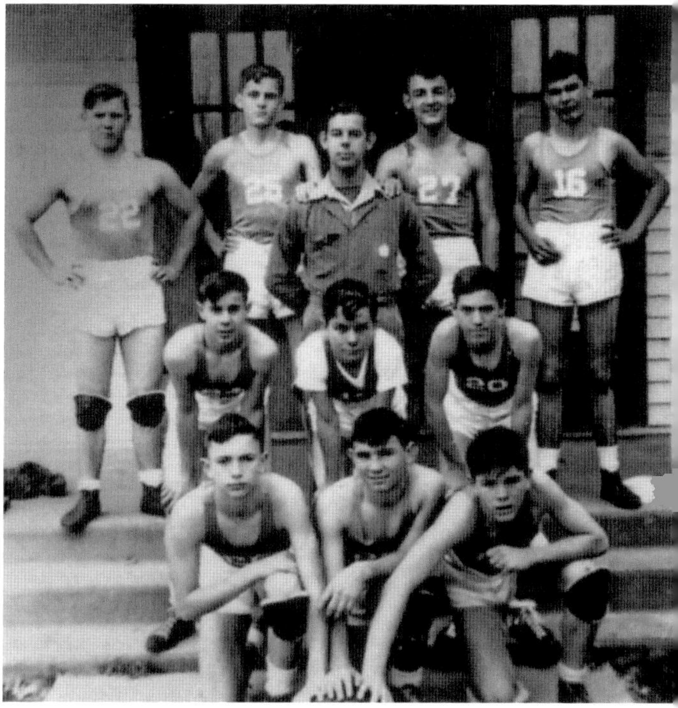

Jesuit High School's Used Uniforms
St. Edmund School's first basketball team took to the court in 1945–1946 wearing hand-me-down uniforms from the Jesuit High School of New Orleans Blue Jays. In their first game against Lawtell High School, the coach told St. Ed's players that Lawtell didn't even have a gym, so they could expect an easy win. Lawtell played on a dirt court. But the final score was a bit lopsided: Lawtell scored 60 points with St. Ed's making only one point. Doug Longman made a free throw in the waning moments of the game to score the Blue Jays' only point and received a standing ovation from Blue Jay fans. To make matters worse, Eunice's future mayor, Curtis Joubert, and local physician, Dr. Sylvan Manuel, played for the Lawtell team. Members of St. Edmund's first basketball team posed in front of the gym for their team photograph. Left to right were (first row) Robert K. Guillory, Doug Longman, and Jack D. Miller; (second row) Larry Manuel, Cliff Bergeron, and Doug Clause; (third row) Coach Gerald Manuel; (fourth row) players R.H. "Bobby" Miller, F.S. DeRouen, Donald Miller, and Rodney Manuel. (Courtesy of Dr. Jack D. Miller Jr.)

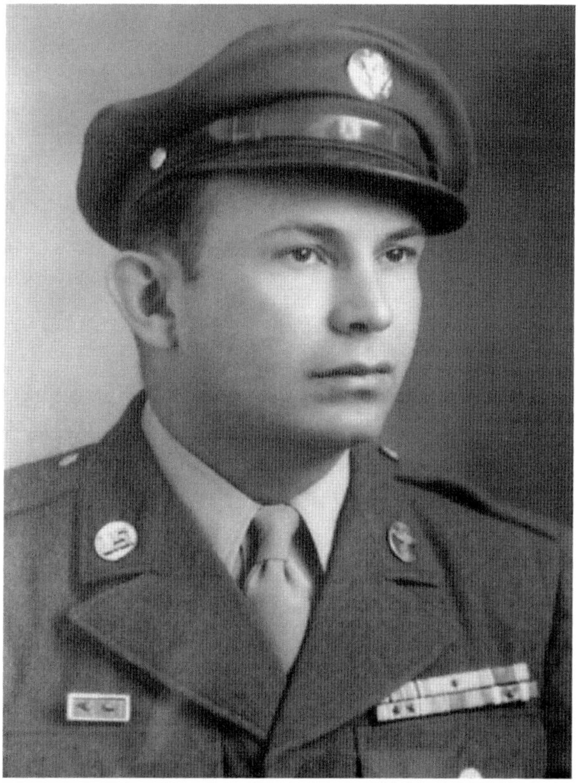

POW in Japan
During World War II, Bruce Miller served in the US Army Air Force in the 16th Bomb Squadron. He was captured by the Japanese at the Mariveles, located at the end of the Bataan Peninsula, in April 1942. Miller survived the brutal Death March, starvation, disease, and torture in Camps O'Donnell and Cabanatuan. He was shipped to Japan on one of the infamous Japanese "Hell Ships," the *Nagato Maru.* Forced to work in coal mines at POW camps near Osaka, Japan, Miller survived to be liberated by US troops in 1945 after atom bombs were dropped on Japan. Discharged as a sergeant, he returned to Eunice to work as a deputy sheriff in St. Landry Parish. (Courtesy of Hazel Miller.)

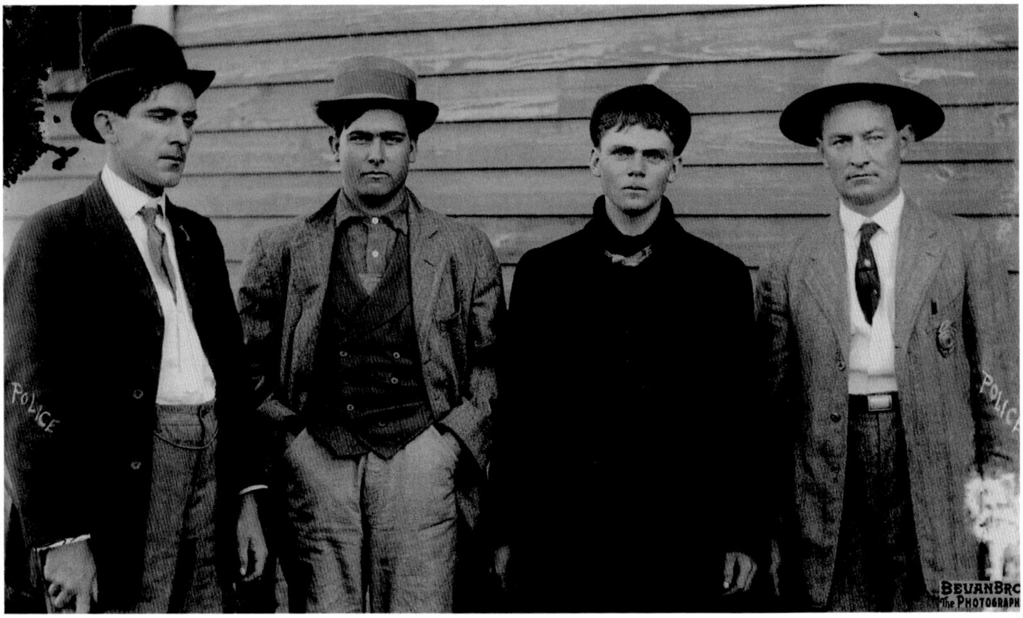

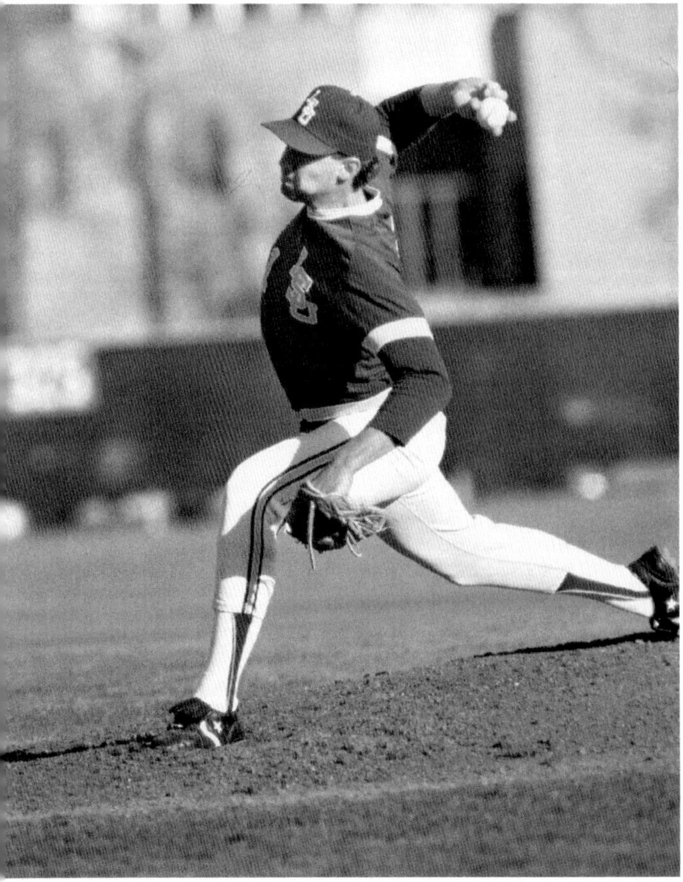

Early City Marshal and Mayor
Henry Landry, born in Opelousas in 1881, was an orphan when he came to live in the Edward DeJean home in Eunice. After his marriage to Ada Ford, Landry proved to be an effective city marshal as recorded in this image with Officer Nat Guillory (left) and two strangers who broke into the Lyman-White Store. In 1908, when Mayor O.E. Vidrine died in office, he was replaced by Henry LaFleur, who resigned. Landry was appointed to fill out the remaining term, which ended with the election of Mayor G. Ardoin in May 1909. (Courtesy of BBHC.)

Three Perfect Games
A son of Raynold and Lynette Loewer, Stanley Loewer was an outstanding high school pitcher. He was an All-Stater and earned Player of the Year honors in 1983. In his 1982 and 1983 seasons, Loewer threw three perfect games. He set records at LSU. The pitcher's best record was in his junior year when he finished 14-4 with a 3.80 ERA. He finished 9-5 with a 4.03 ERA as a senior, striking out 95 in 89.1 innings on the mound. (Courtesy of LSU Sports Information.)

Orphan Train Rider

Ernest Kaplan LeDoux was born in New York in 1904. His mother was a Jewish girl, Sarah Kaplan, who was too poor to provide for the boy. He was admitted to the New York Foundling Hospital of the Sisters of Charity, where he became one of the children whom the hospital baptized Roman Catholic and placed for adoption. Between 1853 and 1929, orphan trains transported children, accompanied by nuns from the Sisters of Charity order, out of eastern cities to rural communities in hope that they would encounter better lives. Onezime and Luscinda Young LeDoux asked for Ernest to be their foster son through the St. Anthony Catholic Church in Eunice. Riding on the orphan train to Opelousas, Louisiana, in May 1907, Ernest was placed with the LeDoux family. He was wearing his #26 ID tag that identified him to his foster parents. It also supplied his name, date of birth, and the name of his foster parents. He became a family member at the tender age of three and a half. Onezime and Luscinda were almost 40 years old when they took Ernest into their family. They had three married sons, Alfred, Arnold, and Alphan, and a daughter, Eugenie, who was 12 years old. In later years when Luscinda was asked why she would take in a small child at her age, she replied, "As the priest said, there is always room for one more and I have a feeling I will be able to rely on him in my old age." As it turned out, her husband Onezime died in 1912 when Ernest was only eight years old, and all the sons died young. Eugenia, the daughter, died while giving birth to a daughter Mae McGee, when she was only 19. In 1945, when Ernest built a home for his family, his mother moved into his home and lived there until she died in 1951. So his adoptive mother's prophecy that Ernest would care for her in her old age became true. Ernest's story was a happy one, but too many children merely became indentured servants to their foster parents. Standing in front are, left to right, Aniese Martel LeDoux and Pearl, Luscinda Young LeDoux, and third from right, Ernest Kaplan LeDoux. Eugenia's daughter, Mae McGee, was sitting in the toy wagon to the left. Others are unidentified. (Courtesy of John E. LeDoux Sr.)

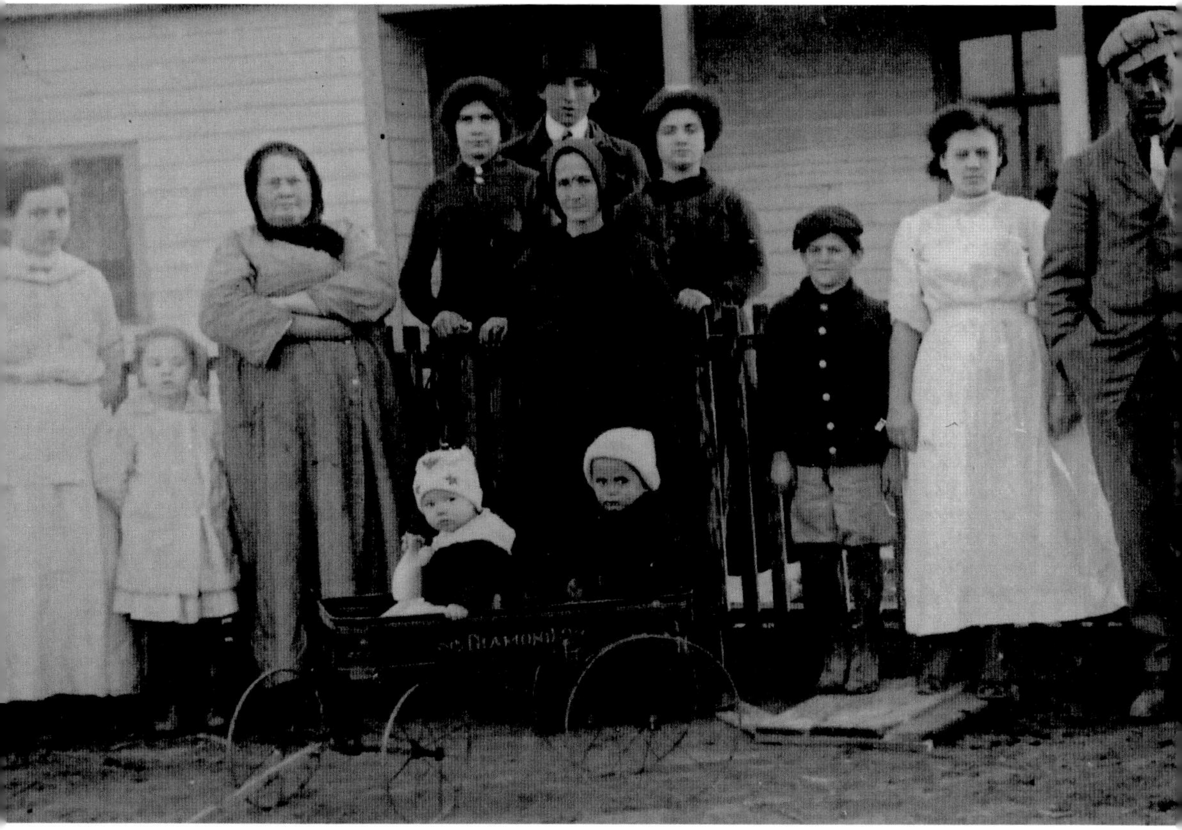

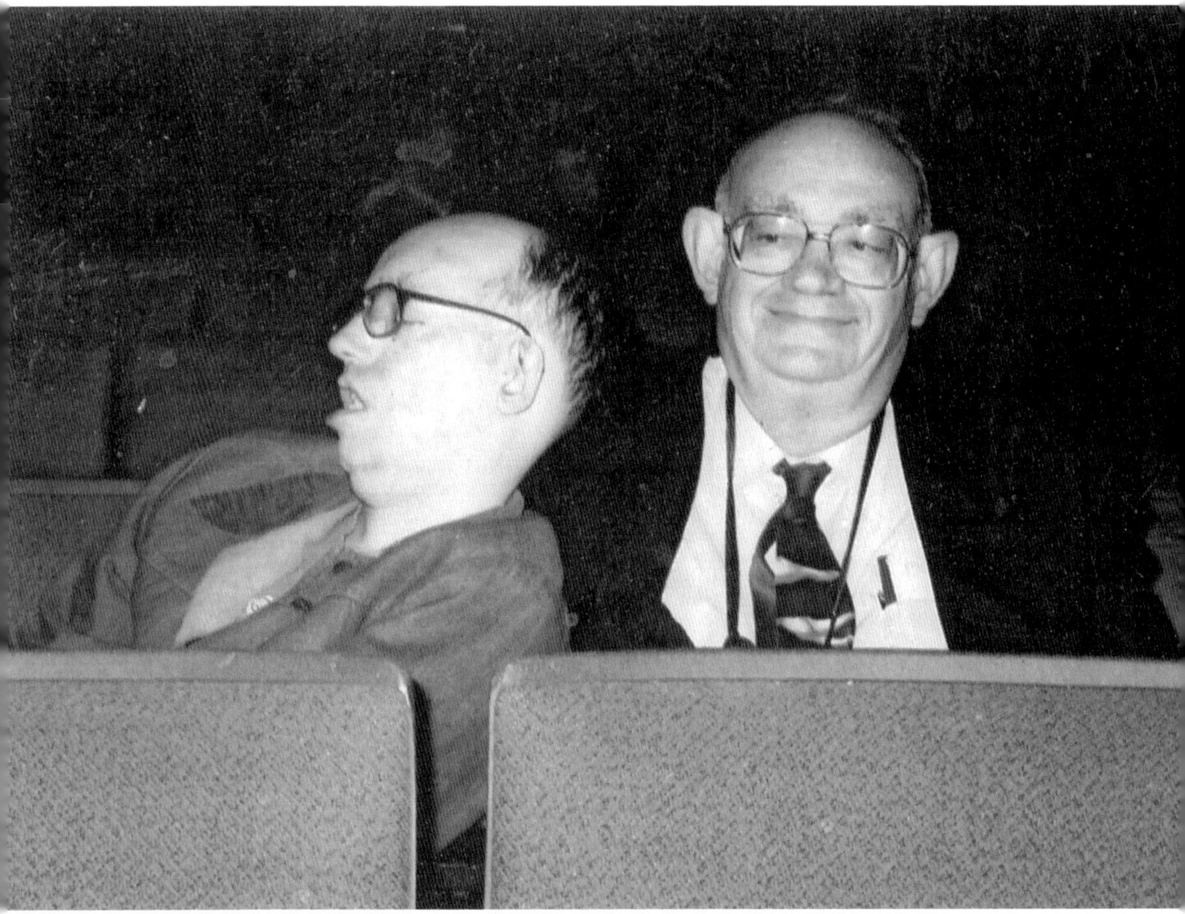

He Practiced What He Preached

Jerry Hoffpauir was never without a broad smile for everyone he encountered. He worked for the *Eunice News* for over 30 years as a news editor and sports editor. A graduate of the University of Southwestern Louisiana in Lafayette, he worked at several newspapers while in school. Hoffpauir was a member of the Eunice Rotary Club and the Cultural Community Service Committee. He was the recipient of many awards such as the Martin Luther King Humanitarian award, the Eunice Players Theater's coveted Tim Wooten Award, the Rotary's Citizen of the Year award in 1993, and the Jaycee's "Jaycee of the Year" award. He served as pastor of the First United Methodist Church in Basile. He also substituted for Methodist ministers in the area if they needed help. Hoffpauir was a longtime friend and supporter of LSU Eunice and was an honorary member of the Volunteer Fireman's Association. Hoffpauir's name has always been synonymous with the town and the newspaper. Individuals in the community respected and treasured his friendship. "Mr. J." was the quintessential good father. When his wife, Barbara, predeceased him and their special needs son, Clifton, Hoffpauir became both mother and father to the young man. People said, "Everywhere Jerry went, Cliff went." He did a remarkable job teaching, befriending, and providing a normal home situation for his son. Clifton Hoffpauir, left, and his father, Jerry, enjoy the evening at a theater production. Hoffpauir was the son of Howard Murrel and Hazel Hoffpauir of Crowley. Hoffpauir left a legacy of community service particularly for his coverage of city activities for the newspaper and his willingness to attend any event if his reporting of it would benefit the community. (Courtesy of Myra Miller.)

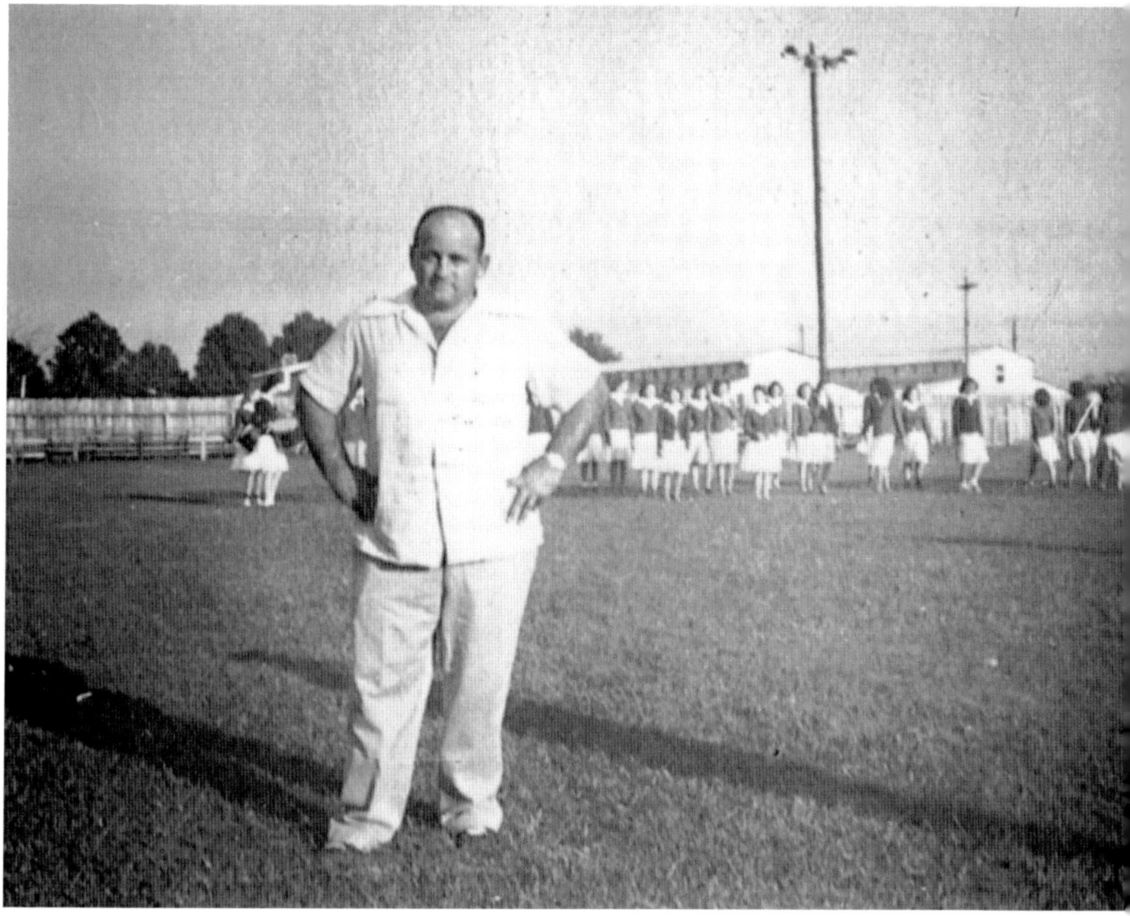

Legendary Coach

Faize Mahfouz, husband of Helen Allen and father of Claire, was the only high school coach inducted into the Louisiana Sports Hall of Fame, yet his high school teams never won a state championship. His coaching career spanned 35 years. A son of Lebanese immigrants, Mahfouz played quarterback on the Louisiana Normal teams in the early 1940s. He compiled an overall record of 127 victories, 80 losses, and four ties in 22 years at Eunice High School where his biggest rival was Opelousas High, coached by his brother, Payne. He spoke at coaching clinics around the United States where his contribution to high school athletics was deemed phenomenal. Mahfouz was known by his peers and sportswriters as an offensive innovator. He was credited with introducing the Wing-T and Split-T to high school football. He was not only a coach, but a counselor and friend. Many are the student athletes who were called "Jugheads" by the best-known coach in high school football. He said, "Life was so much simpler in my day. The biggest thing a kid had to do other than sports was work on his dad's farm. That's hardly a temptation compared to what they have to distract them today." After leading Eunice High to 20 winning seasons in 22 years, Mahfouz gave college coaching a try, but it didn't appeal to him. He took on coaching a New Iberia High School team that had a long losing record just for the challenge. There, he built a winning team. When he was inducted into the Hall of Fame, Mahfouz said, "This award needs to be divided into a zillion pieces so they can give one to each of the kids, and my wife Helen should get the biggest piece for putting up with me for 42 years." He was pictured on familiar turf, the practice field at old Eunice High School, with the 1946 Green Jackets pep squad in the background. (Courtesy of Bettie Brunson Jenkins and Claire Mahfouz.)

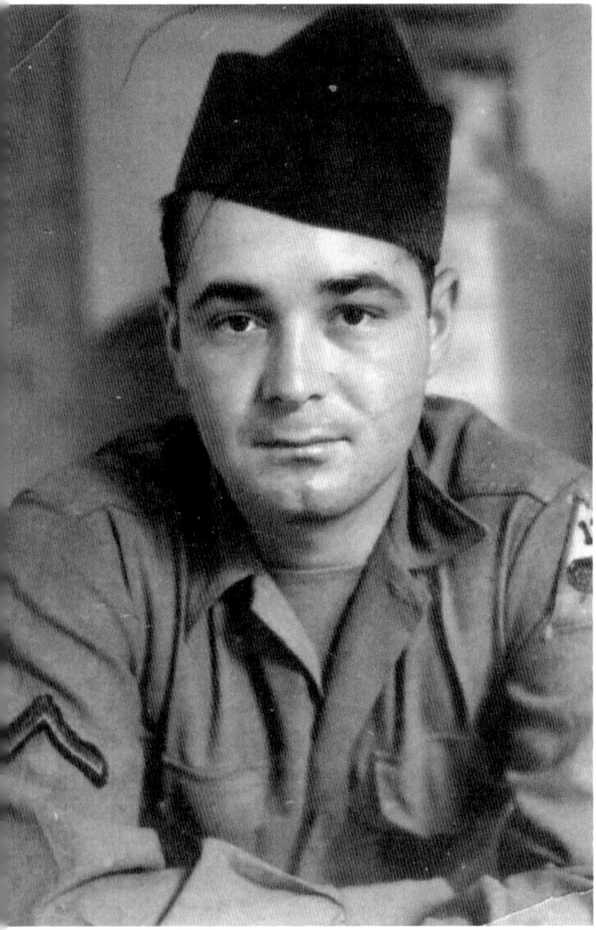

Cajun Translator
Felix Mire served in a unique role during World War II. He was one of the Cajun translators who were as important to the American war effort as the much acclaimed Native American "Code Talkers." Hundreds of French-speaking Cajun men from South Louisiana enlisted in the military. Their linguistic skills and French cultural backgrounds, although ridiculed for years, became vitally important to the American war effort in French North Africa, France, and Belgium. These Cajun servicemen worked with the French Resistance after D-Day and supplied America's most effective means of communicating with French-speaking officials and civilians, thus providing critical support and intelligence to the American forces. Mire died in 2006 in his beloved Cajun Louisiana. (Courtesy of Patrick Mire.)

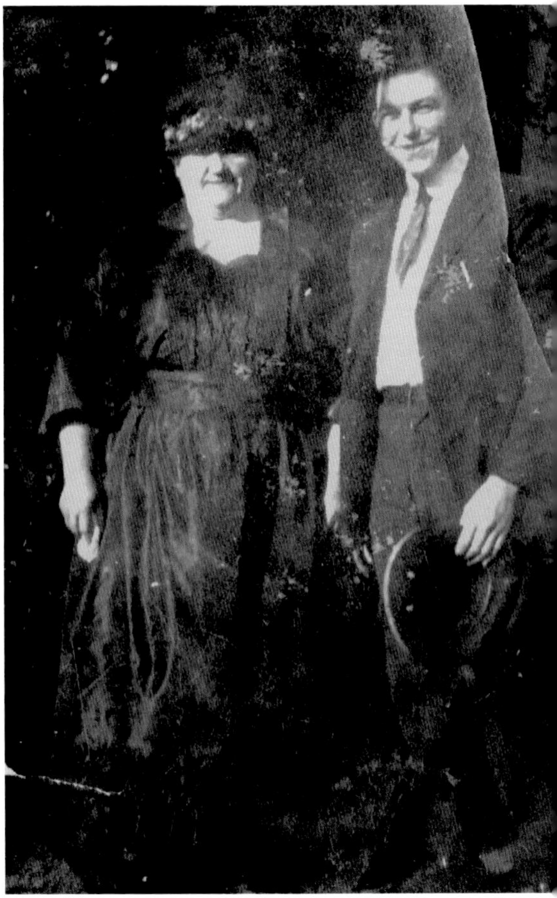

Letter Home
Charles Sanders Jr., with the US Army's 1st Battalion, 41st Infantry (Armored) Regiment in North Africa and Italy, wrote: "In November 1942, we landed in Casablanca, our first invasive action . . . America's first amphibious landing of the war. We went to Algeria by train—100 men and 8 mules to a car. Africa is a memory now, almost as distant as the one we have of America. Then Sicily . . . if we wanted to leave Sicily, we sure as heck wished we were back there when we landed in Italy at a place that will go down in history—Salerno. They threw everything in the book at us on that small beachhead. Those without religion when they got there, sure had it when they came out." Sanders, right, is shown with his mother, Sallie Sanders, prior to the war. (Courtesy of William F. Sanders.)

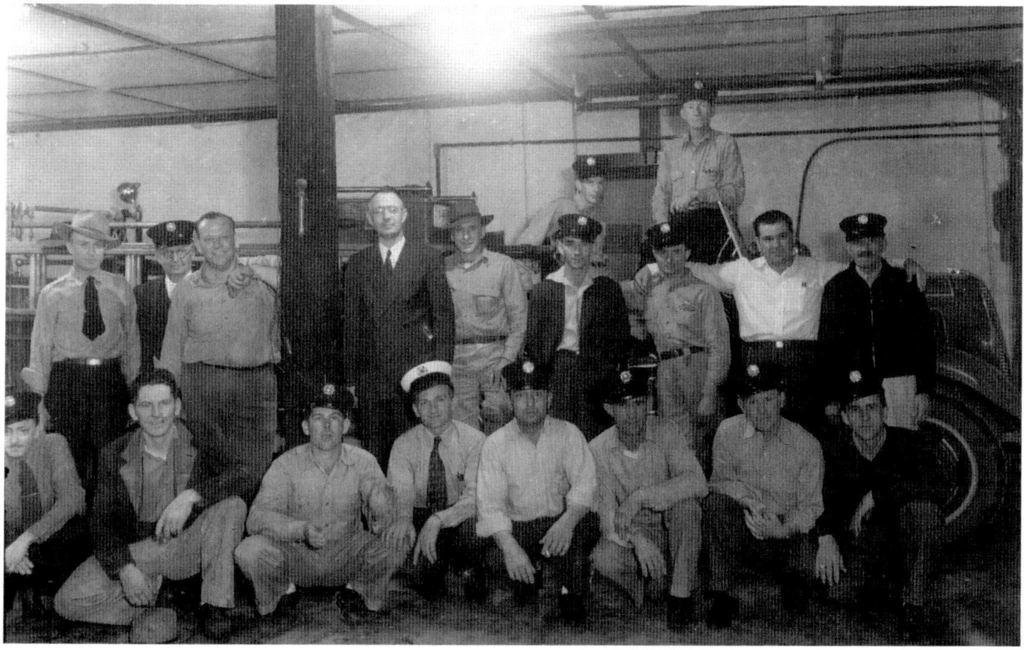

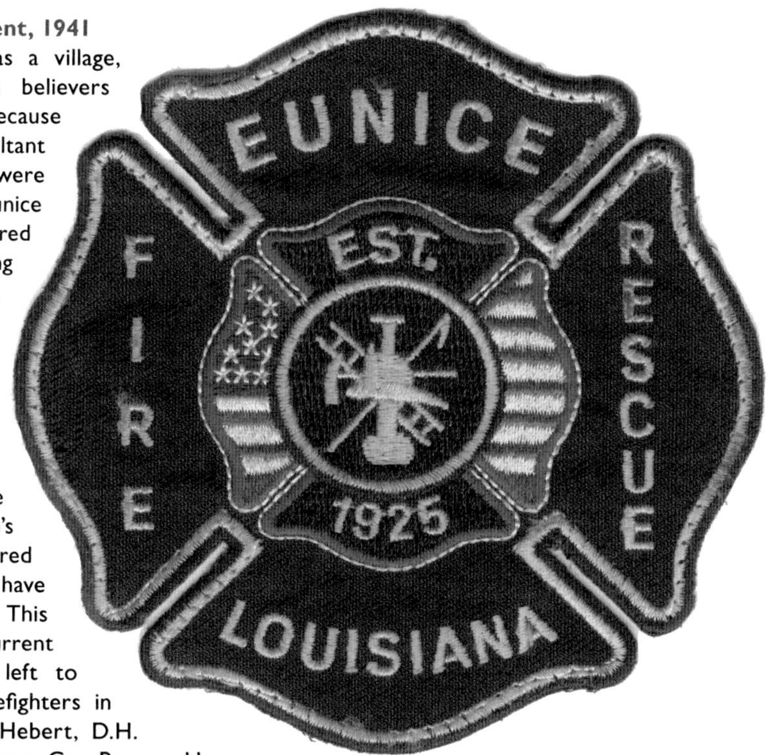

Eunice Fire Department, 1941
At the time Eunice was a village, its citizens were firm believers in fire prevention because fires and the resultant death and destruction were their greatest fear. Eunice residents have rendered their services fighting fires from the bucket brigade to the horse-drawn carts, then to the automobile-drawn carts and, finally, to the modern fire trucks with fully trained and expert personnel. Eunice Fireman's Association's patches have been altered as firefighter's duties have changed since 1925. This patch, right, is the current symbol. Pictured from left to right are the Eunice firefighters in 1941: Edgar Pitre, C.E. Hebert, D.H. McManus, C.A. Mornhinveg, Gus Pesson, Henry Miller, Robert Kleiser Jr., Eddie Brown, M.L. Arnold, Clovis Durio, Katar Moosa, L.S. "Sam" Uzzo, Warren Prudhomme, L. Edgar Meaux, Lannie Frugé, Noah Guillory, Ovid Landry, Aubry Arnold, and Percy McGee. (Courtesy of Eunice fire chief Michael Arnold.)

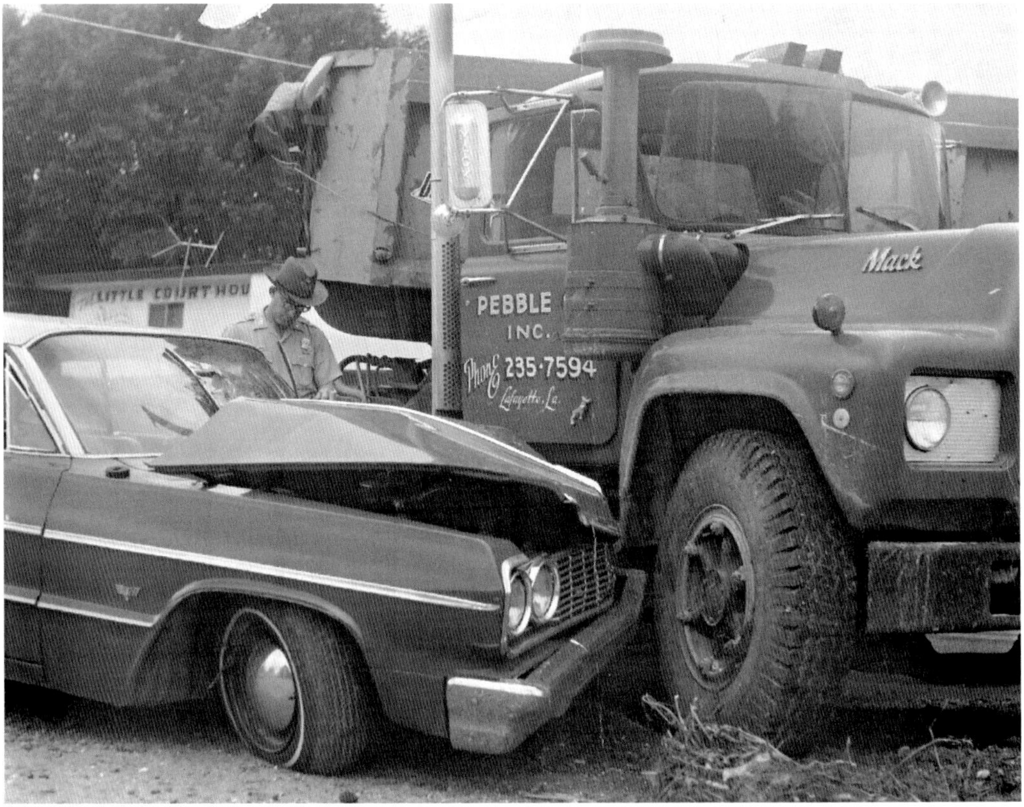

A Trooper

Joseph Clayton "Blinky" Bertrand Jr., son of C.J. and Armildy "Mel" Fusilier Bertrand, attended the Louisiana State Police Training Academy. Assigned to Troop K, he recalls the memory of his first fatality, a youth who burned to death in a wreck. Also, Bertrand remembers pursuing an armed robber who crashed on an "S" curve. Approaching the car and pointing his pistol, Bertrand yelled, "Show me your hands and they'd better be empty!" Ordering the suspect to crawl out of his car, Bertrand saw the man held a pistol against his chest and knew he was in a perilous situation. Bertrand also escorted Louisiana governors John McKeithen and Edwin Edwards at various times. (Courtesy of Clayton Bertrand.)

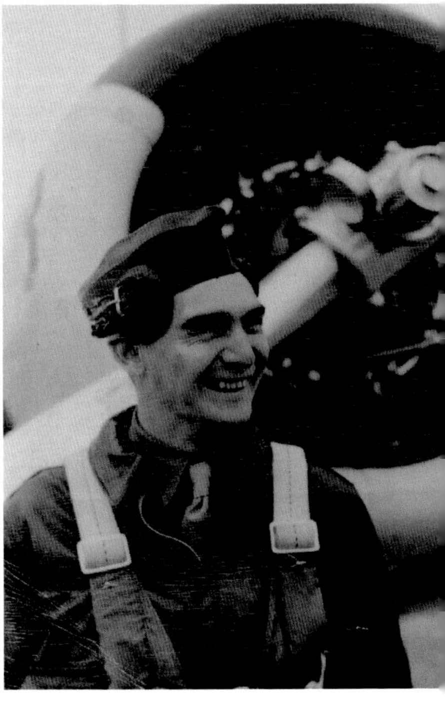

Nazi Prisoner

Harold Gournay, with the 15th Air Force in Foggia, Italy, was shot down over Maribor, Yugoslavia. Captured because his parachute caught in a tree, he was sent to Stalag Luft III. Enduring a 480-mile march to Stalag VII in six inches of snow because of advancing Russians, he was liberated by General Patton in 1945. (Courtesy of Harold Gournay.)

Killed in Action in Vietnam

S.Sgt. Donald Sistrunk began his tour in Vietnam in March 1970; he died one month later. He was assigned to Company B, 501st Infantry, 101st Army Battalion. One of Sistrunk's friends reported his death: "Sgt. Donald Sistrunk was leading his squad of soldiers back to their base camp at Phu Bai, Viet Nam, about 20 miles below the so-called Demilitarized Zone of Viet Nam, when he was killed in a Viet Cong ambush attack. No contact with the enemy had been reported in that area for several months." However, Sistrunk's platoon sergeant, Lyle Kohmetscher of Lawrence, Nebraska, argued that they were "about six to nine miles north of the northern tip of the A Shau Valley at a place we called Re-Up Hill when Donald was killed. Our platoon was on its way to link up with two other platoons of the company when he was shot. Donald was not more than five feet away from me when he was hit in the chest with a single shot from a North Vietnamese sniper. We had already lost an entire squad that day. The platoon went from 28 men to around 14 in 24 hours. They were killed in one afternoon when we thought we were safe after a day of battle where we lost many friends. I have not forgotten him." After talking with other veterans who were in Vietnam with them, Kohmetscher reported that the men agreed that Sistrunk did not die leading his squad back to Phu Bai as the newspaper reported, but he was on Re-Up Hill with the rest of the men who were killed on April 9, 1970. The entire town closed down for Sistrunk's funeral and for his burial at St. Louis Cemetery. He is also honored on the national Vietnam Veterans Memorial, and on the Memorial Wall at the USS *Kidd* in Baton Rouge, Louisiana. (Courtesy of Cat Jamison.)

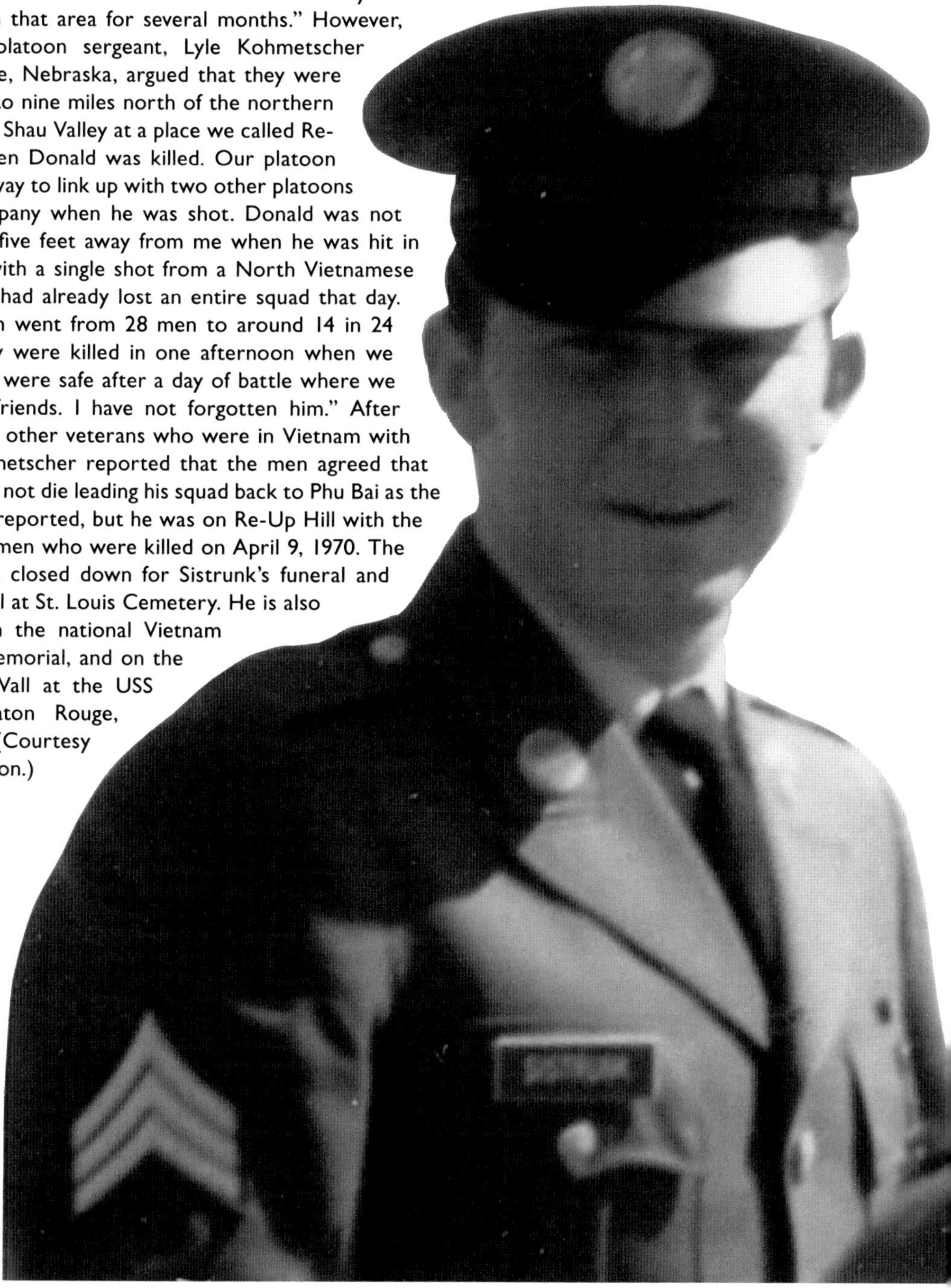

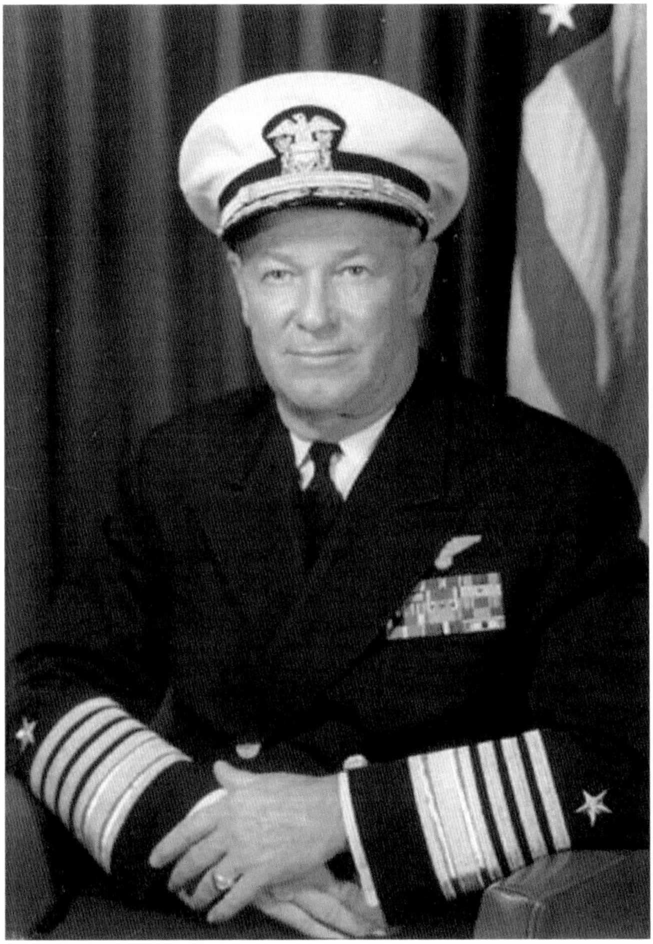

Eunice's Admiral

Born the eldest of 12 children in Big Bend, Louisiana, Adm. Roy Lee Johnson grew up in Eunice, graduating from Eunice High School in 1924 and the US Naval Academy in 1929, where he played varsity football and was on the staff of the academy yearbook. He married Margaret Louise Gross on his graduation day. Johnson rose through the ranks. He served as commander of Carrier Air Group Two in World War II and on the carrier USS *Hornet*. He led attacks against Japanese forces at Palau and Wake Island, receiving the Air Medal for Meritorious Achievement. He also led campaigns against the Japanese at Iwo Jima, Okinawa, and the Philippine Islands. Johnson was the first commander of the USS *Forrestal*, America's first super aircraft carrier, which was a 66,000-ton attack ship on which several Eunice sailors served. In 1951 during the Korean War, Johnson became the commanding officer of the escort carrier, *Badoeng Strait*, affectionately called "Bing Ding" by her crew. After the Korean War, he was assigned to the National War College in Washington, DC, before he was chosen to command the Seventh Fleet later in 1955. As commander of the Pacific Fleet, he ordered American ships, the USS *Maddox* and *Turner Joy*, to return enemy fire in what would be called the Gulf of Tonkin Incident. After the incident, Johnson was named commander-in-chief of naval forces in the Pacific. He retired from the Navy in 1967 and died in Virginia in 1999. Johnson received numerous medals and citations including the prestigious Legion of Merit with gold star and two Distinguished Service Medals. The admiral had two children. His son, Roy, predeceased his parents and sister in 1994. His daughter, Jo Ann Coe, was the first female Secretary of the US Senate and chief of staff for Sen. Bob Dole. (Courtesy of US Navy Historical Association.)

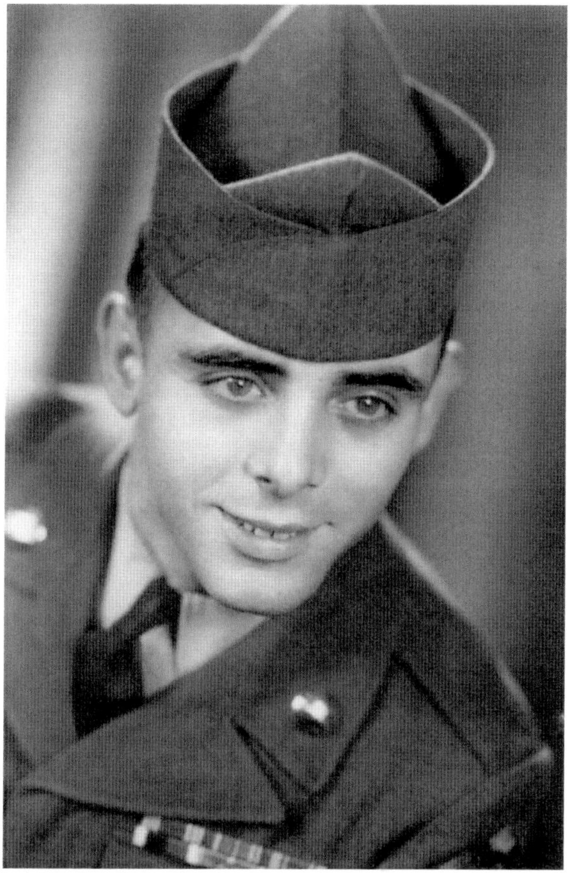

New Yorker
Cpl. Joe Sanfilippo, a native of Wappingers Falls, New York, was the son of Antonio and Maria LoBianco Sanfilippo of Sicily. During World War II, he served in the US Army's 4th Division that invaded Germany. He met his future wife, Verbie Courville, in 1952 at The Rendezvous in Basile. When he saw her with Ruth Courville and Regina Delaune, he knew she was "the one!" (Courtesy of Joe Sanfilippo.)

Scouts at Camp
Boy Scouts gathered each summer at Camp Thistlethwaite to hone their wilderness camping skills. This troop, pictured in the mid-1950s, included from left to right (front row) Calvin Prudhomme, unidentified, Gary Gotreaux, unidentified, unidentified, Roger Caviness, and unidentified; (second row) John "La Pin" Bertrand, Cecil Brown, unidentified, ? Carrier, unidentified, unidentified, unidentified, and unidentified; (last row) Nolan Fontenot, Rodney T. Reed, unidentified, unidentified, J.W. LaHaye, and Rallen Fontenot. (Courtesy of Dr. Rodney T. Reed.)

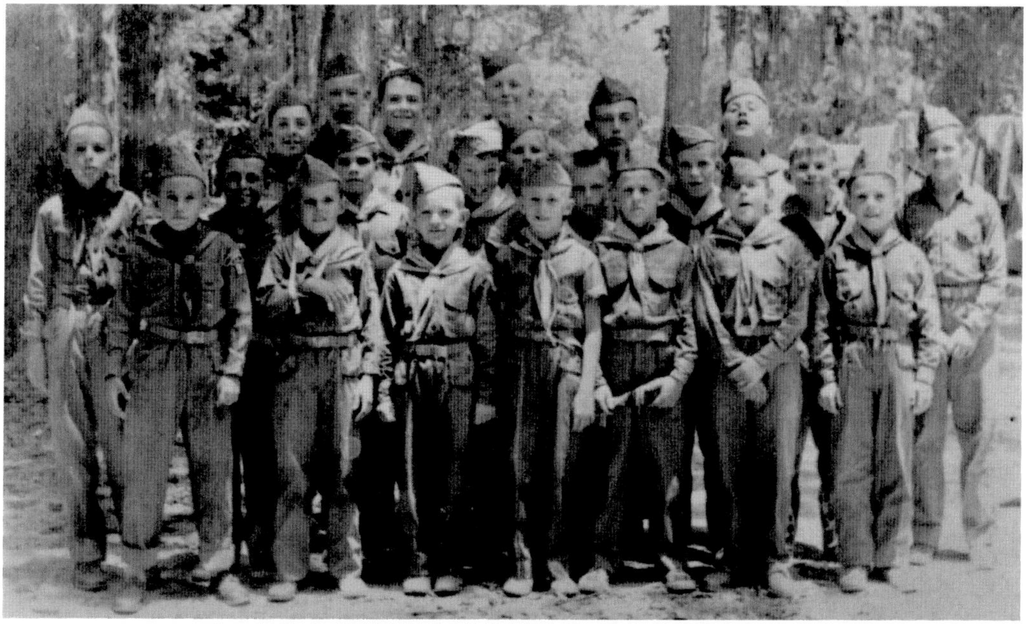

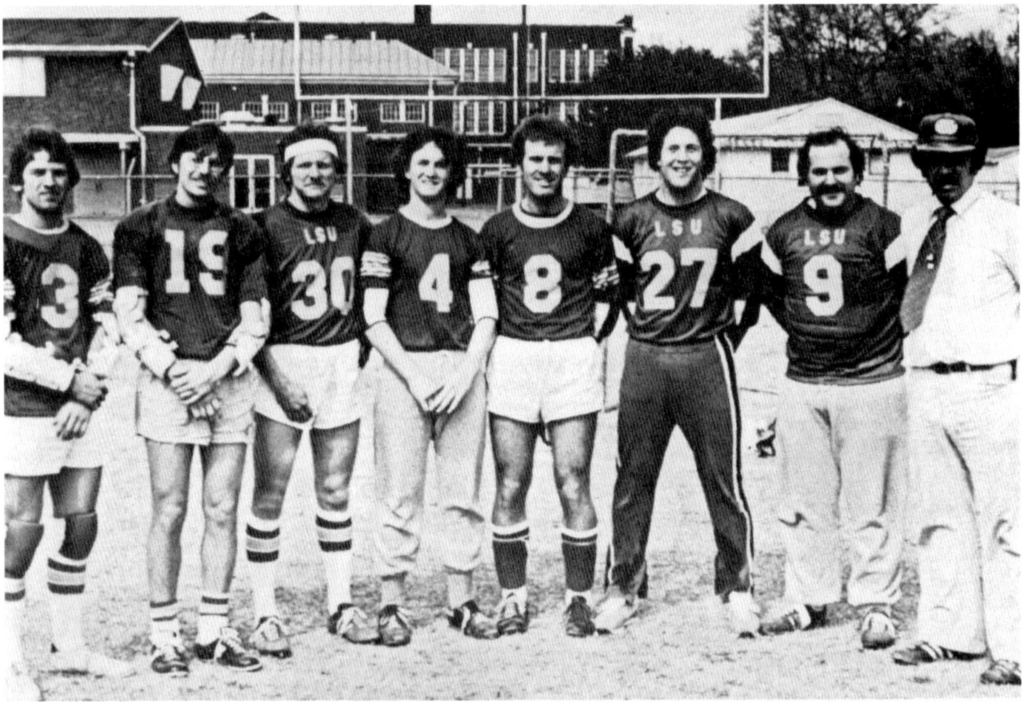

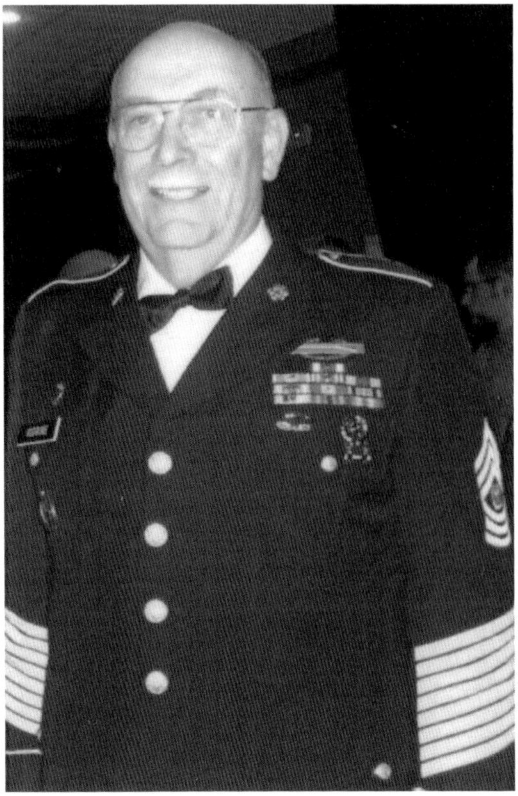

LSU Lacrosse Team
The LSU Lacrosse team played against Texas A&M at the old Bobcat Field on Eighth Street at Maple Avenue in 1978. LSU Eunice vice chancellor for academic affairs, Dr. Stephen Guempel, played on the team. Pictured are the players, left to right, Andre Vizina, Guempel, Rudy Frugé, Tony Vidrine, John Eldred, Hank Cowen, Mitch Kimball, and Ed Kardes. (Courtesy of LSU Eunice.)

Santo Domingo Action
Command Sgt. Major John R. "Randy" Vidrine, son of Kirby Lee and Isola Landreneau Vidrine, was born in Eunice in 1944. He served active duty in the US Army until 1965. In 1975, he joined the Army Reserve, where he achieved many awards. Vidrine fought in combat when the 82nd Airborne Division was deployed to Santo Domingo, Dominican Republic in 1965. He was also called into Operation Desert Storm when the 4073rd US Army Reception Battalion of Reserves was activated and mobilized in 1991. Vidrine achieved the rank of command sergeant major at retirement. (Courtesy of John R. Vidrine.)

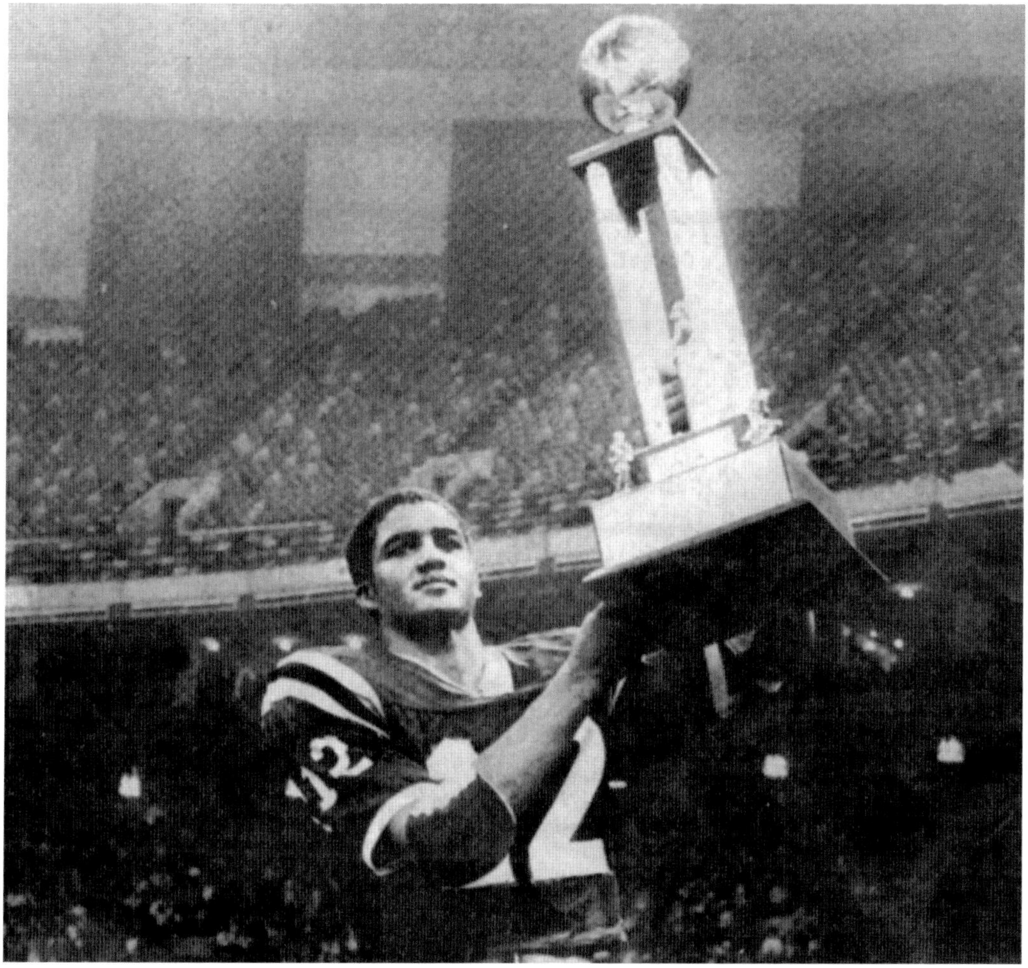

Sports Honors

One of eight sons in a family of 12 children of Freddie and Maggie Tate Carrier, Chris Carrier piled up honors as an athlete at Eunice High School. Pictured above, in 1982, he was both captain of the Eunice High School 3-AAA State Championship football team and the MVP of that game. Carrier was a two-time All-State recipient. Gaining more athletic honors, he made the All–Deep South team and earned Adidas All-American football honors while in high school. He made the All-SEC team in 1986–1987 while at LSU. While playing at LSU from 1983 to 1987, he was a four-year varsity letter winner and started at safety for the Tiger football team. Carrier played in the 1985 Sugar Bowl game, the 1985 Liberty Bowl, 1986 Sugar Bowl, and the 1986 Gator Bowl. Drafted by the Phoenix Cardinals in 1988, he signed as a free agent with the Indianapolis Colts in 1989. He earned a BS from LSU in 1990. Carrier's high school coaching and disciplinary position experience includes stints of nine years at Baton Rouge Catholic High, two years at St. Louis Catholic High in Lake Charles, and seven years as head of in-school suspensions at Dutchtown High School. Carrier also coached for a short time for the Baton Rouge Blaze, an arena football team. He is presently dean of students at Zachary High School. He describes his philosophy of discipline this way: "It is not hard to understand that every student must get to class on time and every student must be doing what they are supposed to do when they are supposed to do it. There's nothing hard about that." Carrier and his wife, the former Wanda Thomas, have two sons, Christopher II and Cameron. (Courtesy of LSU Sports Information.)

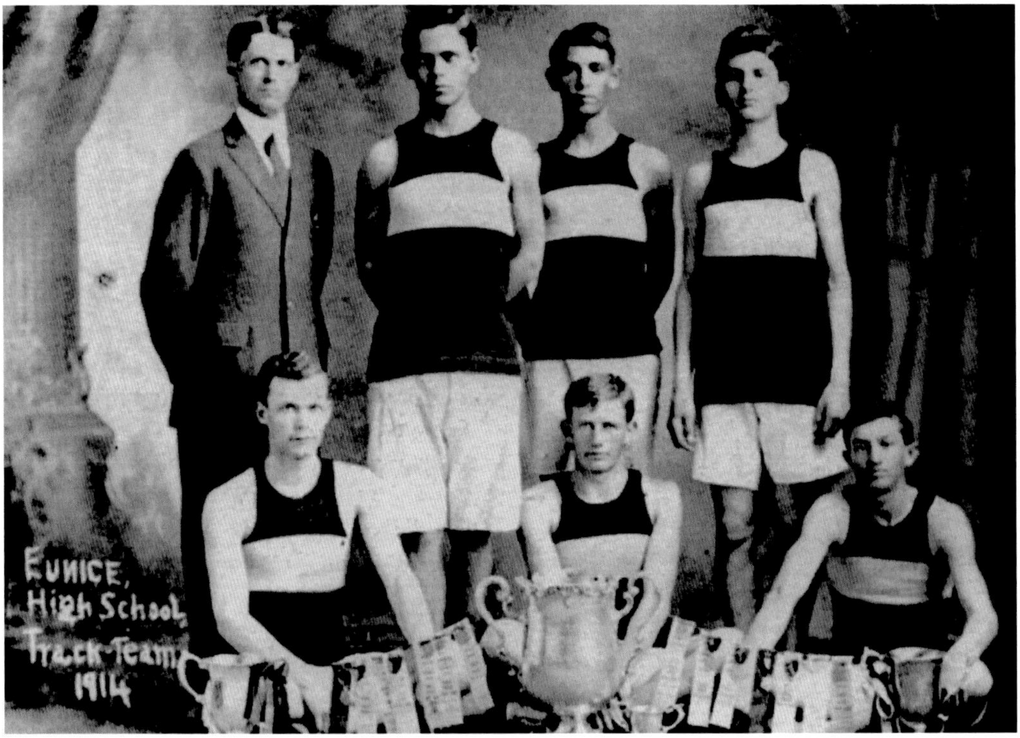

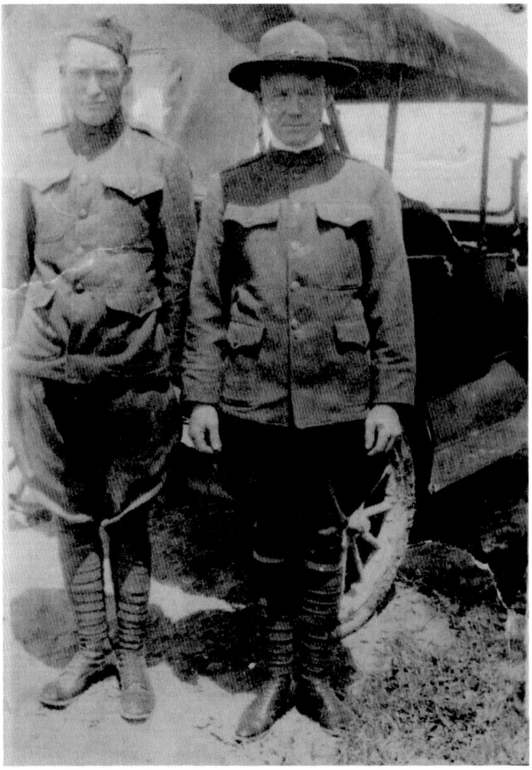

Track Star
Dana Jenkins, first row, center, son of William and Clara Stagg Jenkins, could have been one of the greatest track stars in America, but World War I ended his fabulous career. He starred at Eunice High School and at LSU, where some opponents refused to compete with him because he was so feared. When war was rumored, he was sent to Texas with the National Guard. Jenkins was called to attend the Olympic Trials in 1916 in New Jersey, but his lack of training while in the service led to his loss in the half-mile run. (Courtesy of BBHC.)

Band of Brothers
Arthur "Bud" Arnold, right, and his brother, Milton "Red" Arnold, sons of William and Sarah Elizabeth Herring Arnold, served in the American Expeditionary Force in World War I. Milton was engaged in the Meuse-Argonne offensive in 1918 where he experienced the dreaded trench life. After the war, Arthur was an active Mason. Milton returned to Eunice as a city fireman. (Courtesy of Garland "Bully" Arnold.)

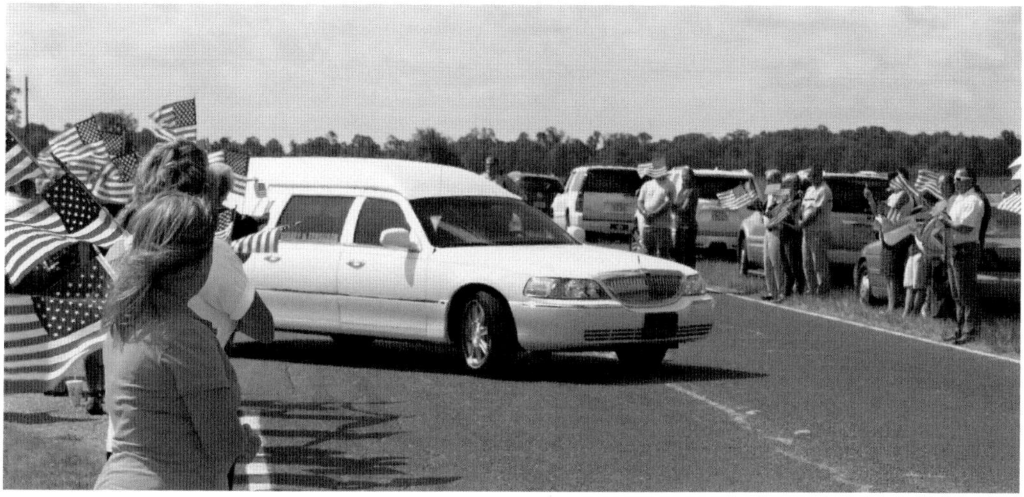

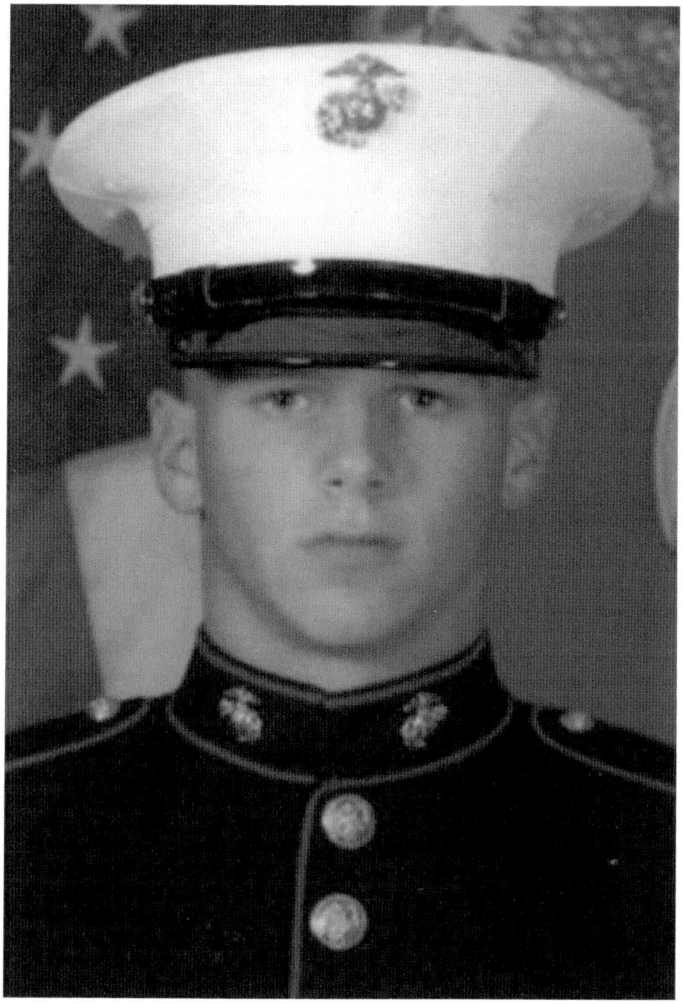

He Died a Marine
Marine Corporal Matthew Richard, son of Jeff and Alicia Richard, was killed in Helmand Province, Afghanistan, in 2011, by an explosive device. Richard was a 21-year-old serving his second tour as an infantryman with Golf Company, 2nd Battalion, 8th Marine Regiment, 2nd Marine Division, II Marine Expeditionary Force from Camp LeJeune, North Carolina. His awards included the Navy and Marine Corps Achievement Medal, National Defense Service Medal, Afghanistan Campaign Medal, Global War on Terrorism Service Medal, and the NATO Medal. His mother noted, "He did die a Marine. . . that's what he wanted." Pictured left is Corporal Richard. Above are citizens awaiting the young Marine's final journey home. (Courtesy of Louisiana State Newspapers.)

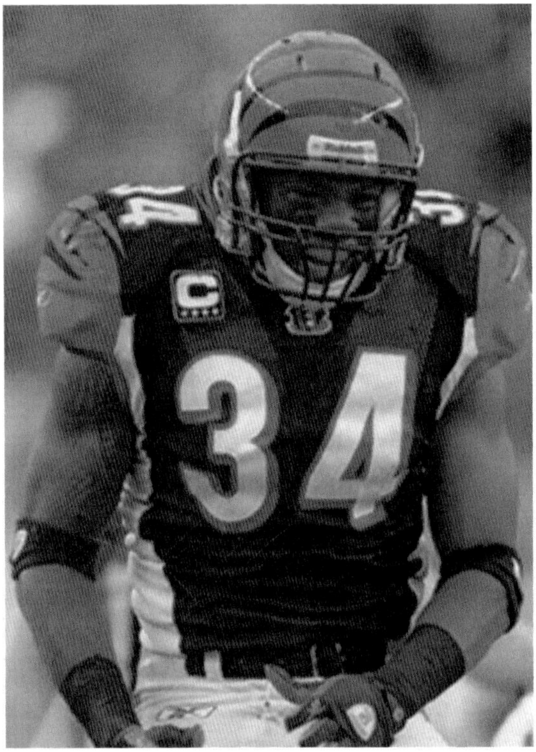

Kyries Cares
NFL football record-holder Kyries Hebert was honored when a street in Eunice was named for him. While playing for the Cincinnati Bengals, he was their captain and held the franchise record for special teams tackles. He also played for the Canadian League. To encourage area youth, his KyCares Foundation sponsors professional sports role models at area football, cheerleading, and dance camps for city youth. (Courtesy of Kyries Hebert.)

Korean War
Rodney Manuel, left, and Jack Miller are pictured clowning around at Fort Sam Houston, a US Army base in San Antonio, Texas, after they were inducted in July 1952 during the Korean War. The men were sent to Fort Bliss in El Paso, Texas, to an Army anti-aircraft artillery unit. Miller and Manuel were in the vanguard of air defense training at the base, where they learned to use anti-aircraft guns to repulse enemy aviation operations and to support the infantry. (Courtesy of Dr. Jack D. Miller.)

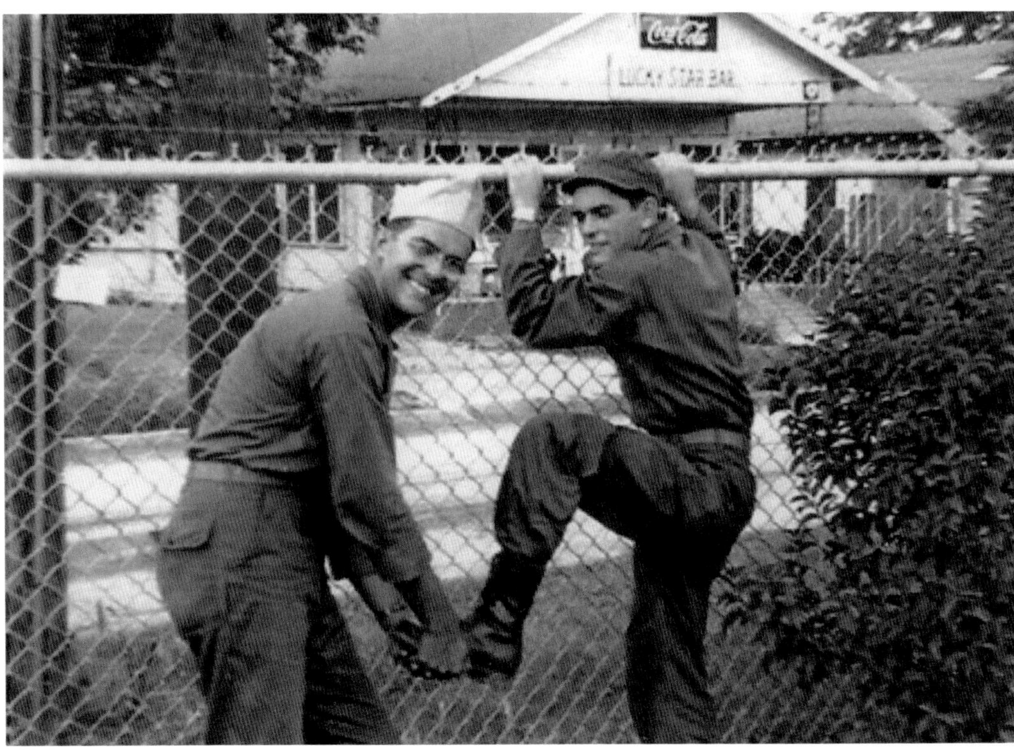

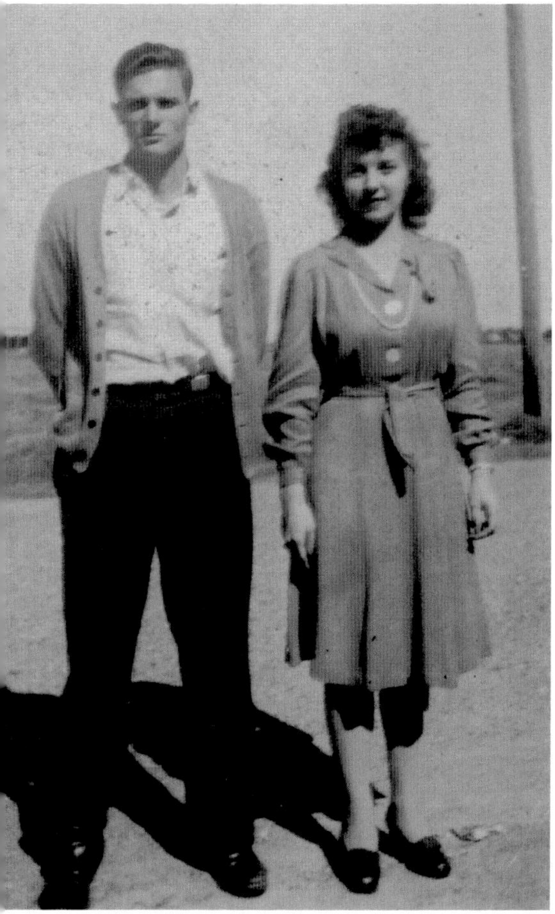

Naval Cadet

Thomas McGowan Dunkin, left, pictured with Marcia Pinckard, was the son of Rev. Curtis O. and Alma Dunkin of the Acadia Baptist Academy, south of town. His family arrived from Oklahoma City, Oklahoma, when his father took the job as dean of men. Dunkin graduated from Acadia Baptist Academy in 1944, and was accepted into the Navy V-5 program to train as a naval cadet at Mercer University in Macon, Georgia. (Courtesy Marcia B. Pinckard.)

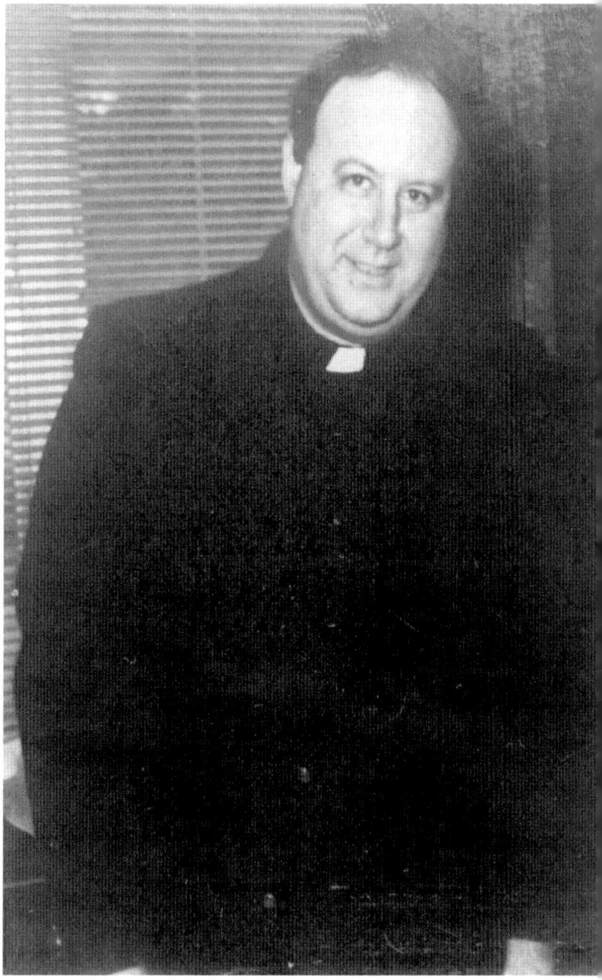

Genealogist, Author, and Priest

Fr. Donald J. Hebert, son of Louis and Marie Mire Hebert, was pastor at St. Anthony's Catholic Church from 1980 to 1985. He became a hero to scores of genealogy researchers when in 1972, Hebert began a project to collect and index every record of baptisms, marriages, and funerals in all churches of the Diocese of Lafayette from 1756 to 1902, including civil records. The project grew into 30 volumes of *Southwest Louisiana Records* that provided invaluable information. Hebert wrote *History of St. Anthony Parish, 1902–1983*. In 1975, he began a new series of volumes of church and civil records from the Diocese of Houma-Thibodeaux, *South Louisiana Records to 1902*. He died at Mire, Louisiana, in February 2000. (Courtesy of authors' collection.)

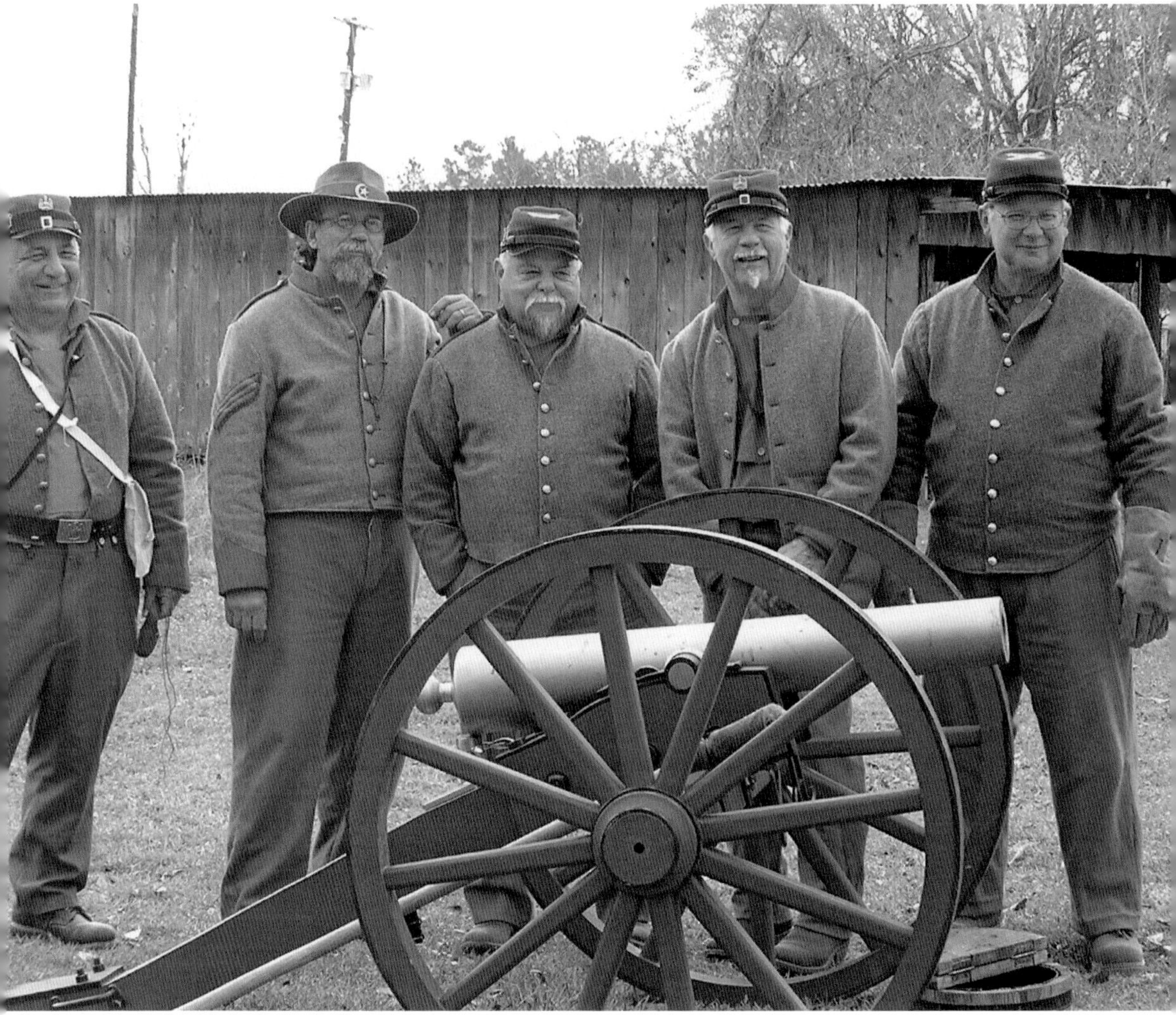

Living History Cannon Crew

King's Artillery, living history reenactors named for a Civil War unit formed in 1861 by Col. Edward King, symbolizes the heroes of the bloody war by portraying the brave men of this unit. Formed in 2005 by Al Krantz and Mike Broussard, the cannon crew has participated in re-enactments in Louisiana, Texas, and Mississippi, living history school demonstrations, soldiers' headstones dedications, placements of historical markers, and in the movie, *In the Electric Mist*, filmed in New Iberia. They are from left to right, Joe Richard, Eunice; Mike Broussard, Breaux Bridge; Johnny Reed, Eunice; Al Krantz, Breaux Bridge; and Preston LaCombe of Iota. (Courtesy of authors' collection.)

CHAPTER SEVEN

Some Notable Visitors

Eunice has attracted myriad visitors—some notable and some forgettable—since 1894. A number of them came to visit family like Brig. Gen. Ernest F.B. Cook, who came from England to visit his uncles and cousins. Some say his mother, Lady Amelia Bult Cook, also came to see her brother, whom she had not seen in over half a century. Entertainers such as bandleaders Jimmy Dorsey and Harry James with their orchestras, or popular musician Papa Cairo performed at the Silver Slipper Supper Club in the late 1940s. Roy Rogers, Lash La Rue, and other stars made appearances at the Liberty Theater. First Lady Eleanor Roosevelt threw dimes to over 3,000 citizens in 1939 as her train pulled out from a "Whistle Stop" event for the March of Dimes. In 1955, Count Yoga, billed as "the man who has revolutionized the greatest science of all sports—golf—into the easiest sport," gave lessons to local golfers. Sadly, his photograph is not available. Other visitors were anthropologist Dr. Margaret Mead, St. Louis Hawks' basketball great Robert Petit Jr., and Johnny Mack Brown, the University of Alabama's great football star who visited his college friend, Dr. B. Rodney Reed. Pres. Lyndon Johnson's daughter, Luci, visited the James Montelaro family and attended mass at St. Anthony Catholic Church. Other visitors came to enjoy the food and festivities. Singer Tim McGraw enjoyed crawfish boils with the Tanny Devillier family. The Winston Atteberry family entertained both Gen. William C. Westmoreland and Dr. Harry Heimlich. Numerous history-making military officers including Generals Eisenhower, Marshall, and Patton spent time in town during the 1941 Louisiana Maneuvers war games. The astronaut and space shuttle pilot Robert L. Crippen was invited by Mayor Curtis Joubert in the 1980s. However, a few visitors were here with nefarious purposes. Rumor had it that Bonnie and Clyde, Lee Harvey Oswald, and Jack Ruby used Highway 190 for their dreadful plans. Numerous other famous people have been spotted in town, but the stories were never verified. The people of Eunice are known for their warm friendliness, hospitality, public spirit, and enthusiasm. Their doors are thrown wide to all visitors.

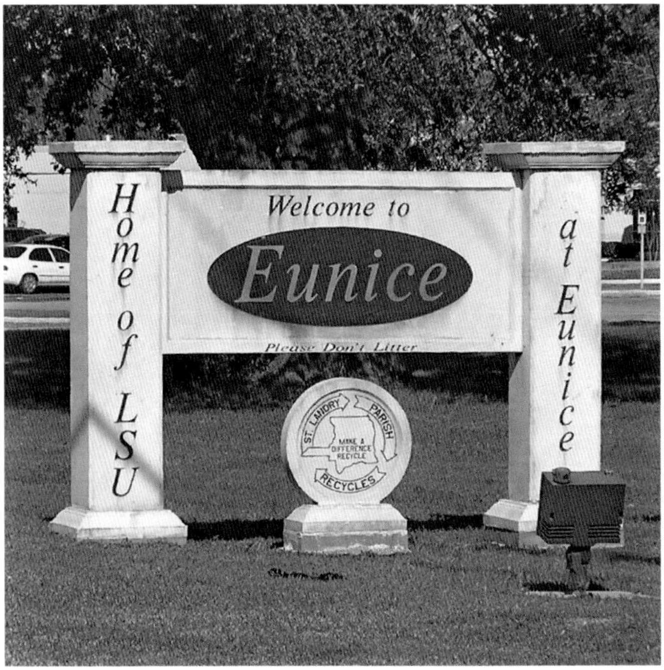

Welcome to Eunice
Eunice residents welcome newcomers to their town. This sentiment is evident in the Welcome to Eunice signs at the city's main entrances. Erected during Mayor Lynn LeJeune's administration, the signs not only greet visitors, they proclaim the people's pride in LSU Eunice and warn against littering. (Courtesy of the authors' collection.)

United States Congressman
Dr. Charles Boustany Jr. (in white shirt) has been the US representative for Louisiana's 7th District since 2005. The affable man takes pride in visiting his constituents as he is shown doing here with unidentified students and Chancellor Nunez at LSU Eunice. Boustany, a heart surgeon, called his program for revitalizing the area's economy his "Prescription for Prosperity." (Courtesy LSU Eunice.)

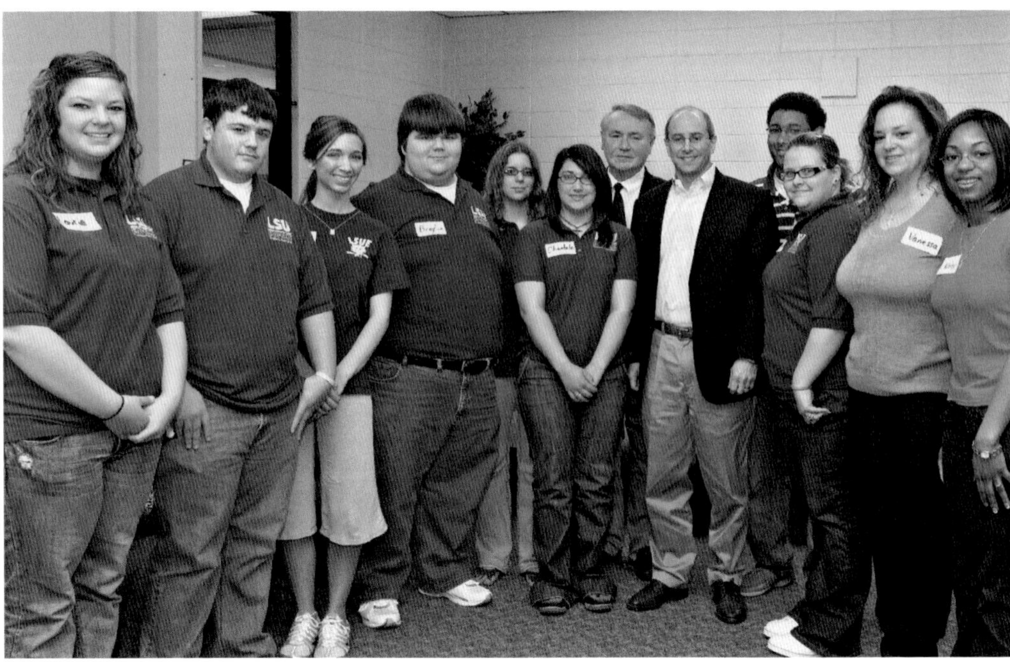

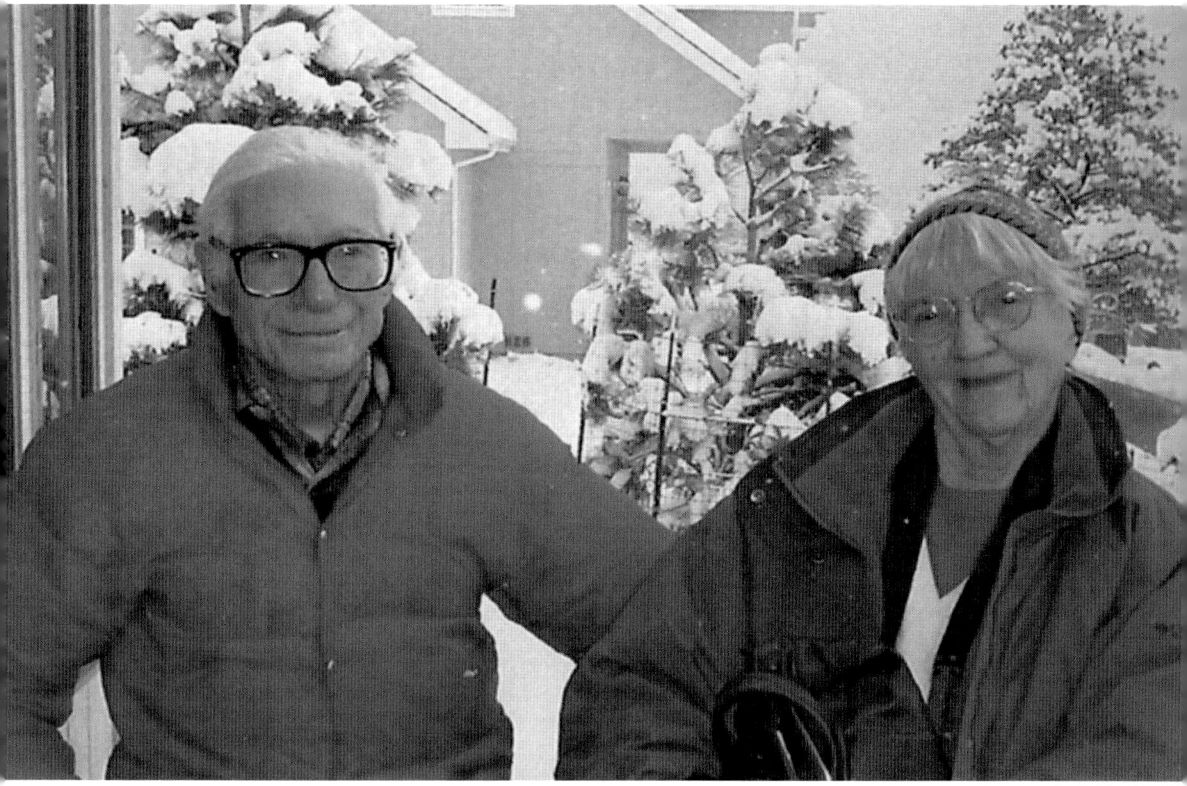

Space Scientist
Dr. William A. "Bill" Rense, a frequent visitor to Eunice since 1942, was professor emeritus of physics at the University of Colorado. Born in 1914 in Massillon, Ohio, the son of German immigrants, Joseph and Rosalia Luther Rense, he developed a love of astronomy that led him to earn degrees at Case Western Reserve University and Ohio State. He held teaching positions at Rutgers, University of Miami, Texas A&M, and LSU, where he met and married Wanda Childs Rense, daughter of Eunice residents Dr. A.B. and Ora Childs, who lived on Maple Avenue next door to the Maxime McGee family. Rense began teaching at the University of Colorado shortly after their marriage. In addition to his first love, teaching, Rense studied polarized light and its implications for the analysis of zodiacal light. In 1952, he obtained the first photographic spectrogram of the solar Lyman-alpha line of hydrogen. Many other scientific successes followed. Rense was the first director of the Laboratory for Atmospheric and Space Physics (LASP). As a devoted amateur naturalist and "birder," Rense worked in collaboration with George H. Lowery, curator of the Museum of Zoology at LSU, to establish the observational ground rules that would enable ornithologists to determine the compass heading, altitude, and density of birds along their nocturnal flyways. He retired from the university in 1980, and relocated to Lafayette, Louisiana, where he and his wife could easily visit family and friends in Eunice. He particularly enjoyed Cajun music, festivals, and beautiful azaleas. Although the Renses traveled extensively, they always found time to visit and enjoy Eunice Mardi Gras activities. Rense and his wife were parents of three sons, Dr. William C. Rense, John Rense, and Charles Rense. (Courtesy of Dr. William C. Rense.)

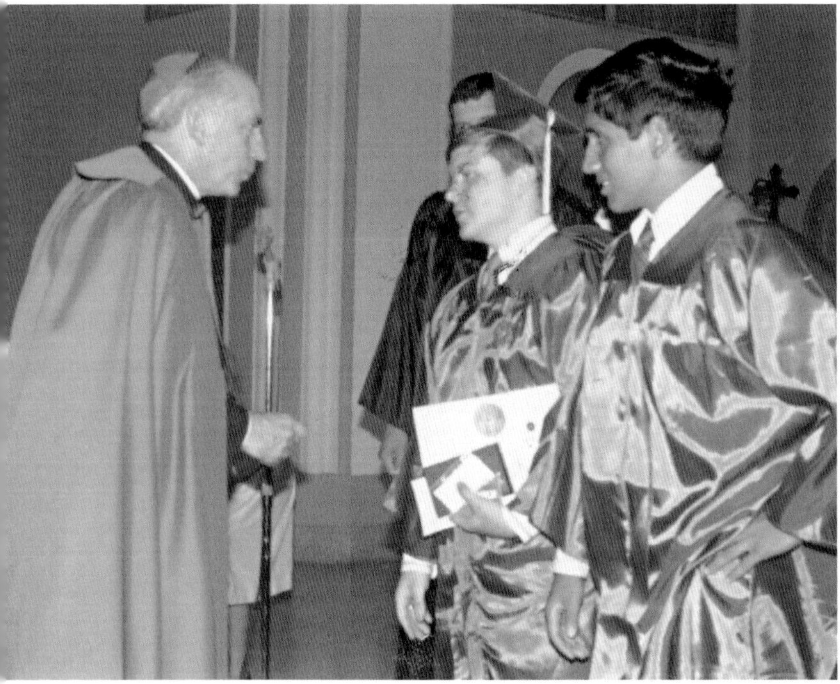

The Archbishop
Bishop Harry Flynn was the coadjutor bishop for the Diocese of Lafayette. Renowned for his kindness and encyclopedic memory, Flynn was pictured at the 1987 St. Edmund High School graduation mass speaking with graduates, Van Reed, left, and Milan Janmeja. In 1994, Flynn became coadjutor Archbishop of the Archdiocese of Saint Paul and Minneapolis. (Courtesy of Valerie Reed Jumonville.)

Ernest Gaines
Pictured, seated, after his presentation at LSU Eunice, Ernest J. Gaines, Writer-in-Residence Emeritus of the Ernest Gaines Center at the University of Louisiana Lafayette, visited with Dr. Stephen Guempel, left, with back to camera, Dr. Huey Guagliardo, right, Ching Wasmuth, right, and other unidentified audience members. Gaines discussed how he based his writings on the African American experience in the rural South. (Courtesy of Dr. David Simpson.)

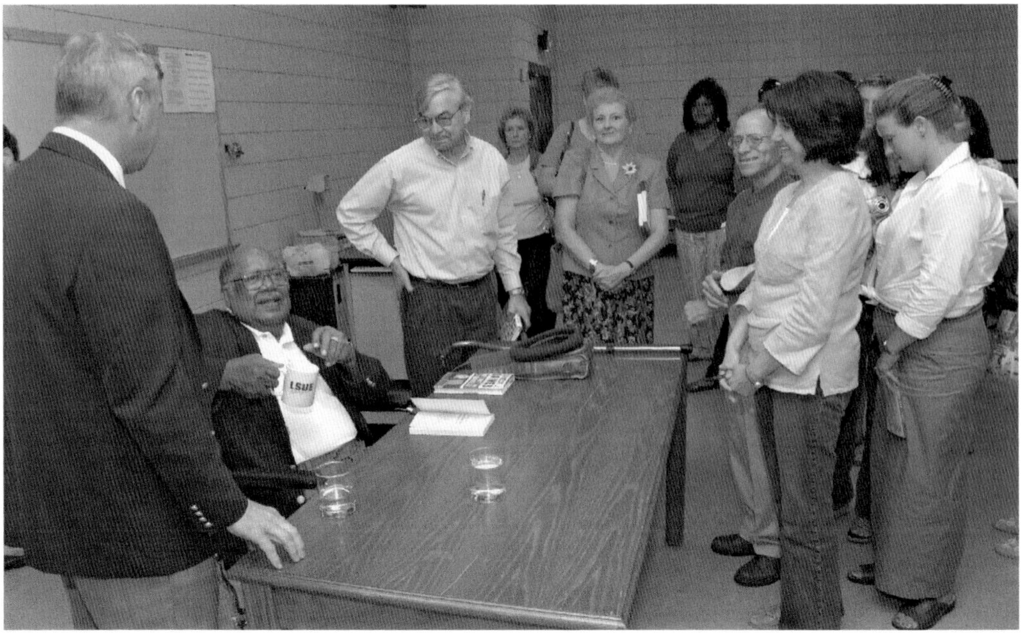

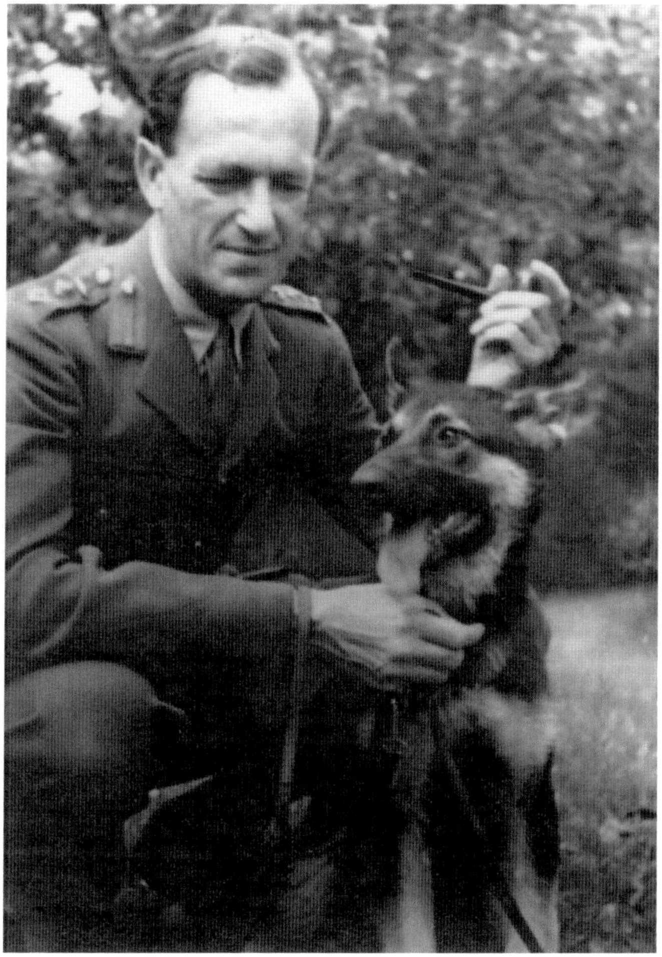

British General Visits

Eunice residents were amazed in 1955 when a British brigadier general appeared in town. On a surprise visit to his relatives, Brig. Gen. Ernest F.B. Cook, his wife the former Patricia Constance Clements, and their daughter, Nicola, all of Worthing, England, came to visit his uncle and other family members. The general was a son of Sir Frederick Charles and Lady Amelia Mae Bult Cook, also of Worthing, England. His mother, Lady Mae, was the sister of Eunice resident James Bult and their late brother, George Bult. Sir Frederick Cook was the chief engineer of roads in England. The general had been in the United States as a member of the British Joint Services Mission in Washington, DC. Their daughter, Nicola, also lived in this country. Cook attended the Royal Military Academy and was commissioned in the Corps of Royal Engineers. He served in India and Canada before being assigned to the British Joint Staff Mission in the United States before spending four years in Germany. The Cook family was entertained at the Samuel Jasper Morris home and by the Frank Bult family at the American Legion Hall where over 65 members of the family gathered to greet the English guests. James Bult, General Cook's uncle, told how he came to the United States over 64 years before the general's visit. He left home at the age of 19 and only went back to settle his father's estate. Some family members claimed that James Bult was a stowaway, since no records of his passage seem to exist. He had not seen his sister, Lady Mae, since his father died. She was 83 years old at that time. The Cook family was delighted with Louisiana cooking and hospitality. (Courtesy of Thomas Morris Jr.)

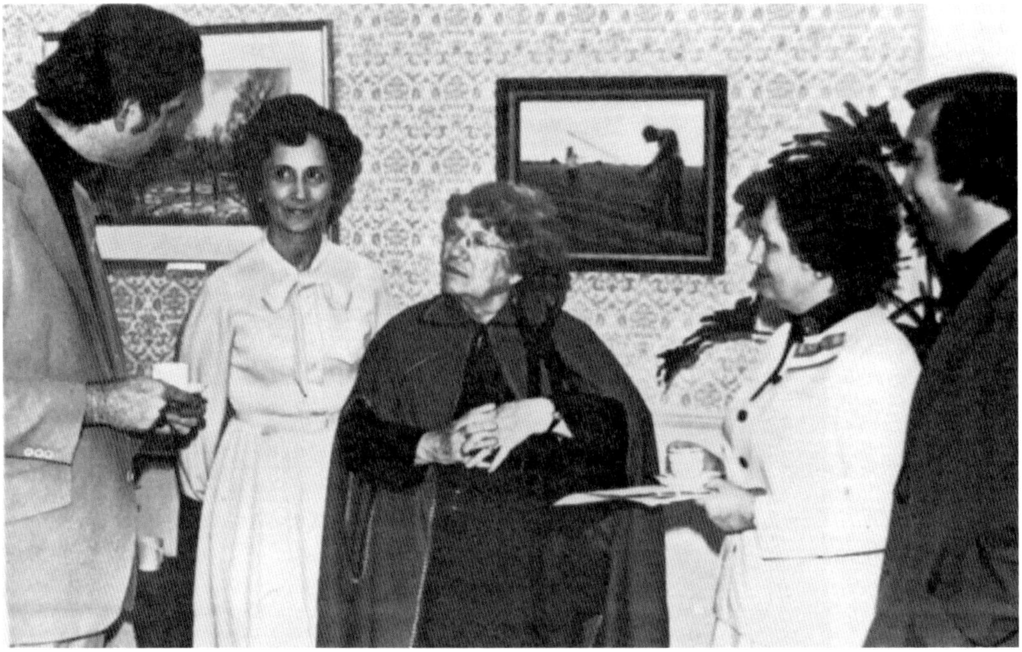

Businesses Closed for Her

A conversation prior to her lecture at LSU in Baton Rouge resulted in an unplanned trip to Eunice for Dr. Margaret Mead, America's foremost cultural anthropologist. In 1976, a citizen mentioned that LSU Eunice would benefit from her lecture. She offered to come, a private airplane was made available, and the entire city of Eunice closed down for her visit. Mead stated, "Never doubt that a small group of committed people can change the world. Indeed, it is the only thing that has." Mead, center, was pictured at a reception at LSU Eunice prior to her standing-room-only talk. Also pictured are, far left, Dr. James Forester, library director; Beverly Lewis, registrar; Joan Hernandez, professor; and Fr. Cary Landry. (Courtesy of LSU Eunice.)

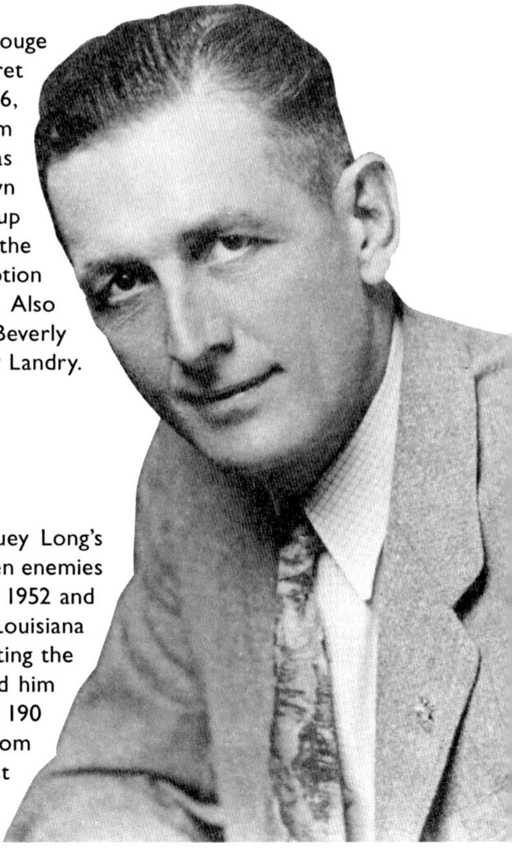

The "Cat"

Elected St. Landry Parish sheriff in 1936 as part of Huey Long's political dynasty, D.J. "Cat" Doucet served until 1940 when enemies of the Long family defeated him. He was elected again in 1952 and served until 1968. Doucet was among the first white Louisiana politicians in the 1950s to endorse civil rights by supporting the registration of African American voters. The FBI accused him of protecting gambling and prostitution on the Highway 190 corridor. His nickname, "Cat," may have originated from the illegal "cathouses" he ignored. He liked to drive fast and likely set speed records on his many visits to Eunice. (Courtesy of Eunice Public Library.)

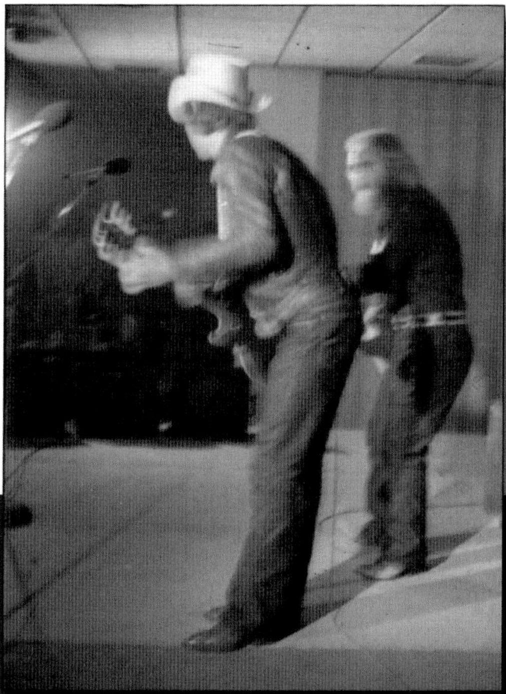

ZZ Top

ZZ Top, an American rock band, formed in 1969 in Houston, Texas, performed for a capacity audience at LSU Eunice in 1973. Their early sound was rooted in blues, but eventually bowed to other influences. Their rhythm and guitar style were unique. For students, the band's lyrics consisting of humor and sexual innuendos made them a hit. Shortly after they appeared in Eunice, the band released an album that propelled them into the mainstream. By the mid-1970s, they were among the most popular touring acts in the nation, breaking concert attendance records. Here they are shown on stage. (Courtesy of Charles Seale.)

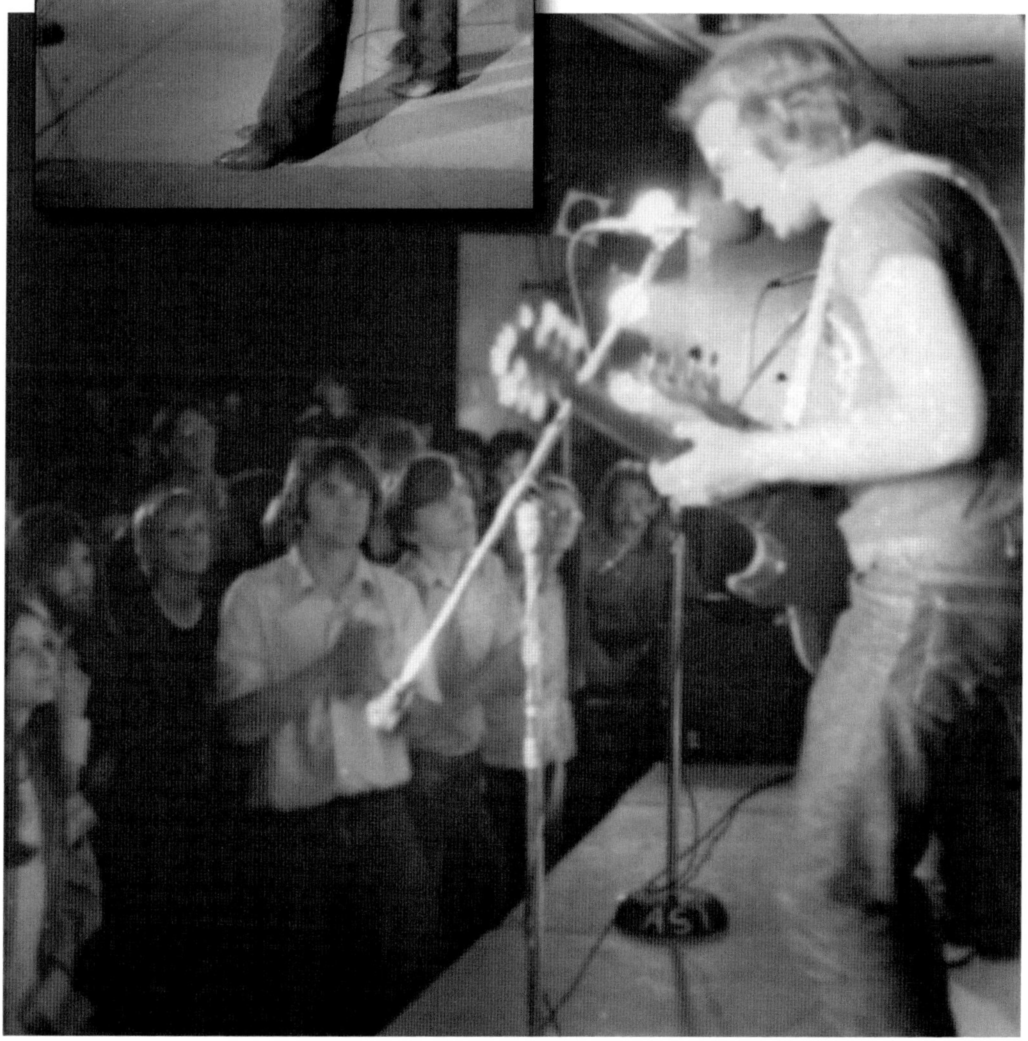

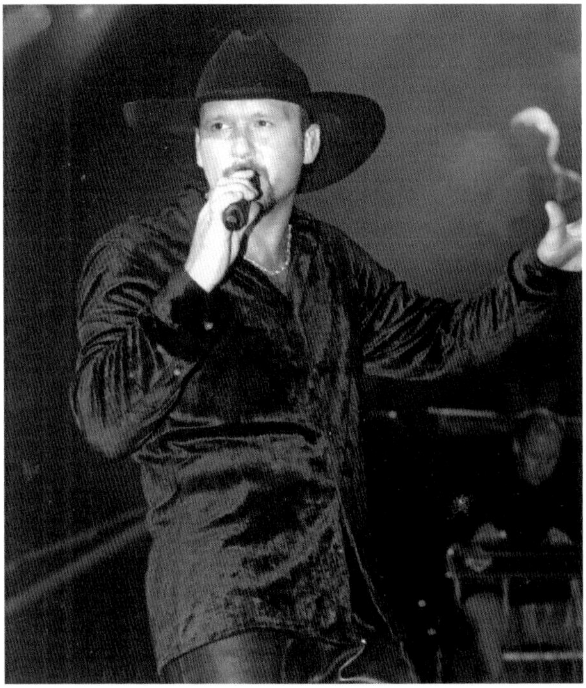

Grammy Awards and a Movie

Tim McGraw, nee Timothy Smith, is the son of former major league baseball pitcher "Tug" McGraw. Born in Delhi, Louisiana, in 1967, he attended Northeast Louisiana University on a baseball scholarship. McGraw's musical career and his reunion with a father who once denied their relationship did not happen quickly. Life improved with McGraw's sales of over 40 million albums and three Grammy Awards. Above, he performed in his home state and below in 2004, McGraw, right, and his assistant, Daine Devillier of Eunice, who met McGraw in college and went on to work for him, paused on the set of *Black Cloud*, a movie in which McGraw played a rural sheriff and Devillier played his deputy. (Courtesy of Maginnis Photography and Daine Devillier.)

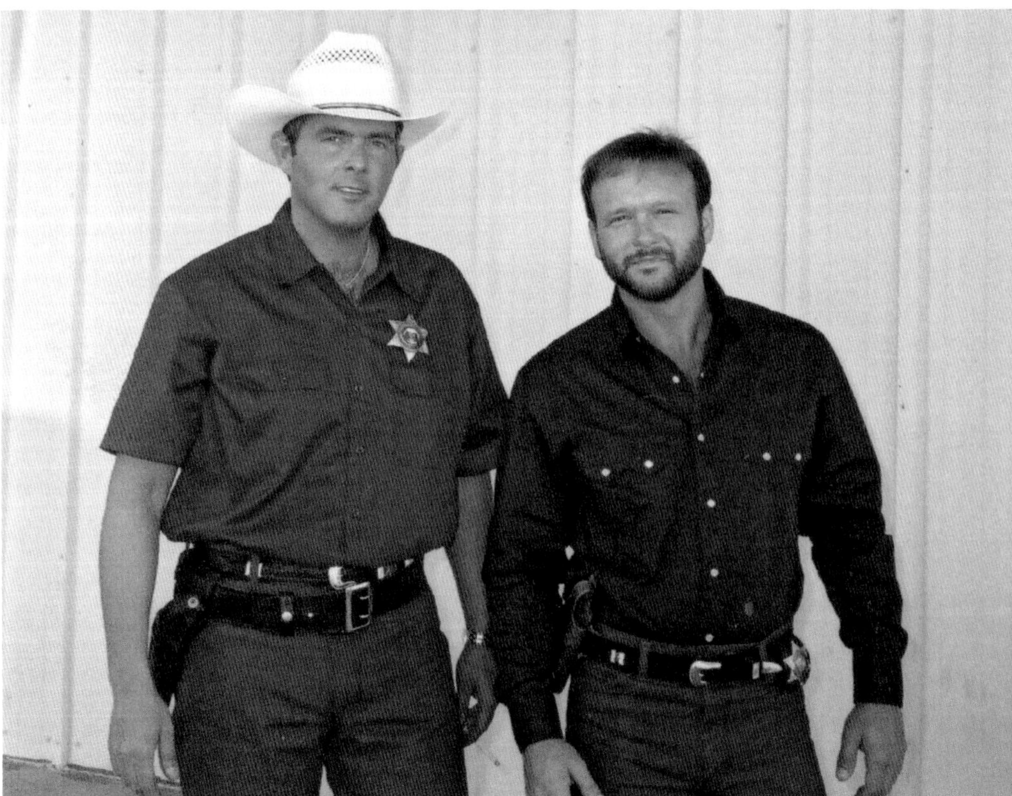

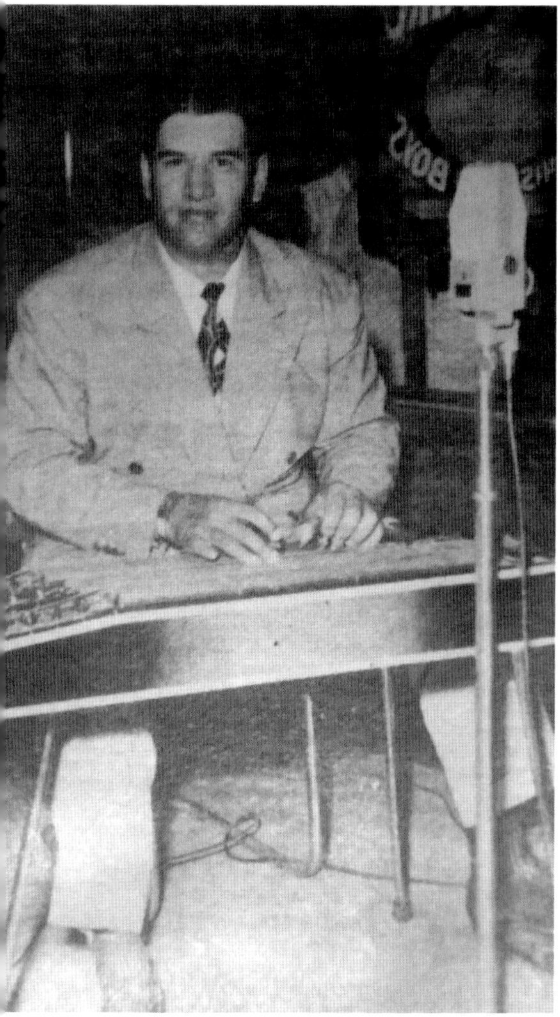

Papa Cairo

Steel guitarist Papa Cairo, born Jules Angelle Lamparez, was so popular that he practically lived in dance halls, including Eunice's Silver Slipper Club, in the 1950s and 1960s. In 1987, he played the renovated Liberty Theater's first show. Having performed with Ernest Tubbs, Jimmie C. Newman, Harry Choate, and Marty Robbins, he enjoyed a 64-year career that began with the New Orleans band the Daylight Creepers in 1935. (Courtesy of Eunice Public Library.)

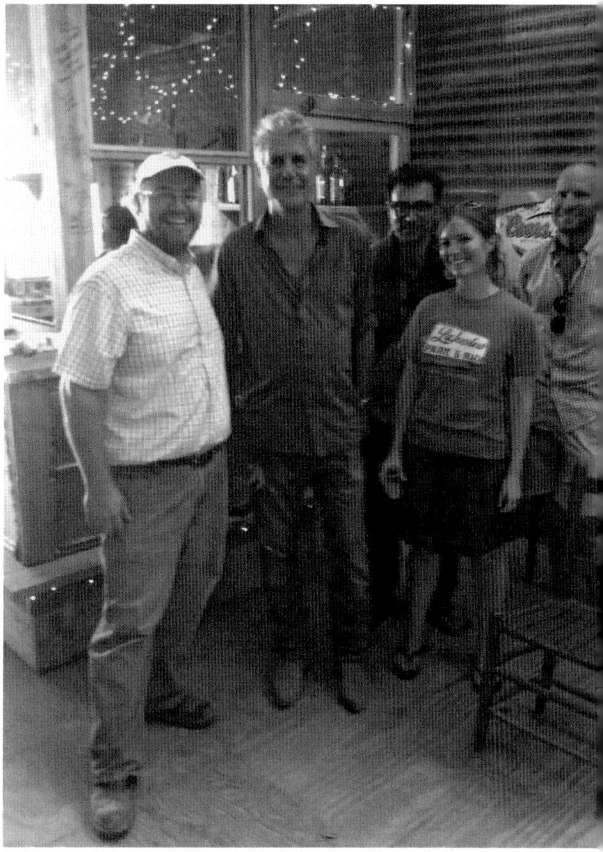

No Reservations

Chef, author, and television personality Anthony Bourdain, who hosts Travel Channel's culinary and cultural adventure program, *Anthony Bourdain No Reservations*, filmed a Cajun *boucherie* (butchering) at Kenneth Pitre's Lakeview Park in 2012. Bourdain is pictured in the huge barn at Lakeview Park with owners Lance Pitre, left, and Bonnie Pitre, right, and two unidentified fans. (Courtesy of Kenneth, Lance, and Bonnie Pitre.)

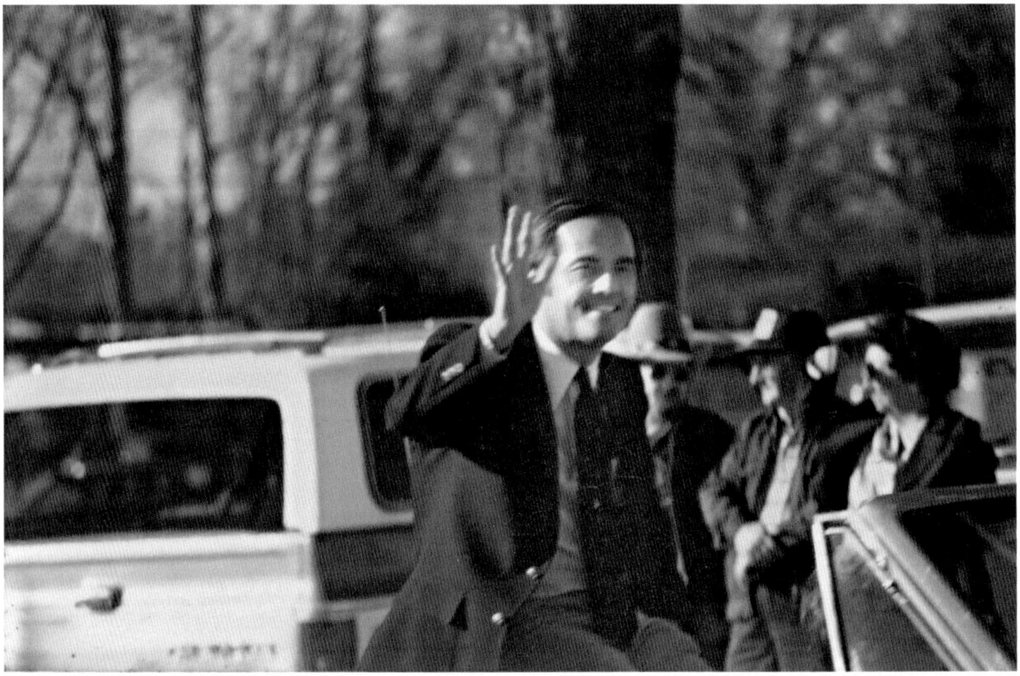

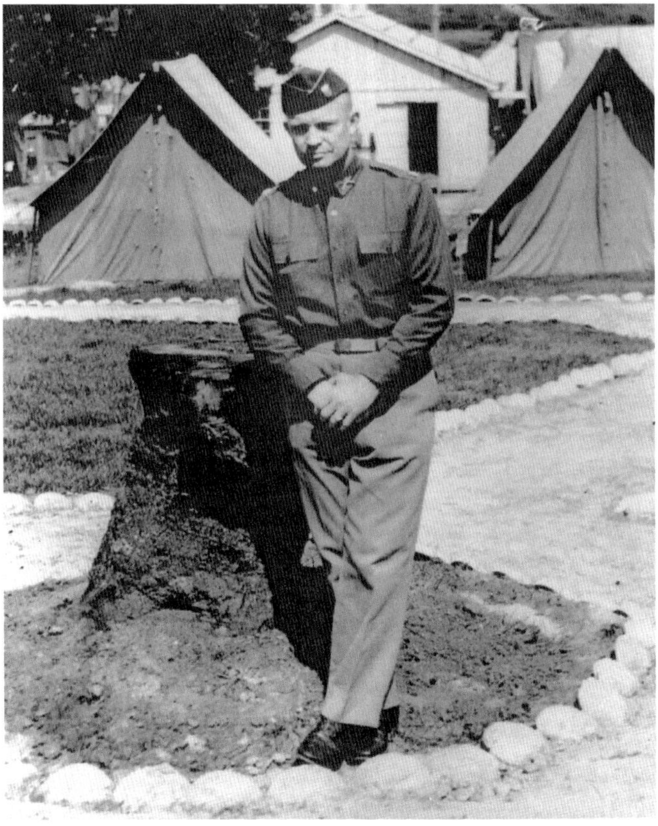

Space Shuttle Pilot
Astronaut Robert L. Crippen visited in 1985 at the invitation of Mayor Curtis Joubert. Crippen piloted the space shuttle *Columbia* in 1981 and *Challenger* in 1983, taking the first American woman into space. He is shown riding in a parade in his honor. (Courtesy of Van Reed.)

Eisenhower Slept Here
General Dwight D. Eisenhower came in 1941 during the Louisiana Maneuvers. His headquarters and barracks were at the old Eunice High School, which burned down in 1982. Eisenhower, along with Generals Marshall and Patton, took part in the massive war games. (Courtesy of the Louisiana Maneuvers and Military Museum.)

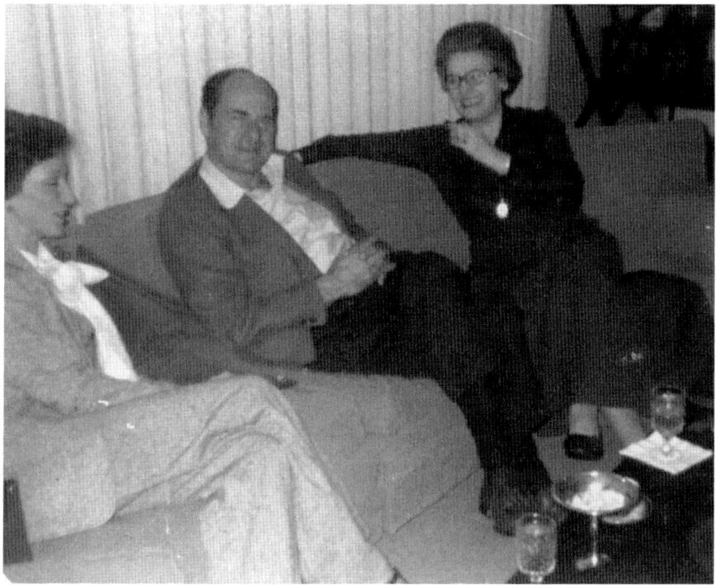

Famed Physician
Dr. Harry Heimlich, who married Jane Murray, daughter of famed dancer Arthur Murray, asked Carrie D Atteberry to sit on his foundation's board after a referral from her physician. A friendship developed between the doctor famed for his anti-choking maneuver and the Atteberry family, resulting in Heimlich's visits to their farm. Pictured in the 1960s were Jane and Dr. Heimlich and Carrie D Atteberry. (Courtesy of William "Mac" Atteberry.)

General Westmoreland
Gen. William C. Westmoreland, who commanded US military operations in the Vietnam War and was Army Chief of Staff until 1972, visited the Winston "Skeet" Atteberry home on July 4, 1976, after attending patriotic programs in Eunice and Crowley. Pictured, left to right, were Mr. and Mrs. Lucien Branch, General Westmoreland, Ruth Barnett, and Winston and Carrie D Atteberry. (Courtesy of William "Mac" Atteberry.)

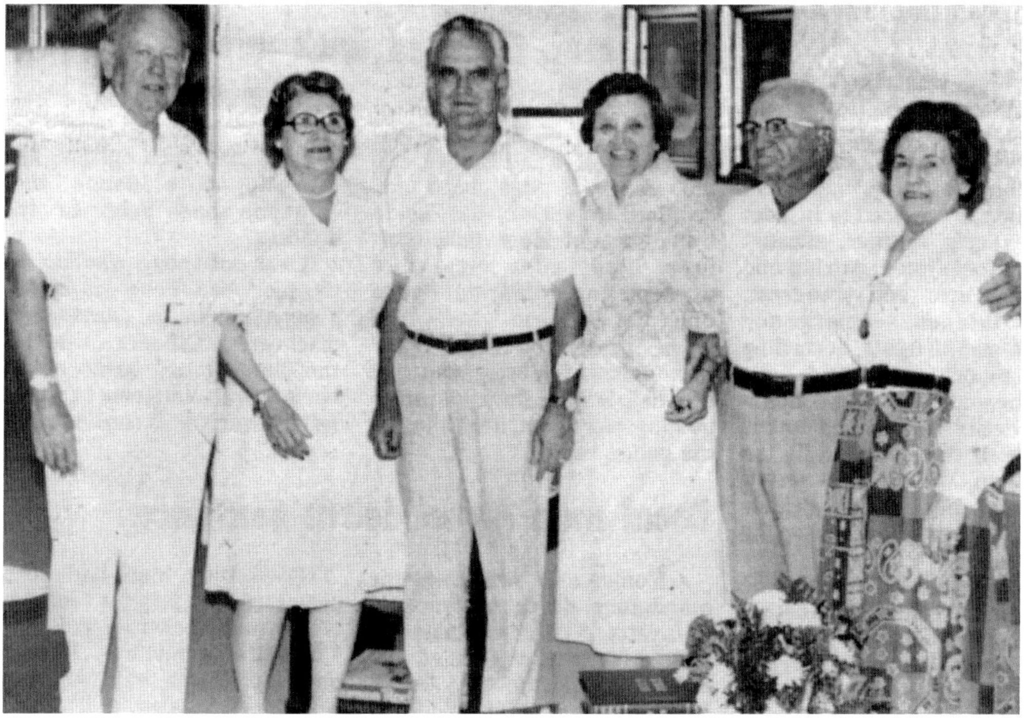

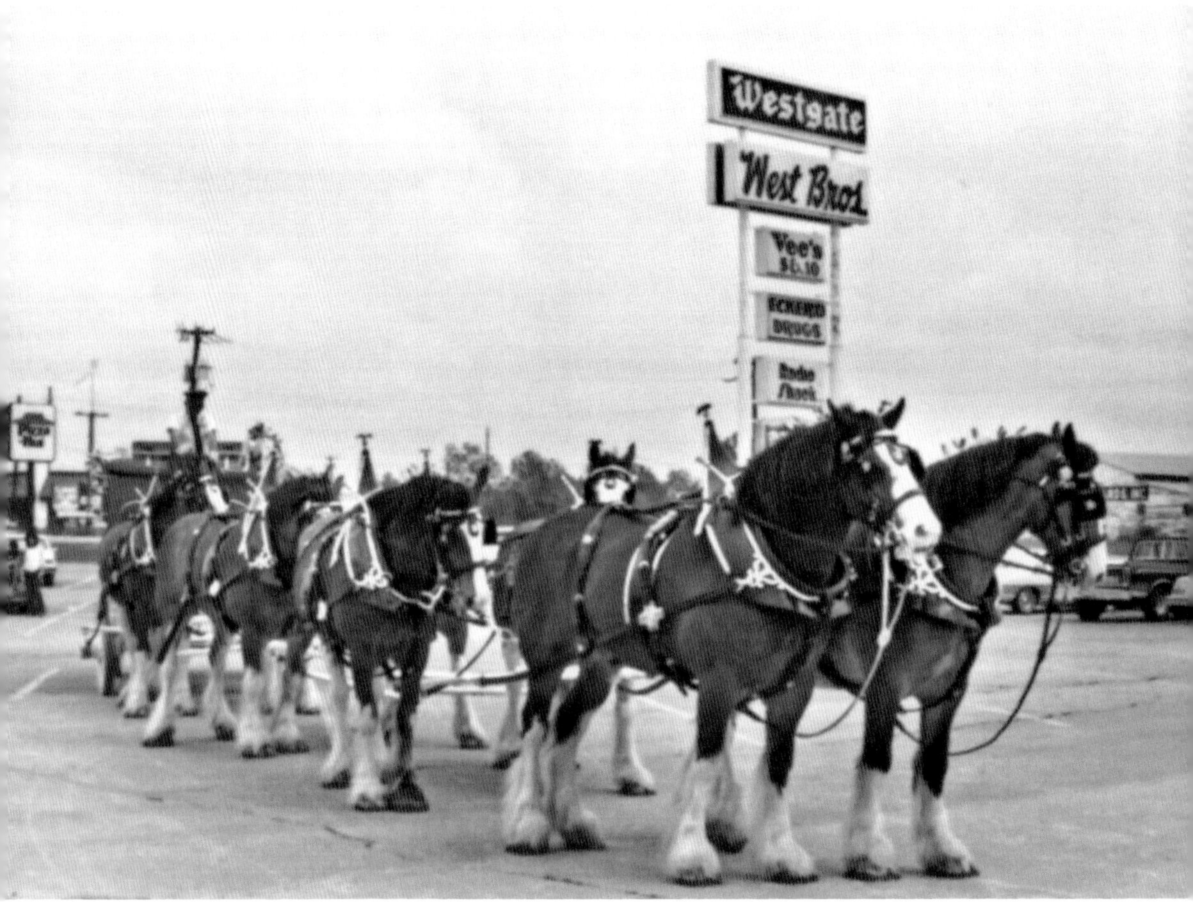

Clydesdale Horses Visit

In 1982, city residents had an opportunity to see the world-famous Budweiser Clydesdales at the local Westgate Shopping Center for a massively advertised promotion. Eight horses weighing about 1,500 pounds each pulled a four-ton antique red, white, and gold beer wagon. Two alternate horses made the trip also. The trademark mascots were first introduced by the Anheuser-Busch owner as part of his aggressive advertising strategy in 1933 to celebrate the repeal of Prohibition. They proceeded to carry the first case of post-Prohibition beer out of the St. Louis brewery. (Courtesy of Leo and Drucilia Quebedeaux.)

INDEX

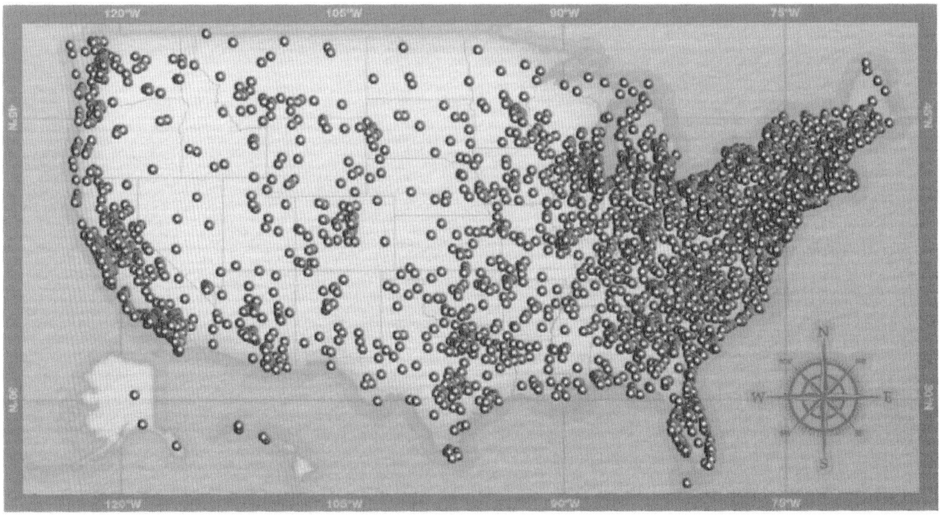

Consistent with our mission to preserve history on a local level, this book was printed in South Carolina on American-made paper and manufactured entirely in the United States. Products carrying the accredited Forest Stewardship Council (FSC) label are printed on 100 percent FSC-certified paper.